STABILITY OF ARCHES.

WOODBURY.

No. 7.

PAPERS

ON

PRACTICAL ENGINEERING,

PUBLISHED BY THE ENGINEER DEPARTMENT,

FOR THE USE OF THE

OFFICERS OF THE UNITED STATES CORPS OF ENGINEERS.

PAPERS ON PRACTICAL ENGINEERING.

No. 7.

TREATISE

ON THE

VARIOUS ELEMENTS OF STABILITY

IN THE

WELL-PROPORTIONED ARCH.

WITH

Numerous Tables of the Ultimate and Actual Thrust.

BY

CAPTAIN D. P. WOODBURY,

U. S. CORPS OF ENGINEERS.

NEW YORK:

D. VAN NOSTRAND.

1858.

INTRODUCTION.

THE first part of this paper, ending with Section V., is devoted mainly to the theory of the arch first proposed by Coulomb, and subsequently developed by Audoy, Petit, Poncelet, and other French authors. New developments and illustrations are here given, and new and extensive tables have been added.

The thrust may be due to the tendency of the upper voussoirs to slide down their beds, or to the tendency of some upper segment of the arch to rotate on the interior edge of its lowest joint. Both of these tendencies are investigated as questions of maxima; and the greatest of the two resulting forces is the true thrust.

In almost all practical cases this true thrust is due to rotation, and is developed at the instant of equilibrium preceding rupture and fall. For convenience we have called this the ultimate thrust. It is obviously much less than the actual thrust of the well-established arch; nor has any relation between the two been hitherto pointed out.

The defective character of this theory was indicated by Coulomb, and has been clearly seen by many authors. Moseley, Méry, and others, have written able treatises in search or support of a better principle, but no one seems to have seized the final idea, or combination of ideas, which places the theory of the actual thrust upon a perfectly definite mechanical basis. We have before us an "Examen historique et critique des principales théories concernant l'Equilibre des Voûtes," by Poncelet, drawn up with the characteristic ability and learning of that great man, in which no allusion is made to any attempt to furnish a definite and exact theory of the actual thrust of circular and elliptical arches. Approximations to this thrust, regarding the curve of pressure or curve of equilibrium as a sort of catenary, and the intrados as nearly parallel thereto, have indeed been attained by English mathematicians of the last century, and, of late, far more completely, it is said, by Yvon Villarceau; and Carvallo, in a beautiful and highly practical treatise, published in the Annales des Ponts et Chaussées, 1853, has given, approximately, the actual thrust and all other elements of semicircular and elliptical arches surcharged horizontally. We say approximately, for Carvallo, to facilitate calculation, regards the joints of the arch as vertical, instead of perpendicular to the intrados, and determines the angle of greatest thrust by supposed rotations of the upper segments upon the intrados, instead of the lowest of the two curves which divide the joints into three equal parts.

The last part of this paper, beginning with Section VI., furnishes an original and probably a new theory of the arch, with numerous tables giving the actual thrust of most arches in common use without calculation. This actual thrust is found to differ largely, in most cases, from the ultimate thrust above mentioned, their ratio varying from 1 to nearly 2.

This new theory is based on the principle that the curve of pressure shall not approach the intrados or extrados within certain prescribed limits, and that it shall touch, at the three or five joints of rupture, so-called, the two curves which pass through those limits. Every case, as in the ultimate thrust, is a question of maxima.

Coulomb pointed out the several modes of rupture to which arches are liable; in one of which the crown rises. Most writers upon the arch repeat his remarks; but no one seems to have given the subject any particular consideration—much less to have determined the limits within which such rupture is possible or probable. Indeed, without a knowledge of the actual thrust no practical or useful solution was possible. The reader will be surprised to learn that most of the light beautiful stone bridges of Great Britain are inclined to this mode of rupture. Our remarks on this subject, in relation to the limits of possible and practicable arches, and in the discussion of Table I, will be found, we trust, both interesting and useful. Every proposed bridge of large span should be investigated in view of this third mode of rupture, in which the arch may fall without disturbing the piers. If not unnecessarily heavy, the bridge will, in general, be in the neighborhood of the *practicability* connected with this mode of rupture.

We have taken great pains to prepare simple and comprehensive formulæ for thickness of piers. These formulæ are the same in form, whether we use the actual or ultimate thrust; the only difference being in the magnitude of the thrust, and in its point of application or lever arm.

Both the ultimate and actual thrusts of many arches consist of two parts: first, the thrust of the arch proper and a certain part of its load; second, the effect of a surcharge of constant vertical depth.

These effects have been investigated separately, and the two maxima, taken directly from the tables, give, when added together, the entire thrust in very slight excess. The accuracy of this method may be proved by comparing the results of Table F with those of a table given by Moseley at the end of his "Mechanics of Engineering."

Although the tables and the reduced formulæ provided for the actual thrust cover most of the cases likely to occur in practice, still the subject admits of further development and illustration, as the field is supposed to be entirely new. Additional tables are desirable to make the theory more completely available, and some of the given tables require enlargement.

In connection with this theory we have said nothing of the sliding thrust; because that had already been disposed of in connection with the ultimate thrust.

The sliding thrust, when it exceeds the actual rotation thrust, is, however, given in the tables at the end of Section VI. Cases of this kind are very rare.

Very few arches conform precisely to the conditions which we are compelled to assume in the preparation of tables and formulæ. The geometrical method, given at the end of the paper, is independent of all conditions, and will furnish in a short time all the elements of the most complex case. It affords facilities for *discussing* the plan of an arch, which can hardly be found in calculation alone.

It can be modified so as to give, by successive approximations, an intrados and an extrados at equal distances from the curve of pressure, with joints proportional to the pressure upon them; the pressure per unit of surface on these joints being constant throughout the arch, and, if we desire it, throughout the pier, which may always be treated as a part of the arch. The segmental arch, bounded by arcs of different circles, is itself, in most cases, a good solution of this problem of least material.

The curve of pressure, in the same arch, at different stages of its load, is liable to great changes. Provided the extreme variations be allowable, comparing the unloaded with the fully loaded arch, all intermediate variations may be kept still nearer the mean by putting on the load, in due proportion, at the several parts of the arch, simultaneously. We are indebted for this idea to M. Carvallo who makes perhaps extreme use of it.

To prevent any change at all in the curve of pressure, in the arch without any load and the same arch fully loaded, he goes so far as to make the depth of the arch in constant proportion to the depth of the load on the same vertical lines. This may be very proper in aqueduct and other heavy bridges; but in light arches without much load at the key—the case of common bridges—it would give an extrados nearly horizontal. Certainly, there is no objection to a change in the situation of the curve of pressure, provided it remain within the limits prescribed by Navier; since, in that case, the change cannot be for the worse, and by allowing it we greatly diminish the quantity of material, without in any degree impairing the stability of the work.

No attempt has been made to investigate the change of form and circumstances which, in some measure, must always result from the compression of the material. If we suppose the piers immovable, the extent of joint everywhere proportional to the pressure, and the curve of pressure everywhere at the middle of the joint, compression will convert the circular into an elliptical arch—a change in most cases favorable to the stability of the light arch, although it increases the thrust. These conditions can only be fully realized under a very peculiar load; they will, however, often be nearly realized, and will cause, approximately, the change above mentioned.

In connection with the actual thrust, Section VI., nothing is said of adhesion of mortar, because this force can never act in the well proportioned arch, the curve of pressure passing within such limits that every part of every joint is compressed.

The reader who may consult this paper for practical purposes only, is advised to begin with Section VI., and to refer to the first part of the work only when necessary to understand the second. He is also advised, as the arch must be regarded from many points of view, to acquire a general knowledge of the whole of that Section, before studying critically the particular parts.

It may be asked, Why not, then, invert the work, and place the more important part first? The reason will be given. The first part was nearly completed before the author had discovered an exact mechanical foundation for a theory of the actual thrust—a foundation on which tables of that thrust could be calculated, and definite results obtained, without any sacrifice of principle to facility of calculation. The second part, contrary to the original intention, began to expand, and finally assumed, well nigh, a character of completeness by itself. It was too late to re-write the whole. The author had neither time nor health to do so. Nor could the first part be dispensed with: it is necessary as a complement to the second. It is to be regretted, however, that the fullness of illustration and demonstration given to the first part of the work has not been given rather to the second.

The great variety of dimensions adopted by different engineers for arches of nearly equal span and rise, is shown by Table I. No better proof could be given of the utility of some little attention to the theory of the arch. The engineer may thereby avoid, on the one hand, a large wasteful expenditure for useless excess of strength, or, at the other extreme, the mortification of seeing his work fall down in consequence of impossible proportions.

The preparation of this paper has involved long and arduous labor, in the reduction of formulæ to numerical forms, and in the calculation of tables. The author gratefully acknowledges the assistance of Dr. D. W. Whitehurst and Mr. George B. Phillips, in making the numerical calculations. Without their efficient aid, he could not have undertaken so large a task.

CONTENTS.

[Such parts as are supposed to be entirely new, are given in italics. The numbers refer to the paragraphs.]

SECTION I.

GENERAL INVESTIGATION WITHOUT REGARD TO PARTICULAR CURVES.

SECTION II.

THE SEMICIRCULAR ARCH OF EQUAL THICKNESS THROUGHOUT.

SECTION III.

THE MAGAZINE ARCH, INCLUDING THE EXTREME CASE IN WHICH THE TWO PLANES WHICH FORM THE ROOF, ARE ONE AND HORIZONTAL, OR THE CIRCULAR ARCH SURCHARGED HORIZONTALLY.

SECTION IV.

SEGMENTAL ARCHES—SCARP WALLS.

SECTION V.

ELLIPTICAL ARCHES.

SECTION VI.

THE CURVE OF PRESSURE, NEW THEORY OF THE ACTUAL THRUST, ETC. ETC., BASED ON KNOWN MECHANICAL PRINCIPLES.

[The whole of this, as a definite system, is supposed to be new: the particulars are not given in italics.]

TABLES

OF THE ULTIMATE THRUST, ETC.

TABLES

OF THE ACTUAL THRUST, ETC. ETC.

ERRATA.

Page 287, line 14 from top, for $K=\frac{d}{r}$ read $K=1+\frac{d}{r}$.

Page 319, over 2d column, for $r=5\frac{1}{2}f$ read $r=\frac{5}{2}f$.

THE

THEORY OF THE ARCH.

SECTION I.

DEFINITIONS AND GENERAL REMARKS.

1. The arch proper consists of several parts, commonly called *voussoirs*, which press upon each other in surfaces meeting at one or more central lines. It is distinguished from the beam by exerting, upon its piers or abutments, an outward thrust.

It may be upright or reversed, horizontal or inclined.

Cylindrical arches are fully represented by a section taken at right angles to their general direction. The surfaces of this section give the relative masses of all the parts of the arch and its piers; and to obtain the actual weight of a unit in width, it is only necessary to multiply the surface, expressed in feet or any other unit, by the weight of a cubic unit of masonry.

The arch, when submitted to calculation for the purpose of determining the requisite dimensions of its piers and other parts, is supposed to be a unit in width.

The *extrados* is the exterior outline of the arch proper, whether made up of curves or straight lines.

The *intrados* is the interior line, and the corresponding surface of the arch is the *soffit*.

The wedge-like pieces of which the arch is composed, are called *voussoirs*.

In this paper it will be taken for granted, unless otherwise specially mentioned, that all arches have a joint at the summit, midway over the opening between the piers, called the key-stone or vertical joint.

The sides of the arch are called the *reins*.

The line or bed at which the arch begins, or springs from its piers, is called the *springing line*.

The blocks of masonry, or other material, which support two successive arches, are called *piers;* the extreme blocks, which generally support, on one side, embankments of earth, are called *abutments*.

A pier strong enough to withstand the thrust of either adjacent arch, should the other fall down, is sometimes called an *abutment pier*.

Besides their own weight, arches usually support a permanent load or *surcharge* of earth or masonry, or both.

2. Common mortar in heavy masses of masonry, hardens very slowly—remaining comparatively soft long after the centering has been removed and the arch left to its own support. We must not, therefore, in our calculations for large arches, look for any element of strength or stability in the adhesion of mortar made of common lime. We must suppose the voussoirs, whether large or small, to press upon each other without adhesion to resist either rotation or sliding. The joints are always rough, and any tendency to sliding is resisted by ordinary friction.

On the other hand, arches of all sizes laid in good hydraulic mortar, and thin arches laid in common mortar, may derive some increase of stability from the adhesion of the mortar which unites the joints.

Fortunately we can, by calculation or geometrical construction, easily determine the whole effect of this adhesion, when we assign to it a particular value, that is, so many pounds per square inch.

Perfectly flat arches, with vertical joints, are entirely supported by this adhesion. They are not properly arches, but beams.

So far as any arch derives strength from the adhesion of its parts to each other, it partakes of the nature of a beam.

The thrust of the arch, due to rotation in the case of actual rupture and fall, is, for convenience, sometimes called the *ultimate thrust.*

THEORY OF COULOMB.

3. We shall now indicate, in its most general terms, the theory of the arch first proposed by Coulomb, and subsequently developed by Audoy, Petit, Poncelet, and other distinguished French engineers; a theory hitherto eminently useful, notwithstanding its great defects.

We shall hereafter, under the head of *curve of pressure*, notice these defects, and try to give a more exact and practical theory of the circular, segmental, and elliptical arch.

FIRST AND ORDINARY MODE OF RUPTURE—ROTATION.

4. Let figure 1, plate 10, represent a section of any symmetrical arch in a condition of stability. We may suppose this to be composed of two equal half-arches, meeting, and mutually supporting each other, at the vertical or key-stone joint. From the perfect equality of the two halves, it is evident that the pressure of the one is counterbalanced by the resistance of the other, and that the two forces are equal, horizontal, and directly opposed.

This mutual pressure is exerted, generally, all along the vertical joint, from the intrados to the extrados. Its resultant is applied at some unknown point ordinarily above the middle of that joint. The position of the resultant, however, becomes known, as we shall soon see, when the arch, no longer able to maintain itself, begins to fall, from insufficient resistance in itself or its supports.

Let fig. 2 represent a section of the arch in a condition of instability—that is, all but able to stand upon its springing lines, and just beginning to fall. Fig. 3 represents the piers as adhering to the lower parts of the arch, and the whole as just beginning to fall. This is by far the most common mode of rupture,—almost the only mode, according to the French authors cited above, to which the circular arch of common use is at all exposed.

5. In this first mode of rupture, the arch divides into four pieces; the crown settles down; the reins spread out; the vertical joint opens at the intrados, the adjacent segments touching only at the extrados; the reins open at the extrados, the adjacent segments touching only at the intrados; the weakest joint below the reins opens on the inside.

The two lower segments revolve, outwardly, on the exterior edge of what we have called the weakest joint below the reins—thereby leaving room for the two upper segments to revolve, towards each other, on the interior edges of the joints at the reins. If the first rotation be prevented, by the weight of the piers or lower parts of the arch, the second rotation will also be prevented; for the crown can not settle down unless the reins spread out.

What we have called the weakest joint below the reins, that is, the joint most disposed to open under the horizontal force or pressure acting at the crown, is, in almost all practical cases, the joint at the base of the pier, or at the springing line if there be no pier.

6. Let us suppose one half of the arch removed, fig. 4, and apply at a, the highest point of the arch proper, a

horizontal force, F, just sufficient to keep the remaining semi-arch in its place. This force is the *thrust* of the arch, and is equivalent to the mutual pressure which before existed. It is evident that the arch, in its tendency to fall, cannot generate a pressure or force greater than that which will prevent its falling.

7. If the semi-arch were in one solid, indivisible piece, standing on its springing line, $A\ B$, the force F would be known at once; for, calling M the moment of the semi-arch, in reference to A, the interior edge of the springing line, we should have

$$F \times aC = M; \text{ or } F = \frac{M}{aC}.$$

8. But the arch is not solid: it may separate at any joint. If we regard any segment of the arch $a\,b\,m\,n\,r\,a$, fig. 4, we see that a certain force, F', is necessary to prevent its fall, or rotation forwards, on the inner edge of the joint $m\,n$.

From g, the center of gravity of the segment of the arch proper and its surcharge, drop the vertical line $g\,g'$ upon the horizontal, $m\,m'$.

Let the surface $a\,b\,m\,n\,r\,a = S$.
" lever arm $a\,m' = y$.
" $m\,g' = p$.

We then have the equation of moments

$$F'y = Sp; \text{ or } F' = \frac{Sp}{y};$$

9. Now, if we suppose the position of the joint $m\,n$ to vary, in succession, from the key to the springing line, the force F', required to prevent the fall of the corresponding segments, will also vary. It will be very small near the summit, gradually increase towards the reins, become a maximum about 50 or 60 degrees from the key, and grad-

ually diminish to the springing line. This maximum value of F', which we shall call F, is the thrust of the arch. As it is sufficient to sustain that segment which required the greatest support, it is more than sufficient to sustain all other segments, including the semi-arch itself.

10. The magnitude of this thrust, and the position of the joint corresponding to the angle of maximum thrust, are, it is easy to see, entirely unaffected by the piers and the lower parts of the arch,—that is, by anything below the joint itself.

This remark is important, for it announces one of the few simple principles on which the whole theory of the arch depends.

11. The tendency of the horizontal thrust is to push over the semi-arch, causing it to turn round the exterior edge of its lowest joint. But if the moment of the thrust taken in reference to that center of rotation, be less than the moment of the semi-arch and pier, in reference to the same point, no motion can ensue: the arch is stable. On the other hand, if the moment of the thrust prevail, the arch will begin to fall as represented in figures 2, 3.

The equation of moments will be

$$F \times l = M;$$

M representing the sum of the moments of the semi-arch and its pier, and l the lever arm of the thrust.

12. If we take into consideration the adhesion of mortar upon the joint of the springing line, or base of the pier, the equation of moments will become, art. 15 and following,

$$F \times l = M + \tfrac{1}{6}ce^2,$$

c representing the force of adhesion upon a unit of surface, and e the length of the lower joint. In this expression there is nothing unknown except the thickness of the pier, which enters into M.

13. If the arch have any surcharge whatever, not already included in S, we can always represent its weight by a *surface* of masonry. Let $S'=aa's's$, fig. $4\frac{1}{2}$, represent such weight in magnitude and position; and let p' represent the horizontal distance of its center of gravity from the vertical passing through m, the center of rotation. The horizontal force necessary to prevent the rotation of any particular segment and its load, will now be

$$F'=\frac{Sp}{y}+\frac{S'p'}{y}.$$

The maximum value of F' as before, art. 9, will be the true thrust.

We might, in arches of large span, wish to ascertain the effect, upon the thrust, of several weights in given positions. Let S', S'' &c., represent their several magnitudes; p', p'' &c., the respective distances of their centers of gravity from the vertical line through m. We have

$$F'=\frac{Sp+S'p'+S''p''+\ldots}{y}$$

14. In general, however, the surcharge is continuous, and bounded by one or more straight lines.

It is hardly necessary to say that, in the equation above given, the weights S', S'', &c., are supposed to be located over the segment $a\ b\ m\ n\ r\ a$, to which F' relates; and that, if the center of gravity of any one of them, as S'', is on the left of the vertical through m, the lever arm, p'', will be negative, and the product $S''p''$, therefore, negative.

The surcharge adds, generally, but little to the difficulty of the investigation, as will hereafter be seen.

15. To complete the general formulæ for the first and most common mode of rupture, it is necessary to add expressions for the adhesion of mortar upon the joints.

The ultimate resistance of mortar to compression is much greater than its resistance to extension. Still, we can, without error, regard these forces as equal, provided we determine their value by experiments upon rectangular prisms of the same material as the arch,—that is, by observing the weight necessary to break a beam supported at one or both ends. The product of this weight by its lever arm makes known the effective resistance opposed by the mortar. The expression $\frac{1}{6}cd^2$, which, as we shall see, measures the entire effect of the mortar when the ultimate resistance to extension is supposed to be equal to the ultimate resistance to compression, is identical in value with the expression $\frac{1}{3}c'd^2$, which measures the effect of mortar when the resistance to compression is infinite, and the neutral axis at the edge of the joint. But c as determined on the first supposition, will be twice as great as c' determined on the last.

Let us suppose, then, the ultimate resistance of mortar to extension and compression to be the same. Let c represent that resistance. When the joint $m\ n$, fig. 4, has so far opened that the mortar at n is about to separate, the adhesion or effective force then applied at that point will be c —the ultimate strength of the cement. At the same instant the mortar will be compressed at m to the full extent of its capacity to resist; and there will be a neutral axis at the middle of the joint, where the mortar is neither extended nor compressed.

The resistance, X, to extension, is proportional to the extension, and increases uniformly from the middle of the joint, where it is nothing, to the extrados, where it is c. It is given, therefore, at any point at the distance x from the neutral axis, by the proportion

$$\tfrac{1}{2}d' : c :: x : X = \frac{cx}{\frac{1}{2}d'}; \ (d' = mn)$$

The elementary force is therefore $\frac{cx}{\frac{1}{2}d'}dx$, and the entire resistance to extension—

$$\int_{0}^{\frac{1}{2}d'} \frac{cx}{\frac{1}{2}d'} dx = \frac{cd'}{4} = R$$

In like manner we find the resistance to compression to be,

$$\frac{cd'}{4} = R'$$

When we refer these two forces, which act in opposite directions, to any center of moments not between their respective resultants, we must regard them as having contrary signs. Referred to m, the common center to which all the forces of the system are referred, the force R, tending to prevent rotation, is negative; the force R', tending to cause rotation, is positive; the lever arm of R is $\frac{5}{6}mn = \frac{5}{6}d'$; the lever arm of R' is $\frac{1}{6}mn = \frac{1}{6}d'$. Their combined moment, tending to prevent the rotation of the voussoir $a\ b\ m\ n\ r\ a$, around the point m, is

$$\frac{cd'}{4}\left(\tfrac{5}{6}d' - \tfrac{1}{6}d'\right) = \tfrac{1}{6}cd'^2$$

In like manner, we find, at the vertical joint, above the neutral axis, a resistance to compression, $\frac{cd}{4}$, acting with the lever arm $(y - \frac{1}{6}d)$, tending to prevent rotation around the center, m; and below the neutral axis, the force $\frac{cd}{4}$, acting with the lever arm $(y - \frac{5}{6}d)$, tending to cause rotation around the point m. The combined moment opposed to rotation is

$$\frac{cd}{4}\left(y - \tfrac{1}{6}d - y + \tfrac{5}{6}d\right) = \tfrac{1}{6}cd^2$$

The two joints, therefore, oppose to rotation the moments $\frac{1}{6}c(d^2 + d'^2)$.

We might have shortened the demonstration by assuming at once this obvious principle, that the algebraic sum of the moments of any two equal, parallel, and opposed forces, is constant for all centers of rotation in the same plane, and always equal to either force multiplied by the distance between their respective directions; a principle which might have a very extensive application in calculating the total effect of certain combinations of timber in wooden bridges and other structures.

The French engineers, regarding the neutral axis as at the edge of the joint, give, as the moment of resistance due to mortar, $\frac{1}{3}cd^2$.

We have been the more particular in the above reasoning, because we differ from Poncelet in estimating the effect of mortar upon the vertical joint.*

---

* Poncelet says, page 201, vol. 12, Mémorial de l'Officier du Génie, after giving as the effect of mortar, $\frac{c(d^2+d'^2)}{3y}-\frac{cd^2}{3(H+h)}$; in which, fig. 4, $d'=mn$; $d=ab$; $y=am'$; $h=EE'$; $H=aC$; $c=$the force of adhesion upon a unit of surface,—

"We are led inevitably to this result, by the principle of virtual velocities, in considering, at the same time, the cohesion on the joint of rupture of the reins, and on that of the key, and in supposing, after Mariotte and Leibnitz, that this force is proportional to its distance from the point of rotation of each joint. The justification of this result presents no difficulty except in that part which relates to the second of these joints, which is not usually considered. Now, we must observe that the resultant of the elementary forces $\frac{cx}{d}dx$, which act along ab, in opposition to a movement of rotation at a, and of which the moment, in reference to that point, is evidently $\int_0^d \frac{cx^2}{d}dx=\frac{1}{3}cd^2$, can, as to this movement, be replaced by a horizontal force $\frac{cd^2}{3y}$, supposed to be applied at the edge of the intrados, m, of the lower joint; and as the latter is opposed, at the same time, to the action of the horizontal thrust, F, in its tendency to overturn the entire system of the semi-arch and its pier around the exterior edge of the base of the latter, with a lever arm, $H+h-y$, whilst that of F is $H+h$, we see that, in relation to this movement, it must, in its turn, be replaced by a horizontal force $cd^2\frac{(H+h-y)}{3y(H+h)}$ acting at a, to resist the movement in question, conjointly with the force which is capable of overcoming the cohesion, on the lower joint $m\ n$, with the lever arm y, and of which the known expression is $\frac{cd'^2}{3y}$. We have, therefore, as the total resistance, the quantity,

$$\frac{cd^2(H+h-y)}{3y(H+h)}+\frac{cd'^2}{3y}=\frac{c(d^2+d'^2)}{3y}-\frac{cd^2}{3(H+h)},$$

16. We must caution the reader that the unit of weight in the foregoing equations, is the weight of a cubic unit of masonry. To make the terms involving c homogeneous with the other terms, we must regard c as the ratio of the strength of adhesion, in pounds, upon the unit of surface, to the weight of the same unit cubed.

For instance, suppose the force required to separate a square foot of mortar to be 3,000 pounds, the cubic foot of masonry weighing 150 pounds, we must have $c = \frac{3000}{150} = 20$.

17. Collecting the above formulæ, we have, as the gen-

---

which makes the position of the joint of rupture at the reins depend upon the height of the arch and that of the pier."

In the above translation we have changed the notation, to suit our diagram and text.

This very distinguished philosopher has, we think, here fallen into an error.

The force $\frac{cd}{2}$, which the mortar opposes to rupture at the crown of the arch, and of which the moment, in relation to the upper edge of the vertical joint, is $\frac{cd^2}{3}$ is not opposed to rotation around m, the inner edge of the joint of the reins. Its whole tendency is to cause such rotation. The equal and opposite force, or resistance to compression, acting at a, the summit of the crown, is alone opposed to rotation. The point of application of the force $\frac{cd}{2}$, or resistance to extension, is situated upon the vertical joint at two-thirds its length from the extrados. Its lever arm, in reference to m, is $(y - \frac{2}{3}d)$; and the lever arm of the equal and opposite force, or resistance to compression, acting at the extrados of the crown, is y. The combined moment, in relation to m, is therefore

$$\frac{cd}{2}\left(y - (y - \tfrac{2}{3}d)\right) = \tfrac{1}{3}cd^2.$$

Wherever we suppose the neutral axis to be, the total resistance to compression must necessarily be equal to the whole resistance to extension; and this does not cease to be true even if we suppose one of these resistances, per unit of surface, to be infinite,—that is, if the neutral axis be at the edge of the joint.

M. Poncelet seems to have fallen, inadvertently, into one or two other errors, which make his final result nearly correct.

The force $\frac{cd^2}{3y}$, which we can substitute for the "resultant of the elementary forces $\frac{cx}{d}dx$," or $\frac{cd}{2}$, in relation to the opening of the joint of the crown, for that very reason we can not so substitute in relation to any other center of rotation.

Finally, we are not at liberty to refer the moments of a system in equilibrium to different centers.

eral value of the horizontal thrust, in the common mode of rupture,

Without surch. or adhesion of mortar,	the maximum value of	$F'=\frac{Sp}{y}$;	(1)
With surcharge,	do	$F'=\frac{Sp+S'p'+S''p''+\ldots}{y}$	(2)
With adhesion of mortar,	do	$F'=\frac{Sp}{y}-\frac{1}{6}\frac{c(d^2+d'^2)}{y}$	(3)
With both,	do	$F'=\frac{Sp+S'p'+S''p''+\ldots}{y}-\frac{1}{6}\frac{c(d^2+d'^2)}{y}$	(4)

And, for the thickness of pier, F representing the thrust, however determined,

Without adhesion of mortar at the base of the pier,	$\delta\times F\times l=M$	(5)
With adhesion of mortar at the base of the pier,	$\delta Fl=M+\frac{1}{6}ce^2$	(6)

e is the thickness of pier, δ the coefficient of stability.

18. No arch could stand in bare equilibrium. Experience has shown that the semi-arch and pier must have a certain excess of stability over the thrust; and the French engineers have provided for this excess, in the equations which determine the thickness of pier, by assigning to the thrust an increased value—multiplying it by the *coefficient of stability*, generally assumed at 1.90 or 2 in the heavy arches of fortifications, but which may be safely assumed at less in establishing the piers of ordinary bridges. We shall give a discussion of this important subject hereafter.

19. The thrust at the crown, due to the mutual action of the semi-arches, though not sufficient to turn over the semi-arch and pier, may under some circumstances cause the whole mass to slide outwardly on the base of the pier. The equation of equilibrium, calling W the whole surface of the semi-arch and pier, and f the friction or ratio of

resistance to pressure, will obviously be, $F = W \times f$; and the practical formula, calling δ' the coefficient of stability, will be $\delta' F = W \times f$.

If we wish, however, to take account of the adhesion of mortar upon the base of the pier, we shall have

$$\delta' F = W \times f + c \times e. \qquad (7)$$

As to this particular danger, the weakest joint is generally at the springing line, or very near it. Applied to that case, W would, of course, represent the surface of the semi-arch, and e its thickness at the springing line.

If the masonry be well constructed, even of poor mortar,—that is, well bonded together,—no sliding can ever take place at the springing line or base of the pier.

The thickness of pier should always be determined in view of rotation alone. In those very rare cases in which any danger of sliding can still remain, care must be taken in the preparation of the foundations to render such motion impossible. The most economical and effective expedient is, probably, that of giving to the base of the pier a slight inclination—say one foot in ten.

SECOND MODE OF RUPTURE—SLIDING.

20. When the thickness of an arch compared with its span is very great, the horizontal thrust no longer arises from any tendency to rotation, the lever arm p, equation (1), being very small, or even negative.

The thrust arises from the tendency of the upper voussoirs to slide down their beds or joints. It is precisely like the thrust of an embankment of earth, and is determined in the same manner, viz., by the "prism of maximum thrust."

Let f represent the friction along the joint $m\ n$, fig. 5.
" a " the angle of friction, measured from a horizontal.

Let v represent the angle between the joint $m\ n$, and a vertical line.
" S " the surface of the segment $a\ b\ m\ n\ a$.
" P' " the horizontal force acting on the joint $a\ b$, necessary to keep the segment from sliding down the joint $m\ n$.

We have, perpendicular to the joint $m\ n$, the force $P' \times \cos. v + S \sin. v$; and, parallel to the joint $m\ n$, the force $S \cos. v - P' \sin. v$; hence the equation of equilibrium, $(P' \cos. v + S \sin. v) f = S \cos. v - P' \sin. v$.

Taking account of the adhesion of mortar along the joint $mn = d'$, we have,

$$(P' \cos. v + S \sin. v) f + c \times d' = S \cos. v - P' \sin. v.$$

We have, therefore, as the general expression of the horizontal thrust,

Without adhesion, the maximum value of $P' = \dfrac{S(\cos. v - f \sin. v)}{\sin. v + f \cos. v} = S \times \text{cotang.}(a+v)$; (8)

With adhesion, do $P' = S \text{ cotang.}(a+v) - \dfrac{cd' \cos. a}{\sin. (a+v)}$; (9)

As in the case of rotation, we must suppose the angle v to vary from the summit towards the springing line, and ascertain the maximum value of P' in (8) or (9). This value, which is the *sliding thrust* of the arch, we shall designate by P.

21. Equations (8), (9), include the case of a surcharge, if we suppose S to take in all the load which rests vertically upon the segment $a\ b\ m\ n$.

22. In arches of common use, this mode of rupture can never take place. The resistance necessary to prevent rotation, which one half of the stable arch necessarily opposes to the other half, is, in almost all practical cases,

greater than the force necessary to prevent sliding. If it were otherwise, if P were greater than F, the former would be the proper thrust of the arch, and would take the place of F in equations (5), (6), (7), arts. 17, 19, when we wish to determine the thickness of pier.

23. We commit an error in favor of stability, in supposing the force P to be applied at a, the extrados at the crown. Its true point of application is always intermediate between a and b, and generally near the middle of that joint.

24. The effect of adhesion on any joint, in resisting a force acting parallel to that joint, we have, in the usual manner, measured by the product of the force of adhesion upon a unit of surface into the length of the joint expressed in the same unit.

It does not follow that the force c, which will separate a square foot of cement when acting at right angles to the joint, will tear asunder neither more nor less when acting parallel to the joint.

The rule, however, is the only one that has been offered, and it is, without doubt, sufficiently correct.

It would perhaps be better, proceeding experimentally, to regard the adhesion solely as giving a greater value to the friction.

THIRD MODE OF RUPTURE—ROTATION.

25. This is still more uncommon than the second.

Gothic arches, fig. 6, and arches very light, and lightly loaded at the crown, and overloaded at the reins fig. 7, are liable to this mode of rupture.

As compared with the usual mode of rupture, arts. 4, 5, figs. 2, 3, every thing is reversed. The crown rises; the reins fall in; the vertical joint opens at the extrados, the adjacent segments touching only at the intrados; the reins open at the intrados, the adjacent segments touching only at the extrados; the arch still divides into four pieces; the upper segments turn outwardly on the exterior edges of the joints at the reins; the lower segments turn inwardly on the interior edges of the lower joints.

The active force which pushes over the upper segments, acts in this case at the intrados of the crown. It is generated entirely by the effort or tendency of the semi-arch, or some segment of the arch above the springing line, to revolve under its own weight, turning on the inner edge of its lowest joint. To obtain the exact value of this thrust, we must determine the maximum value of the expression $\frac{Sp}{y'}$, fig. 4, differing from the horizontal thrust in the first mode of rupture only in the lever arm of the thrust, which is now $bm'=y'$, instead of $am'=y$.

Now, the horizontal force at b, fig. 4, necessary to cause any other segment to commence rising at the crown, turning outwardly upon n, is $\frac{Sg'}{y''}$, y'' representing the lever arm bn', and g' the distance of n, the center of rotation, from the vertical, gg', dropped from the center of gravity of the segment. If any segment be caused to rise, it will obviously be that which offers the least resistance. We must therefore by trial find the *minimum* value of $\frac{Sg'}{y''}$. If the horizontal thrust, as defined above, or rather if the maximum value of $\frac{Sp}{y'}$, which is a little greater than that thrust, exceed this minimum value, the arch will fall. This may take place in very light circular or segmental arches, surcharged horizontally; as will be proved hereafter.

FOURTH MODE OF RUPTURE—SLIDING.

26. The thrust at the key, generated by the mutual action of the semi-arches, might, it would seem, cause the arch to slide outwardly upon some of its lower joints. The horizontal force at the key, necessary to cause such movement is $S\,\text{cotang.}\,(v-a)$: for notation, see art. 20. Its least value, in practice, is always at the springing line, where, if anywhere, sliding will take place.

The equation of equilibrium of the semi-arch upon its springing line, supposed to be horizontal, has already been given, art. 19.

SECTION II.

27. We have given in the first section, the theory of the arch in its most general terms.

We shall hereafter give geometrical methods of determining the thrust at the crown, and all the other elements of any case that is likely to arise, in terms equally general; that is, independently of the particular nature of the curves of the extrados and intrados.

As circular arches are by far the most common, and admit of the most precise calculations, we shall first apply the theory to them.

The tables calculated by M. Petit, Capitaine du génie, and the more extensive tables prepared for this work and now published for the first time, will enable us to dispense with calculations in many cases, and greatly abridge them in nearly all.

The brevity and simplicity which characterize the general expressions of the horizontal thrust, unfortunately vanish when we submit the most simple cases to calculation.

CIRCULAR ARCHES, INTRADOS AND EXTRADOS PARALLEL.

28. Referring to fig. 8, let R be the radius of the extrados; r that of the intrados; v the arc which, in the circle whose radius is unity, measures the angle of any joint $m\ n$ with a vertical.

Resume equation (1), $F''=\frac{Sp}{y}$. We have,* $S=\frac{1}{2}v(R^2-r^2)$; $p=r \sin. v-\frac{2}{3}\frac{(R^3-r^3)(1-\cos. v)}{v(R^2-r^2)}$; $y=R-r\cos. v$;

These values substituted give

$$F''=\frac{Sp}{y}=\frac{3r(R^2-r^2)v\sin. v-2(R^3-r^3)(1-\cos. v)}{6(R-r\cos. v)}; \quad (10)$$

an expression of the horizontal force F'' which, applied to the extrados of the key, can prevent the voussoir $a\ b\ m\ n\ a$, corresponding to the angle v, from turning round the point m.

This we can simplify by introducing the ratio of the two radii, $K=\frac{R}{r}$, which gives

$$F''=r^2\frac{\frac{1}{2}(K^2-1)v\sin. v-\frac{1}{3}(K^3-1)(1-\cos. v)}{K-\cos. v}; \quad (11)$$

The value of v, or the inclination of the joint of rup-

---

* Distance from the center of the circle, fig. 8, on the bisecting line Cg, of the center of gravity of the sector $C\,a\,n=\frac{2}{3}\frac{R\times R\,2\sin. \frac{1}{2}v}{vR}=\frac{2}{3}R\frac{2\sin. \frac{1}{2}v}{v}=d$

" " $C\,b\,m=$ - - - $=\frac{2}{3}r\frac{2\sin. \frac{1}{2}v}{v}=d'$

" ring $a\,b\,m\,n\,a=\frac{\text{surf. } c\,a\,n\times d-\text{surf. } C\,b\,m\times d'}{\text{surf. of ring.}}$

$=\frac{2}{3}\frac{(R^3-r^3)2\sin. \frac{1}{2}v}{v(R^2-r^2)}$;

$p=mg'=mm'-g'm'=r\sin. v-Cg\times\sin. \frac{1}{2}v=..$ as above

Surface $C\,a\,n=\frac{1}{2}vR^2$; $2\sin.^2\frac{1}{2}v=1-\cos. v$.

ture which corresponds to the maximum value of F'', may be obtained in the usual way by differentiation. The numerator placed equal to zero, gives, by reduction,

$$\cos. v+(1-K\cos. v)\frac{v}{\sin. v}=K-\tfrac{2}{3}\frac{K^3-1}{K+1}; \qquad (12)$$

and the corresponding value of F'' is

$$F=r^2\Big(\tfrac{1}{2}(K^2-1)(1+\frac{v}{\sin. v}\cos. v)-\tfrac{1}{3}(K^3-1)\Big) \quad (13)$$

These expressions establish the highly important generalizations that, in all similar arches having the ratio K of the two radii constant,—

1st. The thrust is proportional to the square of the radius of the intrados, or to the square of any other linear dimension;

2d. The angle of rupture is constant.

Let u represent the numerator of the second member of equation (11).

Let z represent the denominator of the second member of equation (11).

The condition that F'', $=\frac{u}{z}$, shall be a maximum, gives

$zdu-udz=0$; or $\frac{u}{z}=\frac{du}{dz}$. In this way (13) was obtained.

The value of v obtained by trial from (12) and substituted in (13), gives the true thrust. In this way, M. Petit has calculated table A, giving, either directly or by proportional parts, the horizontal thrust and the angle of rupture for all values of K; that is, for all semi-circular arches which have a constant thickness, or the intrados and extrados parallel.

29. To illustrate the march of F'' through the quadrant, as we assign to K a particular value, and to v in equation (11) a succession of values, we have calculated

the following table, of which the last column, to make the results more tangible, gives the values of F'' in pounds; r being taken at 10 feet, and each unit multiplied by 150, the assumed weight of a cubic foot of masonry. $K=1.20$; $r=10$ feet; $R=12$ feet.

$v=10°$	$F''=r^2\times.013855=$	$10\times10\times150$	$\times$	$.013855=$ 208.00	pounds.
" 20°	" $r^2\times.044678=$	15000	$\times$	$.044678=$ 670.00	"
" 30°	" $r^2\times.075111=$	15000	$\times$	$.075111=1127.00$	"
" 40°	" $r^2\times.096668=$	15000	$\times$	$.096668=1450.00$	"
" 50°	" $r^2\times.108370=$	15000	$\times$	$.108370=1625.55$	"
" 55°	" $r^2\times.110980=$	15000	$\times$	$.110980=1664.70$	"
" 57°	" $r^2\times.111470=$	15000	$\times$	$.111470=1672.05$	"
" 60°	" $r^2\times.111700=$	15000	$\times$	$.111700=1675.50$	"
" 63°	" $r^2\times.111390=$	15000	$\times$	$.111390=1670.85$	"
" 65°	" $r^2\times.110746=$	15000	$\times$	$.110746=1661.19$	"
" 70°	" $r^2\times.108160=$	15000	$\times$	$.108160=1662.00$	"
" 80°	" $r^2\times.099360=$	15000	$\times$	$.099360=1490.00$	"
" 90°	" $r^2\times.085660=$	15000	$\times$	$.085660=1285.00$	"

The angle of maximum thrust is about 60°, and near that angle the variations of F'' are very small,—only $53\frac{1}{2}$ pounds from 50° to 70°. The exact value of the angle of rupture or angle of maximum thrust, is a matter of no importance.

30. If we suppose $v=0$ in equation (10), the thrust becomes nothing. The same supposition, $v=0$, in (12) gives.

$$3K^2-K^3=2$$

from which we deduce two positive roots,

$$K=1\text{; and, }K=2.732$$

For these two values of K, there is no thrust, and no angle of rupture, except that of the key.

The first value, $K=\dfrac{R}{r}=1$, corresponds to an arch infinitely thin, without weight, and therefore without thrust.

The second value, K=2.732, corresponds to arches of great thickness, in which, however small we make the angle v, there can be no thrust, because the center of gravity of the segment resting on any joint, will fall within the intrados of that joint.

For all values of K greater than 2.732, the thrust would be negative; that is, it would require a positive force to turn over any voussoir if one half the arch were to stand by itself. We are here speaking of rotation. Such arches have a very decided thrust from the tendency of the upper voussoirs to slide upon their beds.

EFFECT OF MORTAR.

31. Let us now resume equation (3).

$$F''=\frac{Sp}{y}-\tfrac{1}{6}c\frac{(d^2+d'^2)}{y};$$

an expression of which the maximum value will give the thrust as modified or diminished by the adhesion of mortar.

We have $d=d'=R-r=r(K-1)$; and $y=r(K-\cos. v)$; hence $\frac{c(d^2+d'^2)}{6y}=\tfrac{1}{3}rc\frac{(K-1)^2}{K-\cos. v}$.

To illustrate the effect of the mortar, let us again take up the arch corresponding to $K=1.20$, art. 29. Let us suppose the adhesion of mortar to be 3000 pounds per square foot, and the weight of a cubic foot of masonry 150 pounds;

giving, art. 16, $c=\frac{3000}{150}=20$; and reducing

$$\tfrac{1}{3}rc\frac{(K-1)^2}{K-\cos. v} \text{ to } r\frac{0.8}{3}\times\frac{1}{1.20-\cos. v}$$

Recapitulating the table given in art. 29, and subtracting from each value of F'' the effect of mortar corresponding to the same value of v, we have—

			Pounds.	Pounds.	Pounds.
$v=10°$	$F'=$	$r^2\times.013855-r\times1.2392=$	$208.00-$	$1651.00=$	-1443.00
" 20°	"	$r^2\times.044678-r\times1.0244=$	$670.00-$	$1537.00=$	$-\ 867.00$
" 30°	"	$r^2\times.075111-r\times\ .8000=$	$1125.00-$	$1200.00=$	$-\ 75.00$
" 40°	"	$r^2\times.096668-r\times\ .6145=$	$1450.00-$	$922.00=$	$+\ 528.00$
" 50°	"	$r^2\times.108370-r\times\ .4800=$	$1625.55-$	$720.00=$	$+\ 905.55$
" 60°	"	$r^2\times.111700-r\times\ .3810=$	$1675.50-$	$571.50=$	1104.00
" 70°	"	$r^2\times.108160-r\times\ .3110=$	$1622.00-$	$467.00=$	1155.00
" 80°	"	$r^2\times.099360-r\times\ .2600=$	$1490.00-$	$390.00=$	1100.00
" 90°	"	$r^2\times.085660-r\times\ .2200=$	$1285.00-$	$330.00=$	955.00

The true thrust or greatest value of F'' corresponds now, we see, to about 70°, and is reduced from 1675 pounds to 1155 pounds.

32. We simplify the calculation, without any sensible error, by supposing v, in the term involving the adhesion of mortar, equal to 60°, which, in general, differs but little from the angle of maximum thrust. This gives cos. $v=\frac{1}{2}$. We shall therefore be able, with little labor, to correct the thrust, as given by the 4th column of table A, or obtained by a direct calculation, when we assign to the adhesion of mortar a particular value.

Let C represent the decimal of that column, or the decimal obtained by calculation,—such that $r^2\times C$ is equal to the maximum thrust without regard to mortar. We have, as the thrust diminished by mortar,

$$F=r^2\times C-\tfrac{2}{3}rc\frac{(K-1)^2}{2K-1} \qquad (14)$$

The numerical factor, $\frac{2}{3}\,\frac{(K-1)^2}{2K-1}=C'$, is very easily calculated when we know the value of K. For instance, $K=1.20$, gives $C'=.01905$; and (14) becomes, substituting for C' this value, and for C the value given by table A,—

$$F=r^2\times.1114-r\times c\times.01905,$$

which reduces, when $c=20$, to $F=r^2\times.1114-r\times.381,$

" " " $r=10$ feet to $F=11.14-3.81=7.33=1100$ pounds,

differing slightly from the thrust above given for the same case; our calculation not giving precisely the tabular value of the thrust.

33. Equation (14), which can be put under the form $F=r^2\times C-r\times cC'$, leads to this generalization.

While the thrust of similar arches ($K=\frac{R}{r}$ being constant), independently of the mortar, increases as the square of the radius of the intrados, the effect due to the mortar increases only as the first power of that radius. Consequently, in arches of large span, the effect of mortar becomes insensible; and in arches of small span, this effect may reduce the thrust to nothing.

Placing the second member of (14) equal to zero, we have at once the radius of the intrados corresponding to an arch without thrust,

$$r^2C=\tfrac{2}{3}rc\frac{(K-1)^2}{2K-1} \text{ giving } r=0\text{; and } r=\frac{c}{C}\times\frac{\frac{2}{3}(K-1)^2}{2K-1}=c\times\frac{C'}{C}$$

If K=1.20, we have, from table A, $C=.1114$, and by calculation $C'=.01905$. If we furthermore suppose $c=20$, we have $r=3'.42$.

This corresponds to an arch of 6'.84 span and a little more than 8 inches thick.

If $K=1.50$; $c=20$, we have as the radius of an arch without thrust, $r=9'.66$.

If $K=2$; $c=20$, we have $r=34'.14$.

The general principles announced above relative to the effect of mortar upon similar arches of different spans, are, it is evident, of universal application, whatever be the curves of the extrados and intrados.

EFFECT OF SURCHARGE.

34. Equation (2)

$F' = \frac{Sp + S'p' + ..}{y} = \frac{Sp}{y} + \frac{S'p' + S''p'' + ..}{y}$, gives the force F' necessary to sustain any supposed segment of the arch when the extrados is loaded with the weights S', S'', &c., with their centers of gravity in vertical lines at the distances p', p'', &c., from the center of rotation, or point m of the intrados.

If the surcharge be continuous, and nearly constant in vertical depth, find in table A the value of

$$\frac{Sp}{y} = r^2 C, \text{ and to this add } \frac{S'p' + S''p'' + \&c.}{R - r \cos. v}$$

calculated according to the circumstances of the case. The sum will be, with sufficient exactness, the thrust increased by the surcharge.

Let the surcharge, reduced in depth, if necessary, to give it the density of the masonry, be of the constant vertical depth t. We shall have—

$$p' = \sin. v(r - \tfrac{1}{2}R) = r \sin. v(1 - \tfrac{1}{2}K);\ S = rtK \sin v;$$

and $\frac{S'p'}{y} = \frac{rtK(2-K)}{2} \times \frac{\sin.^2 v}{K - \cos. v}$; which becomes zero, for all values of v, when $K = 2$, or $R = 2r$. The center of gravity of the surcharge then falls upon m.

The variable factor, $\frac{\sin.^2 v}{K - \cos. v}$, we find by differentiation to be a maximum when $\cos. v = K - \sqrt{K^2 - 1}$; and $\frac{\sin.^2 v}{K - \cos. v} = 2(K - \sqrt{K^2 - 1})$.

We have, therefore, with a very slight error in favor of stability, for the thrust increased by a surcharge of uniform depth,—

$$F = r^2 C + rt \times K(2-K)(K-\sqrt{K^2-1}) \quad (15)$$

in which C is obtained from table A, for the given value of K, and the numerical factor $K(2-K)(K-\sqrt{K^2-1}) = N$, is easily calculated when we know the value of K.

Example; $K=1.20$, which gives $N=.5152$. Table A gives $C=.1114$; hence $F=r^2\times .1114 + rt\times .5152$; suppose $t=\frac{1}{5}r$; we have $F=r^2.1114+r^2.1030=r^2.2144$; that is, when $K=1.20$ the thrust is nearly doubled by a surcharge of uniform thickness $t=\frac{1}{5}r$.

The value of v, which renders $\frac{\sin.^2 v}{K-\cos. v}$ a maximum, never differs more than four degrees from the value of v corresponding to the same value of K in table A; and it is the property of a maximum to exceed but little the adjacent values of the same function. We may therefore regard equation (15) as exact.

Table F gives the values of N for all values of K between 1.02 and 1.42; these values being the same in all circular arches of equal thickness throughout, whatever load they may sustain in addition to this surcharge of constant depth.

Tables A and F, therefore, give the thrust required without calculation. See discussion and use of those tables.

35. Let us take up another variety of the surcharge. Suppose a single column, represented in weight by a surface one unit in width and H in height, to rest upon the crown of the arch. We have, $F'=\frac{Sp}{y}+\frac{H\sin. v}{K-\cos. v}$.

The maximum value of $\frac{Sp}{y}=r^2C$, is given, without regard to surcharge, by table A. The maximum value of $\frac{H\sin. v}{K-\cos. v}$, obtained by the calculus, is $\frac{H}{\sqrt{K^2-1}}$. The true thrust, therefore, with some error in excess, is

$$F = r^2 C + \frac{H}{\sqrt{K^2 - 1}} \qquad (16)$$

It is remarkable that this addition to the thrust, caused by a weight upon the crown of the arch, is independent of r, the radius of the intrados, and therefore constant while K remains the same—that is, in all similar arches. This is also evident from general considerations.

Example. On the crown of an arch, 20 feet in span and 2 feet thick, we wish to throw a column one foot square and 10 feet high, one half being supported by each semi-arch.

We have $K = 1.20$; C, from table A, $= .1114$; $\frac{5}{\sqrt{K^2 - 1}} = 7.54$; $F = r^2 .1114 + 7.54 = 18.68$.

The angle v, in table A, corresponding to $K = 1.20$, is $59°.4$′.

The angle v which renders $\frac{\sin. v}{K - \cos. v}$ a maximum, is given by the relation $\cos. v = \frac{1}{K} = \frac{r}{R} = .83333$; or $v = 33°. 35'$.

The true thrust would correspond to $v =$ about $50°$.

In the above example we commit an estimated error in excess, or in favor of stability, of about five per cent. The error will be less as K increases or H diminishes.

The effect upon the thrust, of a weight placed upon the crown of an arch, is evidently the same in all circular arches, whether otherwise loaded or not.

THRUST OF SEMI-CIRCULAR ARCHES, SLIDING.—INTRADOS AND EXTRADOS PARALLEL.

36. Resume equation (8), art. 20. $P'=S\cot.(a+v)$, an expression for the horizontal force required to prevent the segment whose surface is S from sliding down its bed or lower joint $n\,m$ fig. 5. We have

$$S=\tfrac{1}{2}v(R^2-r^2)\text{ ; and, substituting } Kr \text{ for } R,$$
$$P'=\tfrac{1}{2}r^2(K^2-1)\ v\cot.(a+v).$$

The angle of friction according to Boistard is 37°. 14′; according to Rondelet, 30°. Admitting the latter value, as more favorable to stability, we have.

$$P'=\tfrac{1}{2}r^2(K^2-1)\times v\times\cot.\,(v+30°) \qquad (17)$$

The angle v, corresponding to the maximum value of P', deduced by trial from the condition $\frac{1}{2}\sin.\,2(v+30°)=v$, or directly from equation (17), is a little over 26°, and it is obviously the same for all circular arches which have the extrados and intrados parallel, whatever be the relative parts.

Giving to v this value, 26°, in equation (17), we have,

$$P=r^2\times(K^2-1)\times.15304\,; \qquad (18)$$

from which M. Petit has calculated the sliding thrusts in table A.

It will be seen in that table, of which a full discussion will be given hereafter, that the thrust due to rotation is greater than that due to sliding, for all values of K from 0 to 1.44; and that the thrust due to sliding exceeds the other for all values of K greater than 1.44. This value of K corresponds to an arch of 20 feet span and 4′.40 thick throughout.

EFFECT OF MORTAR.

37. Resume equation (9) :—

$$P' = S \cot.(a+v) - \frac{cd' \cos. a}{\sin.(a+v)},$$

which now becomes

$$P' = \tfrac{1}{2} r^2 (K^2 - 1) v \cot.(a+v) - \frac{cr(K-1)\cos. 30°}{\sin.(v+30°)},$$

let us suppose $K=1.50$, $r=10'$, $c=2$, and find the maximum value of P'.

		POUNDS.
$v=20°$	$P'=r^2 \times .18306 - r \times 1.1305 = 18.306 - 11.305 = 7.001$	$=1050$
" 26°	" $r^2 \times .19130 - r \times 1.0444 = 19.130 - 10.444 = 8.680$	$=1302$
" 30°	" $r^2 \times .18890 - r \times 1.0000 = 18.890 - 10.000 = 8.890$	$=1333$
" 35°	" $r^2 \times .17803 - r \times .9555 = 17.800 - 9.550 = 8.250$	$=1237$

The angle v, corresponding to the maximum value of P', is now about 30°. The effect of the mortar for that angle is $rc(K-1)$; and it is nearly the same for $v=26°$. We have, therefore, this simple formula for the sliding thrust diminished by the adhesion of mortar :—

$$P = r^2 C - rc(K-1); \tag{19}$$

in which C is taken directly from the fifth column of table A, and c is the adhesion of mortar upon a unit of surface —art. 16.

The remarks made in art. 33, relative to the effect of mortar upon similar arches of different spans, are equally applicable here. The second member of (19) placed equal to zero, gives, as the radius of an arch without sliding thrust, $r=0$, and $r=\frac{c(K-1)}{C}$.

For $c=2$; $K=1.50$, which gives, table A, $C=.19130$; we find $r=5'.227$;
For $c=2$; $K=1.20$, " " " $C=.06733$; " $r=5'.940$.

If we suppose c=20, as in art. 33, we have, as the

radius of an arch without sliding thrust, for $K=1.50$, $r=52'.27$; for $K=1.20$, $r=59'.4$.

The effect of mortar to prevent sliding is, we see, far greater than its power to resist rotation. In the latter case it has full effect only at the outer edges of the opening joints, and its influence is in most cases still further reduced by the small leverage with which it acts.

38. It is only in heavy arches, in which the thickness is nearly half the radius of the intrados, that the effective thrust is determined by any tendency to sliding.

And in such arches we can not rely upon any adhesion of joints, unless the mortar is strongly hydraulic, and considerable time has been allowed for it to set before removing the centering.

EFFECT OF SURCHARGE UPON THE SLIDING THRUST.

39. The general equation applicable to this case is

$$P'=S\cot.(v+30°)+S'\cot.(v+30°).$$

We can always suppose the vertical depth of the surcharge, as far, say, as 25° or 30° from the crown, to be constant. Let t be that depth. We have $S'=R\sin.v\times t$ $=rtK\sin.v$, and $S'\cot.(v+30°)=rtK\sin.v\cot.(v+30°)$. The maximum value of this expression corresponds very nearly to $v=25°$; while the maximum value of $S'\cot.(v+30°)$ corresponds to $v=26°$.

Adding the two maxima together, we have, with a very slight error in favor of stability, the sliding thrust increased by a surcharge of uniform vertical depth,—

$$P=r^2C+rtK\times.29592. \qquad (20)$$

C is to be taken from the fifth column of table A, opposite the given value of K.

The numerical coefficient $K \times .29592$ is given in the last column of table F, for values of K ranging from 1.35 to 1.50, corresponding to arches of large span in which the sliding exceeds the rotation thrust.

The thrust, increased by surcharge and diminished by mortar, is,

$$P = r^2 C + rtK \times .29592 - rc(K-1), \qquad (21)$$

C being taken, as before, from the fifth column of table A.

Example. $K=2$; $c=2$; $t=5'$; $r=10'$; weight of a cubic foot of masonry = 150 pounds. Table A gives $C=.45912$.

$$P = r^2 \times .45912 + rt \times 2 \times .29592 - 2r$$
$$= 45.912 + 29.592 - 20. = 8325 \text{ pounds.}$$

If $c=o$, $P=11325$ pounds.

40. Table A begins with $K=2.732$, above which the *rotation* thrust is less than nothing. The sliding thrust, however goes on increasing as K increases.

Equation (21), expressed more generally, becomes

$$P = r^2 \times (K^2-1) \times .15304 + rtK \times .29592 - rc(K-1) \quad (21)'$$

in which r, K, t, c, may have any values whatever: t is the mean depth of the surcharge, whether consisting of one or more masses; but in estimating the value of t, we should confine our attention to that part of the surcharge which is over the extrados within 30° of the summit.

41. In the investigation of the true thrust, as modified by surcharge and mortar, three distinct cases may arise.

I. It may be evidently due to rotation. See art. 31, and following.

II. It may evidently be due to sliding. See art. 36, and following.

III. It may be doubtful, and require an investigation of both cases.

The greatest of the forces, F, P, required respectively to prevent rotation and sliding, will, in all cases, be the true thrust.

The third or doubtful class will be very small in the hands of those who have made themselves somewhat familiar with the subject, and especially with the tables contained in this paper.

THICKNESS OF PIER.

42. The horizontal thrust at the key enters as an element into two questions: 1st, the thickness of the pier; 2d, the ability of the material of the arch to stand the pressure at the summit and at the reins. The latter question we shall take up hereafter.

We have shown how to obtain this thrust, both for rotation and sliding. The greatest of these two, which are found all calculated in table A, is the true thrust.

We defer for the present the supposition of any adhesion of mortar, or of a surcharge.

Let F represent the thrust; C the greatest of the decimals in columns 4, 5, opposite the given value of K. We have $F=r^2\times C$.

Let h represent the height of the pier from the base to the springing line, fig. 8; l the lever arm of the thrust; e the thickness of the pier, δ the coefficient of stability. We have $l=h+Ca=h+Kr$.

We must give to the pier such dimensions that its moment, increased by the moment of the semi-arch, shall be equal to the moment of the thrust multiplied by the coefficient of stability.

Let $n=\frac{1}{4}\pi(K^2-1)$; $m=\frac{1}{3}(K^3-1)$;

then nr^2=surface of semi-arch;

mr^3=moment of semi-arch in reference to C;

$(n-m)r^3$=moment of semi-arch in reference to A;

$nr^2\times e+(n-m)r^3$=moment of semi-arch in reference to E or E'.

We have, therefore, expanding equation (5),—

$$\tfrac{1}{2}he^2+nr^2e+(n-m)r^3=\delta Cr^2(Kr+h) \qquad (22)$$

of which the solution gives

$$\frac{e}{r}=-n\frac{r}{h}+\sqrt{n^2\frac{r^2}{h^2}+2(\delta CK+m-n)\frac{r}{h}+2\delta C} \qquad (23)$$

Table B, calculated by M. Petit, gives the reduced form of this equation for all values of K between 1.10 and 2, on the supposition of strict equilibrium, $\delta=1$; the value of C being taken in each case from table A. To modify any one of these equations by introducing the coefficient δ, we have only to add, under the radical, to the coefficient of $\frac{r}{h}$, $2CK(\delta-1)$, and to substitute for the term independent of $\frac{r}{h}$, the same term multiplied by the coefficient of stability.

Example. $K=1.50$. C, being always the greatest of the decimals in columns 4, 5, is .19130

The coefficient of $\frac{r}{h}$, under the radical, is .19370

To this we must add $2CK(\delta-1)=$ $(\delta-1)\times.57390$

The term independent of $\frac{r}{h}$, is .38260

For this we must substitute $\delta\times.38260$

The equation will then read,

$$\frac{e}{r}=-.9817+\frac{r}{h}\sqrt{.9638\frac{r^2}{h^2}+(.1937+(\delta-1).5739)\frac{r}{h}+\delta\times.3826}.$$

LIMIT THICKNESS OF PIERS.

43. Mere inspection of equation (23) shows that when the height of the pier becomes infinite, we have

$$e=r\times\sqrt{2\delta C}$$

that is, the thickness of the pier whose height is infinite must be equal to the square root of double the horizontal thrust multiplied by the coefficient of stability.

This interesting principle was discovered experimentally by Rondelet. It is universal—applicable to arches of every form, and under every variety of circumstances. The moments of the thrust and of the pier increase in nearly the same proportion with the height of the pier.

This limit thickness is not very much greater than the thickness required for moderate heights. Slightly changing his radius, we take from M. Petit the following illustration; $r=10'$; $R=12'.50$; $K=1.25$.

	Strict equilibrium.	Coefficient of 1.90.
$h=7.60$ feet.	$e=2.5000$ feet.	$e=5.6111$ feet.
" 10.00 "	" 2.8190 "	" 5.7995 "
" 15.00 "	" 3.3180 "	" 6.0887 "
" 20.00 "	" 3.6407 "	" 6.2640 "
" 25.00 "	" 3.8657 "	" 6.3825 "
" 50.00 "	" 4.4012 "	" 6.6550 "
" 250.00 "	" 4.9235 "	" 6.9147 "
" infinite.	" 5.0687 "	" 6.9865 "

The whole increase of the practical thickness, $\delta=1.90$, from $h=10$ feet to $h=$infinity, is but little more than 14 inches.

Table A gives the limit thickness for all values of K from 1.10 to 2.00, both for strict equilibrium and for a coefficient of 1.90—$\delta=1$, and $\delta=1.90$.

We thus have the means of criticising many existing cases, and may often be spared much labor and research.

44. If we wish to take into account the adhesion of mortar, or a load upon the back of the arch, the thrust, r^2C, which enters equations (22), (23), will no longer be furnished by table A alone, but must be determined according to the circumstances of the case, as already fully explained in this section.

45. If we take into consideration the effect of mortar only, the thrust is given by the greatest of the two forces—

$F=r^2C-\frac{2}{3}rc\frac{(K-1)^2}{2K-1}$; eq. (14), art. 32; C from column 4, table A.

$P=r^2C-rc(K-1)$; eq. (19), art. 37; C from column 5, table A.

F representing the greatest of these forces, the thickness of pier is given by (23), when we have substituted F for r^2C, or $\frac{F}{r^2}$ for C. (23) becomes

$$\frac{e}{r}=-n\frac{r}{h}+\sqrt{n^2\frac{r^2}{h^2}+2\left(\frac{\delta FK}{r^2}+m-n\right)\frac{r}{h}+\frac{2\delta F}{r^2}} \qquad (23)'$$

The effect of surcharge upon the thickness of pier, will come up in the discussion of other arches.

DISCUSSION OF TABLE A.

46. This table gives, either directly or by proportional parts, for all values of $K=\frac{R}{r}$ between 1 and 2.732.

1st. The angle of rupture.—Rotation.

2d. The ratio, C, of the thrust to the square of the radius of the intrados, in the case of rotation and the case of sliding.

3d. The ratio, $\sqrt{2\delta C}$, of the limit thickness of pier to the radius of the intrados, for the case of strict equilibrium, and for the coefficient of stability of 1.90,—$\delta=1$, and $\delta=1.90$.

It will be seen that the angle of rupture, beginning with zero for $K=2.732$, becomes $54^\circ\ 27'$ for $K=2.10$, attains its greatest value, 64° 9′ for $K=1.50$, varies between 54° 27′ and 64° 9′ for all the fortification arches in common use, that is, for all the values of K between 2.10 and 1.12, and ends with zero again for $K=1$.

It will also be seen that the thrust due to sliding is greater than the thrust due to rotation, for all values of K greater than 1.44; and that the former is less than the latter, for all smaller values of K. We must in all cases, to obtain the true thrust, select the greatest of these two values.

Calling the greatest of these values (or the greatest of the decimals in columns 4, 5) C, the limit thickness of pier is

$e=r\sqrt{2C}$ for strict equilibrium.
$e=r\sqrt{3.80C}$ for the coefficient of stability 1.90.
$e=r\sqrt{2\delta C}$ for any coefficient of stability δ.

As we have $r\sqrt{2\delta C}=r\sqrt{2\delta}\times\sqrt{C}$, it is obvious that, while the thrust increases in a geometrical ratio, the limit thickness increases only in an arithmetical ratio; and that a small error in the thrust becomes much smaller in the pier.

We are at liberty to suppose r, the radius of the intrados, to remain the same throughout the table. Assuming this, we see that the greatest possible thrust that can be caused by rotation in any arch of the radius r, is $r^2\times.17535$, and corresponds to $K=1.58$.

For instance, if $r=10$ feet, we shall have $K=1.58$, $R=15'.80$, and $R-r$, or the thickness of the arch $=5'.80$.

We must not fail, however, to notice that the greater thrust, when $K=1.58$, is given in the column of sliding.

47. By means of this table, M. Petit has settled this question: What is the thinnest arch that can stand upon its springing lines?

It is evidently necessary that the moment of the thrust should not exceed the moment of the semi-arch, both taken in reference to the exterior edge of the joint of the springing lines.

Now, the moment of the semi-arch is

$$r^3(\tfrac{1}{4}\pi K(K^2-1)-\tfrac{1}{3}(K^3-1))$$

The thrust is r^2C; its moment r^3KC.

Value of $K=\frac{R}{r}$.	Ratio of the diameter to the thickness.	Moment of stability of the semi-arch upon its springing lines.	Moment of the horizontal thrust.
2.000	2.000	$r^3\times 2.379075$	$r^3\times 0.918240$
1.500	4.000	$r^3\times 0.680956$	$r^3\times 0.286250$
1.300	6.666	$r^3\times 0.305502$	$r^3\times 0.186290$
1.200	10.000	$r^3\times 0.172024$	$r^3\times 0.133608$
1.150	13.333	$r^3\times 0.117659$	$r^3\times 0.105528$
1.120	16.666	$r^3\times 0.088806$	$r^3\times 0.087763$
1.114	17.544	$r^3\times 0.083320$	$r^3\times 0.083434$
1.100	20.000	$r^3\times 0.071093$	$r^3\times 0.074292$
1.050	40.000	$r^3\times 0.031954$	$r^3\times 0.040034$
1.010	200.000	$r^3\times 0.005844$	$r^3\times 0.008980$

The inspection of this table shows that the arch has abundant stability for $K=1.30$ and upwards; that its moment is in equilibrium with the moment of the thrust, for $K=1.114$ nearly; and that the thrust prevails more and more for smaller values of K.

This value, $K=1.114$, corresponds to an arch of which the span is a little more than $17\frac{1}{2}$ times the thickness; and that is the thinnest or lightest arch that can possibly stand upon its springing line. A thinner arch would be impossible.

This fact has been confirmed by experiment.

SECTION III.

SEMI-CIRCULAR ARCHES OF 180° WITH A ROOF-SHAPED SURCHARGE UPON THE CROWN.

48. The powder-magazine arch, fig. 9, belongs to this class. To make the inclosure bomb-proof, a surcharge of concrete, or other hard material, and sometimes of earth, also, is added to the covering of the arch proper.

We suppose, for the present, the plane of the roof on each side of the central ridge, to be tangent to the proper extrados of the arch, as it frequently is in practice, and the the joint of rupture to rise vertically above the extrados through the surcharge. We also suppose the thrust to act always at a, the extrados at the crown, the mass of masonry or other material above acting only as a weight.

Let I be the angle between the slope of the roof and a vertical; v still the angle between the joint of rupture and a vertical; r the radius of the intrados; R the radius of the extrados, supposed to be equally distant from the intrados throughout; $K=\frac{R}{r}$.

We have, as the general expression of the horizontal force required to keep any voussoir $A'\,a\,b\,m\,n\,p\,A'$ from falling by rotation round the point m,

$$F'=r^2\frac{\sin.^2 v}{6(K-\cos. v)}\left\{\frac{K^2}{\sin. I}\Big(6-3K-(3-2K)\sin.(I+v)\Big)-\left(\frac{3v}{\sin. v}-\frac{1}{\cos.^2\frac{1}{2}v}\right)\right\}^* \qquad (24)$$

* Fig 9. $CA'=\frac{R}{\sin. I}=B$; $np=\frac{R-R\sin.(I+v)}{\sin. I}=B'$; $R\sin. v=h=$ perpendicular distance between CA' and np; $h\frac{B+2B'}{3(B+B')}=$the distance of the center of gravity of $CA'pn$ from CA'; $h\times\frac{B+B'}{2}\left(r\sin. v-h\frac{(B+2B')}{3(B+B')}\right)=$moment of trapezoid $CA'pn$ on $m=\frac{1}{6}\left(\frac{2R-R\sin.(I+v)}{\sin. I}\times R\sin.^2 v\times 3r-R^2\sin.^2 v\left(\frac{3R-2R\sin.(I+v)}{\sin. I}\right)\right)=\frac{1}{6}r^3\sin.^2 v$

The maximum value of this expression must be found for any particular arch by trial.

M. Petit makes an application of this formula, to the powder magazine of Vauban, of the following dimensions, viz.: $I=49°.\ 7'.\ 17''$; $R=5.035$ metres$=16.5148$ feet; $r=4.0605$ metres$=13.3184$ feet; $K=1.24$.

These values of I and K substituted in the preceding equation, give

$$\text{for } v=53° \ldots F''=0.229290\times r^2;$$
$$\text{“ } v=54° \ldots F''=0.229381\times r^2=F;$$
$$\text{“ } v=55° \ldots F''=0.229295\times r^2.$$

Near the angle of maximum thrust, and as far as six or eight degrees on both sides of that angle, the variations of F'' are very small. The exact determination of that angle is not important. It may be regarded in the present case as 54°. The thrust is $F=0.229381\times r^2=40.69$ feet.

If one cubic foot of the masonry weigh 150 pounds, the thrust is equivalent to the effort necessary to sustain 40.69 $\times 150$ pounds$=6103$ pounds.

EFFECT OF MORTAR UPON THE ROTATION THRUST.

49. To obtain the thrust diminished by the adhesion of mortar upon the joints, we have only to subtract from the value of the second member of (24), corresponding to each assigned value of v, the expression (see equation (3) and art. 15, 31),—

$\left\{\frac{K^2}{\sin. I}(6-3K-(3-2K)\sin. I+v)\right\}$. Moment of sector, $C\,b\,m$, on $m=\frac{1}{2}vr^2\left(r\sin. v - \frac{2}{3}\times\frac{r^2 2\sin.^2\frac{1}{2}v}{rv}\right)=\frac{1}{6}r^3\sin.^2 v\left(\frac{3v}{\sin. v}-\frac{1}{\cos.^2\frac{1}{2}v}\right)$; $4\sin.^2\frac{1}{2}v=\frac{\sin.^2 v}{\cos.^2\frac{1}{2}v}$; $F''\times am'=F''\times r(K-\cos. v)$=moment of trapezoid $C\,A'\,p\,n$—moment of sector $C\,b\,m$; hence F''=as above, (24).

$$\frac{c(d^2+d'^2)}{6y}=\frac{rc(K-1)^2}{3(K-\cos. v)}$$

The resulting maximum will be the true thrust.

But we can simplify this expression, as in art. 32, by supposing v, in the term involving the adhesion of mortar, to be always 60°, which differs but little from the angle of maximum thrust in heavy semi-circular arches, however loaded. See the various tables contained in this paper.

Suppose we have obtained by direct calculation, or from tables A, C, D, or F, the thrust r^2C without regard to mortar. The thrust diminished by mortar is given by equation (14),

$$F=r^2C-\tfrac{2}{3}rc\frac{(K-1)^2}{2K-1} \tag{14}$$

The effect of adhesion depends solely upon the dimensions of the arch proper, and is not affected by its load. It is, therefore, the same in all equal arches however different may be their loads; and the general conclusions of art. 33 are applicable to all arches, as already stated.

If the joints are unequal, as often happens, we may still suppose $v=60°$, and d' representing the length of the joint of rupture, d the length of the vertical joint, the thrust will be

$$F=r^2C-\frac{c(d^2+d'^2)}{6(d+\frac{1}{2}r)} \tag{14)$'$}$$

C being the number which, multiplied by r^2, gives the thrust independently of mortar; c the force, in pounds, required to separate a square unit of the joint, divided by the weight of a cubic unit of masonry.

Example: the magazine of Vauban, art. 48.

$$F=r^2C-\tfrac{2}{3}rc\frac{(K-1)^2}{2K-1}=r^2\times0.229381-r\times0.519=40.69$$

feet $-$ 6.91 feet $=$ 6103 pounds $-$ 1036 pounds $=$ 5067 pounds.

THE EFFECT OF SURCHARGE UPON THE ROTATION THRUST.

50. To obtain the thrust as modified by a load or surcharge of the density of the masonry, and of the constant vertical depth t, we must add to the second member of (24), see art. 34,

$$\frac{S'p'}{y}=\frac{rtK(2-K)}{2}\times\frac{\sin.^2 v}{K-\cos. v}$$

of which the maximum value is, art. 34,

$$rtK(2-K)(K-\sqrt{K^2-1})=rtN.$$

The effect of this surcharge depends solely upon the dimensions of the arch proper, and is not affected by any other load. Suppose we have obtained by calculation, or from tables A, C, D, or F, the thrust r^2C without regard to surcharge, we have

$$F=r^2C+rtN. \qquad (15)'$$

We have given, in the 13th column of table F, the values of N corresponding to all values of K between 1.02 and 1.42, applicable to all semi-circular arches, whatever load they may carry in addition to the surcharge of constant depth.

This mode of treating the surcharge, leads to a small error in excess, or in favor of stability; for while r^2C is the thrust independently of surcharge, calculated at a particular angle, rtN is the maximum effect of the surcharge, corresponding, generally, to some other angle.

The true thrust would correspond to some intermediate angle, and would be somewhat less than the sum of the two maxima. The difference, however, in the two angles, is very small; in the heavy arches of fortifications never exceeding six or eight degrees.—See table F. The error, therefore, always in excess, is very small, it being the property of a maximum to exceed but little the neighboring values of the same function. This principle has been illustrated in art. 29.

51. The weight of a single column resting upon the crown of the arch, we can always represent by a surface one unit in width and H in height.

The thrust increased by such a weight, see art. 35, is, $F=r^2C+\frac{H}{\sqrt{K^2-1}}$, r^2C being the thrust independently of surcharge, obtained from table F or by direct calculation.

For a more extended discussion of this case, see art. 35. All the remarks there made are equally applicable here.

THE SLIDING THRUST.

52. The general expression of the horizontal force necessary to prevent the segment whose surface is S, from sliding down its lower joint $n\ m$, is, equation (8), $P'=S$ cot. $(a+v)$; which, in the present case, becomes, fig. 9,

$$P'=r^2\frac{\sin. v}{\sin. I \text{ tang. } (a+v)}\left\{K^2\left(1-\tfrac{1}{2}\sin. (I+v)\right)-\tfrac{1}{2}\sin. I\frac{v}{\sin. v}\right\}^{*} \ldots (25)$$

Assuming $a=30°$, I and K being known by the conditions of the problem, we must find, by assigning, in succession, different values to v, the maximum value of P' in (25).

The greatest of the two maxima, F, P, (24), (25), will be the true thrust.

$$* \; S=\tfrac{1}{2}\left(\frac{R}{\sin. I}+\frac{R-R\sin. (I+v)}{\sin. I}\right)\times R\sin. v-\tfrac{1}{2}vr^2.$$

THE EFFECT OF MORTAR UPON THE SLIDING THRUST.

53. The sliding thrust diminished by the adhesion of mortar, is the maximum value of P' in equation (9)— $P'=S \cot. (a+v)-\frac{cd' \cos. a}{\sin. (a+v)}$. The angle v which renders S cot. $(a+v)$ a maximum, or which corresponds to the true sliding thrust independently of mortar, varies in the several arches, from 29° when the roof is horizontal, to 22° when the roof is inclined 45° on each side of the central ridge. As in art. 37, we can, without sensible error, suppose v, in the term involving the adhesion of mortar, always equal to 30°. We have then, this formula for the sliding thrust diminished by the adhesion of mortar,

$$P=r^2C-rc(K-1),$$

in which C is taken from table C, D, or F, or obtained by direct calculation, and the last term is the effect of mortar. For illustration of this subject, see art. 37.

The effect of adhesion depends solely upon the length of the joint, and is therefore the same in all equal arches however loaded.

The above formula will seldom be needed; for it is only in very heavy arches that the sliding can exceed the rotation thrust, and in such arches it would hardly be safe to rely upon any adhesion of mortar.

EFFECT OF SURCHARGE UPON THE SLIDING THRUST.

54. The general equation applicable to this case is $P'=S \cot. (v+30°)+S' \cot. (v+30°)$. We can always suppose the surcharge S', which is entirely above the roof of the arch, to have a constant vertical depth as far as 25° or 30° from the crown. Let t be that depth. We have

$S'=t\times R\times \sin. v=rtK \sin. v$; and $S' \cot. (v+30°)=rtK \sin. v\times \cot. (v+30°)$, of which the maximum value, corresponding very nearly to $v=25°$, is, $rtK\times 0.29592$. Adding the two maxima together, we have, with a slight error in favor of stability,

$$P=r^2C+rtK\times 0.29592 \qquad (20)'$$

r^2C being the sliding thrust independently of surcharge, obtained from tables C, D, or F, or by direct calculation. This formula has already been given, art. 39, equation (20), and is applicable to all circular arches however loaded—always giving a result slightly in excess.

We have given in table F the value of $K\times 0.29592$, corresponding to values of K which render the *sliding* greater than the *rotation thrust*, applicable to all semicircular arches, tables A, C, D, F, and to segmental arches which have the angle at the center greater than 25°.

This mode of treating the surcharge is precisely like that adopted in art. 50. Here too, the error, always in excess, is very small; for the angle v, which gives the sliding thrust without regard to surcharge, varies, in the several arches, from 22° to 29°, never differing more than 4° from the angle 25°, which renders the effect of the surcharge a maximum.

The true thrust will be the greatest of the two maxima F, P, (15)', (20)'.

GENERAL REMARKS ON TABLES C, D, F.

55. M. Petit has applied the general equations (24), (25), to the two extreme cases in which the roofs are, respectively, horizontal and inclined 45°; limits between which probably all powder-magazine arches are comprised. Tables C and D contain his results. We have filled up the interval, between $I=45°$ and $I=90°$, with eight

columns, I varying at intervals of 5°. The results are embodied in table F, which gives directly, or by proportional parts, the thrust of all circular arches of common use, whose loads are bounded on top by two symmetrical planes extending as far, at least, as from the crown to the reins, or angle of rupture—applicable to all semi-circular roof-covered magazine arches, and to almost all full-circle stone and brick bridges. See discussion of that table.

For the purpose of general illustration, and as introductory to tables C and D, we give the application of (24), (25), to the two cases mentioned above, $I=45°$, and $I=90°$.

ROOF INCLINED FORTY-FIVE DEGREES.

56. Make $I=45°$ in equation (24). It becomes..

$$F'=r^2\frac{\sin.^2 v}{6(K-\cos. v)}\left\{K^2\sqrt{2}\Big(6-3K-(3-2K)\sin.(45°+v)\Big)-\left(\frac{3v}{\sin. v}-\frac{1}{\cos.^2 \frac{1}{2} v}\right)\right\} \quad (26)$$

Suppose, furthermore $a=30°$ in equation (25), and for v substitute 22°, which corresponds, very nearly, to the maximum value of P', or the horizontal sliding thrust, we have

$$P=r^2(0.2234\times K^2-0.14999) \quad (27)$$

By means of these two formulæ, and of another, $e=r\sqrt{2\delta C}$, art. 43, M. Petit has calculated table C, analogous to table A, giving, for all values of K between 1.05 and 2, the angle of rupture, the thrust—rotation and sliding, and the limit thickness of pier required for strict equilibrium and for the co-efficient of stability 2. See discussion of that table.

M. Petit has proved conclusively, by a course of reasoning like that given in art. 47, that this kind of arch,

$I=45°$, is always stable upon its springing line; that is, that however thin the arch may be, the moment of the thrust is always less than the moment of the semi-arch in relation to the exterior edge of the springing line.

ROOF HORIZONTAL.

Figure 4.

57. Make $I=90°$ in equation (24). It becomes

$$F'=r^2\frac{\sin.^2 v}{6(K-\cos. v)}\left\{K^2(6-3K-(3-2K)\cos. v)-\left(\frac{3v}{\sin. v}-\frac{1}{\cos.^2\frac{1}{2}v}\right)\right\} \quad (28)$$

Make $I=90°$, $a=30°$, in (25), and for v substitute $29°$, which corresponds very nearly to the maximum value of P', we have

$$P=r^2(0.16391\times K^2-0.15206) \quad (29)$$

By means of these two formulæ, and of another—$e=r\sqrt{2\delta C}$, M. Petit has calculated table D analogous to tables A and C. See discussion of that table.

By a table similar to that given in 47, M. Petit has demonstrated that the moment of the semi-arch exceeds the moment of the thrust, both taken in reference to the exterior edge of the springing line, for all values of K greater than 1.0435; and that the moment of the thrust is the greater for all smaller values of K. The thinnest arch therefore, of this kind, having a surcharge limited to the horizontal line tangent to the extrados at the crown, figs. 4, 7, that can stand upon its springing lines, is one whose span is about 46 times its thickness.

DISCUSSION OF TABLE C—THE ROOF INCLINED FORTY-FIVE DEGREES.

58. After explaining the use of tables C, D, and F, we shall show how to apply the results to the determination of the thickness of pier.

Table C gives, either directly, or by proportional parts, for all values of K between 1.05 and 2 :—

1st. The angle of rupture, or of maximum thrust.—Rotation.

2d. The decimal C, column 4, which, multiplied by the square of the radius of the intrados, gives the horizontal thrust on the supposition of rupture by rotation.

3d. The decimal C, column 5, which, multiplied by r^2, gives the thrust on the supposition of rupture by sliding.

4th. Columns 6, 7; the value of the radical, $\sqrt{2\delta C}$, which, multiplied by the radius of the intrados, gives the limit thickness of pier in the case of strict equilibrium, $\delta=1$, and with the "stability of Vauban," $\delta=2$.

It will be seen that the thrust due to sliding is greater than the thrust due to rotation for all values of K greater than 1.42, and that the rotation thrust is the greater for all smaller values of K.

Calling the greatest of these values (or the greatest of the decimals in columns 4, 5) C the limit thickness of pier, or the thickness required for an infinite height, is

$$e=r\sqrt{2C}; \text{ for strict equilibrium; } \delta=1.$$
$$e=r\sqrt{4C}; \text{ for the stability of Vauban; } \delta=2.$$

The greatest of the decimals in columns 4, 5, must always be selected as giving the true thrust.

The thrust given in table C for $K=1.29$, is double the thrust in table A for the same value of K. For larger values of K the thrusts of table C are more than double, and for smaller values of K less than double, the thrusts of table A.

Of all arches having the same span and radii, the magazine arch has the greatest thrust. Its span, however, is small, seldom exceeding 30 feet.

DISCUSSION OF TABLE D—THE SURCHARGE HORIZONTAL.

59. Table D, analogous to A and C, gives directly or by proportional parts, for all values of K between 1 and 2.

1st. The angle of rupture, or of maximum thrust.—Rotation.

2d. The decimal C, columns 4 and 5, which, multiplied by the square of the radius of the intrados, gives the horizontal thrust on the supposition of rupture by rotation, and by sliding.

3d. The value of the radical $\sqrt{2\delta C}$, columns 6, 7, which, multiplied by the radius of the intrados, gives the limit thickness of pier in the case of strict equilibrium, $\delta=1$ and, with the "stability of Lahire," $\delta=1.90$.

It will be seen that the thrust due to sliding is greater than the thrust due to rotation for all values of K above 1.34, and that the former is less than the latter for all smaller values of K. We must in all cases, to obtain the true thrust, select the larger of these two values.

The angle of rupture for all the usual values of K, in which the thrust is due to rotation, that is, from $K=1.10$ to $K=1.34$, differs from 60° by only 5°; while, for the most common values of K, the difference is less.

The thrust given by table D is equal to the thrust of table A when $K=1.30$.

The thrusts of table D exceed those of table A when K is less than 1.30.

The thrusts of table A exceed those of table D when K is greater than 1.30.

The greatest possible thrust that can be caused by rotation in any arch of the radius r, is

$$r^2 \times 0.14506, \text{ and corresponds to } K=1.36.$$

The thrust of table C is about double the thrust of table D when $K=1.34$.

DISCUSSION AND USE OF TABLE F.

60. Columns 3 and 12 have been extracted from tables C and D, calculated by M. Petit. The remaining columns have been calculated for this paper.

This table gives directly, or by proportional parts, the thrust, for all values of K between 1.02 and 1.50, of all semi-circular arches which carry loads of masonry, or of equal weight with masonry, rising to two planes meeting along a central ridge, and tangent to the extrados of the arch, or to surfaces parallel to such tangent planes.

Column 3 gives the thrust for that case in which the two planes become one and horizontal, tangent to the extrados at the crown.

Column 4 gives the thrust for $I=85°$, the two planes making each an angle of 5° with a horizontal, and being each tangent to the extrados 5° from the vertical or central joint.

Column 5 gives the thrust for $I=80°$, the two planes making each an angle of 10° with a horizontal and touching the extrados 10° from the summit.

Columns 6, 7, 8, 9, 10, 11, and 12, give the thrust for $I=$successively, 75°, 70°, 65°, 60°, 55°, 50°, and 45°.

Column 13 gives the addition to the thrust (rotation) caused by a surcharge of uniform vertical depth t above the roof.

Column 14 gives in like manner the addition to the *sliding* thrust caused by a surcharge of uniform depth, t, above the roof.

Near the top of each column of thrusts, will be seen a horizontal line. Below that line, the true thrust is due to rotation; above, to sliding. When the ratio of the two radii, $\frac{R}{r}=K$, places the thrust below that line, the addition A, caused by surcharge, must be taken from column 13. If the thrust is found above the horizontal line, A must be taken from column 14.

Columns 3, 9, and 12 give the angles of maximum thrust: for sliding, down to the horizontal line; for rotation, below. These angles, for want of room, are not given in the other columns.

In columns 3, 9, and 12, the thrusts are calculated within ½ degree of the angle of maximum thrust; in the other columns within one degree.

Columns 13 and 14 give results generally a little in excess, never too small.

Column 13 gives the angles corresponding to the maximum effect of the surcharge in the case of rotation. Comparing these angles with the angles of maximum thrust, in columns 9 and 12, we see that, from $K=1.10$ to $K=1.42$, they differ in no case more than 9°, while the mean difference is much less. We therefore know that the error in excess, arising from adding these two maxima together, is exceedingly small. The difference in these angles is very small in all the *magazine* arches in common use, never, it is believed, exceeding 7°. It is only in very light arches, $K=1.02$, 1.03, &c., loaded nearly or quite horizontally, that the error becomes of any consequence.

The error in excess in using column 14, is never of any consequence.

RULES FOR USING TABLE F.

61. From the dimensions of the given arch, determine the ratio $\frac{R}{r}=K$, the angle I, and the elevation E of the ridge above the springing line. If K, and I or E, are found in the table, the thrust is given at once at the intersection of the two columns. But one or both of these quantities, K, and I or E, will generally be intermediate between the tabular numbers. The thrust must then be determined by proportional parts.

We suppose the thrust to vary uniformly between any two successive horizontal columns, say from $K=1.20$ to $K=1.21$; and also uniformly between any two successive vertical columns, say from $I=50°$ to $I=45°$, or rather from $E=R\times1.30541$ to $E=R\times1.41421$. This sort of interpolation can offer no difficulty to those who understand common arithmetic.

Rule I. Suppose I, of the given arch, to have one of its values in table F, K being between two tabular values of that ratio.

Under the given value of I, take the difference of the decimals opposite the adjacent values of K. Call that difference $d\,d$ (difference of decimals); let $d\,K$ represent the difference between the adjacent values of K, and $d'\,K$ the excess of the given value of K over the adjacent smaller value of K. The proportion

$$d\,K : d\,d :: d'\,K : x$$

gives the correction; which must be *added* to the decimal under I and opposite the smaller adjacent value of K, when the decimals *increase* ascending; subtracted when they *decrease* ascending.

Rule II. Suppose K, of the given arch, to have one of its values in table F, I or E coming between two tabular values of those quantities.

Opposite the given value of K, take the difference of the decimals under the greater and less adjacent values of I or E. Call that difference $d\,d$. Let $d\,E$ represent the difference between the adjacent values of E, and $d'\,E$ the excess of the given value of E over the adjacent smaller value. The proportion

$$d\,E : d\,d :: d'\,E : x$$

gives the required correction; which must be added to the decimal opposite K and under the smaller adjacent value of E, when the decimals increase from left to right; subtracted, when they decrease from left to right. We may use I or E according to convenience. Using the former, the proportion will be

$$5^\circ : d\,d :: d'\,I : x.$$

The results will be nearly the same. As I diminishes from left to right, $d'I$, in this last proportion, will be the excess of the preceding adjacent value of I over the given value of I, expressed in degrees and decimals of a degree.

Rule III. Suppose K and I both to be intermediate between tabular values of those quantities.

By rule I. determine the decimal corresponding to the given value of K and the preceding adjacent value of I or E; then by the same rule determine the decimal corresponding to the given value of K, and the following adjacent value of I or E. Call the difference between these two decimals $d\,d$. Let $d\,E$ represent the difference between the adjacent values of E, and $d'\,E$ the excess of the given value of E over the preceding adjacent smaller value. The proportion.

$$d\,E : d\,d :: d'\,E : x,$$

gives the required correction, to be added when the decimals increase from left to right, subtracted when they decrease from left to right.

If we use I instead of E, the proportion will be

$$5^\circ : d\,d :: d'\,I : x.$$

Calling C the final value of the decimal, we have the thrust $\mathbf{F}=r^2\times C$.

In practice, the roof is hardly ever more inclined than 45°. Still, we can, if necessary, obtain from the table the thrust corresponding to smaller values of I, on the principles above explained.

The rate of variation from $I=50^\circ$ to $I=45^\circ$, we may, without sensible error, suppose continued a few degrees below 45°.

Rule IV. If there be a surcharge in masonry rising to the lines $R'\,D'$, $R'\,F''$, fig. 10, draw the parallel lines $R\,D$, $R\,F$, tangent to the extrados of the arch.

Then determine the thrust of the arch $R\,b\,A\,E\,D\,R$, limited by these tangent lines, by the rules already given; and add, for surcharge, from columns 13, 14, as directed in those columns. The addition to be made is $A=rt\times$ decimal, in which $t=R'R=D'D$; $r=$the radius of the intrados. The decimals in columns 13, 14, are the same for all values of I, but are supposed to increase or diminish uniformly between any two consecutive values of K. They must be corrected by rule I. when the ratio, K, of the given arch is not found in the table.

Rule V. If there be a surcharge of earth above the masonry, reduce its thickness over the key and over the reins, in the proportion of its density divided by the density of the masonry.

We can then regard all that comes below the reduced line as composed of masonry alone, and the case falls under rule IV.

62. If the two sides of the arch be unequally loaded, look for the thrust on that side which carries the greatest load,—for the thickness of pier on that side which carries the least.

63. Example 1. The magazine of Vauban.

$r = 13'.3184$; $R = 16'.5148$; hence $K = \frac{R}{r} = 1.24$ very nearly; $I = 49° 7' 7''$; $E = 21'.85 = R \times 1.32258$.

Referring to rule II. and to columns $K = 1.24$; $I = 45°$, $I = 50°$, we have

$d\,E$		$d\,d$		$d'\,E$		
1.41421		.26850		1.32258		
1.30541		.22219		1.30541		
.10880	:	.04631	::	.01717	:	$x = .00731$
						.22219
						$\mathbf{F} = r^2 \times 0.22950$

M. Petit gives, from an independent calculation, ... $\mathbf{F} = r^2 \times 0.22938$

The difference $r^2 \times 0.00012$

is in effect nothing. Had we interpolated in reference to I, the result would not have been quite so accurate, as the thrust varies rather with the elevation of the ridge than with the angle I.

Example 2. The magazine at Fort Jefferson.

$r = 14'$; $R = 17'.50$; $K = 1.25$; tang. $I = \frac{26}{17.5}$; $I = 56°.3' 23''$; $E = \frac{R}{\sin. I} = R \times 1.20542 = 21'.0948$.

Referring again to rule II. and to columns $K = 1.25$, $I = 60°$, $I = 55°$, we have

$d\,E$		$d\,d$		$d'\,E$		
1.22078		.19027		1.20542		
1.15470		.16492		1.15470		
.06608	:	.02535	::	.05072	:	$x = 0.01946$
						0.16492

The thrust is . . $r^2 \times 0.18438 = 36.13848$

Brot. forward, 36.13848

To this we must add for a surcharge 5′.90 deep (see column 13, opposite $K=1.25$),

$A=14.\times 5.90\times 0.46875=38.71875$

Giving as the total thrust, say, . $\mathbf{F}=74.86000$

Example 3. An arch constructed at Fort Porter, fig. 11. This arch has a surcharge, both of masonry and earth.

Reducing the height of the latter in the proportion of 2 to 3, supposed to be the relative weights of a cubic foot of earth and masonry, we find the reduced ridge to be 14′.28 above the springing line, and the reduced roof, on the side most loaded, to make an angle of 86° 46′ with a vertical line. The data are

$r=6'$; $R=7'.668$; $K=1.278$; $I=86°\,46'$; $E=\frac{R}{\sin. I}=R\times 1.00137=7'.68$; $t=14'.28-E=6'.60$.

This case comes under rules III. IV. V.

By rule I.

$dK=1 : dd=.00085 :: d'K=.8 : x=0.00068$

Add . . 0.14101

Giving, as the decimal for $K=1.278$, $I=90°$, ... 0.14169=0.14169

Find, in like manner, the decimal for $K=1.278$, $I=85°$, . . . 0.13486

$dd=$ 0.00683

$dE=.00382 : dd=.00683 :: d'E=.00137 : x=$. 0.00245

Giving as the thrust, without surcharge, $r^2\times 0.13924$

$=5.01264$

To this add for surcharge $A=6\times 6.60\times 0.44495=17.62000$

Total thrust, $=\mathbf{F}=22.63000$

THICKNESS OF PIER, THE ROOF HAVING ANY INCLINATION.

Figure 9.

64. We suppose the surcharge, if partly of earth or any light material, to be reduced in height in the proportion of its density compared with the density of the arch proper. Let

h=the mean height of the pier from its base to the surface of the reduced surcharge over its top=$E' D$, fig. 4; $O O'$, fig. 10; to be estimated if not known.

E=the elevation of the reduced ridge above the springing line=$C a$, fig. 4; $C R'$, fig. 10, 11.

E'=the depth of the arch and its reduced surcharge at the springing line=$A a'$ fig. 10; =Ca or E, fig. 4.

n=the surface of that part of the arch and its reduced load which lies directly over the half-span.

m=the moment of that surface in relation to the interior edge of the joint of the springing line.

l=the lever-arm of the thrust=$a q$, figs. 4, 10.

F=the horizontal thrust however determined.

r=the half span=the radius of the intrados in semicircular arches.

x=the distance between the exterior edge of the base of the pier, and the intersection of this base with the curve of pressure, that is, the point of application of the resultant of all the forces which act upon the base.

δ=the coefficient of stability.

e=the unknown thickness of pier.

We have in all arches

$n=\frac{1}{2}r(E+E')$—the curvilinear surface $A\ b\ C$, figs. 4, 10.

$m=r^2(\frac{1}{3}E+\frac{1}{6}E')$—the moment on A of the surface $A\ b\ C$, figs. 4, 10.

Let the resultant pass through the exterior edge of the base, $x=0$; we have

$$\tfrac{1}{2}he^2+ne+m=\delta Fl;\text{ giving} \qquad (30)$$

$$e=-\frac{n}{h}+\sqrt{\frac{n^2}{h^2}-\frac{2m}{h}+\frac{2\delta Fl}{h}}; \qquad (31)$$

All the other quantities being known, the value of x is

$$x=\frac{\frac{1}{2}he^2+ne+m-Fl}{eh+n}; \tag{32}$$

Let the resultant pass through the base at $\frac{1}{3}$ its length from the exterior edge, $x=\frac{1}{3}e$; and let $\delta=1$; we have

$$\tfrac{1}{6}e^2h+\tfrac{2}{3}ne+m=Fl \tag{$30\frac{1}{3}$}$$

$$e=-2\frac{n}{h}+\sqrt{4\frac{n^2}{h^2}-6\frac{m}{h}+6\frac{Fl}{h}}; \tag{$31\frac{1}{3}$}$$

Let $x=\frac{2}{5}e$, and $\delta=1$; we have

$$\tfrac{1}{10}e^2h+\tfrac{6}{10}ne+m=Fl \tag{$30\frac{2}{5}$}$$

$$e=-3\frac{n}{h}+\sqrt{9\frac{n^2}{h^2}-10\frac{m}{h}+10\frac{Fl}{h}}; \tag{$31\frac{2}{5}$}$$

Let the resultant pass at any proportional distance, pe, from the exterior edge, $x=pe$, and let $\delta=1$, we have

$$(\tfrac{1}{2}-p)e^2h+(1-p)ne=Fl \tag{$30p$}$$

$$e=-\left(\frac{1-p}{1-2p}\right)\times\frac{n}{h}+$$

$$\sqrt{\left(\frac{1-p}{1-2p}\right)^2\times\frac{n^2}{h^2}-\frac{2}{1-2p}\times\frac{m}{h}+\frac{2}{1-2p}\times\frac{Fl}{h}}; \tag{$31p$}$$

Let the resultant pass through the middle of the base, $x=\frac{1}{2}e$, and let $\delta=1$, we have

$$\tfrac{1}{2}ne+m=Fl \tag{$30\frac{1}{2}$}$$

$$e=2\left(\frac{Fl}{n}-\frac{m}{n}\right) \tag{$31\frac{1}{2}$}$$

The values of e drawn from (31), ($31\frac{1}{3}$), ($31\frac{2}{5}$), ($31p$), differ only in the numerical coefficients of $\frac{n}{h}$, $\frac{n^2}{h^2}$, $\frac{m}{h}$, $\frac{Fl}{h}$; so that, having solved one of these equations, we can readily solve others.

It has been customary in large arches, to assign to δ, the coefficient of stability, the value of 1.90 or 2, and determine the thickness of pier from an equation equivalent to (31). But this is not always enough. We may still want to know where the resultant of the thrust and of the weight of the semi-arch and pier cuts the base. This is given by (32) for any assigned values of h and e.

When we have determined e from (30), (31), for any particular coefficient of stability δ, we can substitute, in the numerator of the second member of (32), for $\frac{1}{2}he^2+ne+m$, the equivalent (30), δFl, which gives to (32) a form more convenient for computation, viz.:

$$x=(\delta-1)\frac{Fl}{eh+n} \tag{32δ}$$

When $\delta=2$, its usual value, we have $x=\frac{Fl}{eh+n}$

Giving to h and l in (32) the particular values which correspond to the springing line, we learn where the curve of pressure cuts that line.

If we suppose l, the lever-arm of the thrust, to be variable in ($31\frac{1}{2}$), e also being variable, that formula becomes the equation of a right line, very easy to construct, whose intersection with the base gives the middle of the pier.

The thickness of pier should never be less than that which is given by ($31\frac{1}{3}$); for if the resultant cuts the joint of the base within one third of its length from the exterior edge, that joint will open, or tend to open, at its inner edge.

According to the rule deduced by Audoy, from an examination of the magazine of Vauban, we suppose the thrust to be doubled, assume $\delta=2$, and determine e from equation (31). This rule is perfectly safe in almost all practical cases; but it gives, to piers of great height, a thickness too small, by causing the curve of pressure to pass within the proscribed limit just mentioned, and by leaving the surface of the base too small to bear the superincumbent weight.

To piers of small height, the rule gives a thickness unnecessarily large.

Poncelet recommends as a rule for piers of small height, that the resultant should pass through the middle of the base. The required thickness is then given by the very simple formula ($31\frac{1}{2}$), which we here repeat,

$$e=2\left(\frac{Fl-m}{n}\right).$$

This last rule would seem to be a good one, so far as the pier is concerned, provided the thickness thus determined is sufficient for the superincumbent weight; but Poncelet did not intend that this rule should be followed blindly. It will often give results much too small. At the springing line of most segmental arches, it becomes illusory, for there we have $Fl=m$, or, by the rule, $e=0$.

If we knew the real acting pressure at the crown and its point of application, the rule would be perfect.

To construct ($31\frac{1}{2}$): on the profile of the magazine of Vauban, fig. 13, from a', the intersection of the inner face of the pier with the horizontal $a\,a'$, lay off $a'\,n=\frac{m}{n}$; on the horizontal $a\,a'$ prolonged lay off $n\,p'=F$, and, on the vertical through n, lay off $n\,p=n$. The diagonal $n\,q$ is the required line.

It is easy to give to (31) such a form as to establish, in its utmost generality, the principle already announced for a particular case, art. 43, relative to the limit thickness of pier. Calling i the difference between h and l, we have

$$\frac{2\delta Fl}{h}=\frac{2\delta F(h\pm i)}{h}=2\delta F\pm\frac{2\delta Fi}{h}.$$

Suppose h=infinity; (31) becomes $e=\sqrt{2\delta F}$. In like manner, we find the limit thickness to be,

when $x=\frac{1}{3}e$, ($31\frac{1}{3}$), $e=\sqrt{6F}$;

" $x=\frac{2}{5}e$, ($31\frac{2}{5}$), $e=\sqrt{10F}$;

$$\text{when } x=pe,\ (31p),\ e=\sqrt{\frac{2}{1-2p}F};$$

$$\text{"}\quad x=\tfrac{1}{2}e,\ (31\tfrac{1}{2}),\ e=\text{infinity}.$$

The formulæ given in this article are all of universal application, whatever be the load, and whatever the curves of the arch, circular, elliptical, segmental, &c. But the values of n and m, given above, are based on the supposition that the surface of the reduced surcharge over the half-span is a single plane. Should that surface be irregular, it is only necessary to say that n is the sum of all the surfaces over the half-span, and m the sum of the moments of all those surfaces in reference to A, figures 4, 10, the interior edge of the joint of the springing line. Should the value of e resulting from (31), show that we have not estimated h very correctly, we shall be able to correct the estimate and calculate e anew. Strictly speaking, h is not precisely the same in (31), (32), ($30\frac{1}{3}$), &c. In (32), h is properly the mean height; in (31), fig. 10, the height measured along a vertical cutting the base of the pier at $\frac{1}{3}$ its thickness from the interior face. It would be easy in any particular case to make the proper correction; but such correction will hardly ever be necessary, for e changes very little with small variations of h.

THICKNESS OF PIER.—THE INTRADOS A SEMICIRCLE.

65. The formulæ of the preceding article all remain unchanged: but we have (figs. 4, 10),

the curvilinear surface $A\ b\ C$, $=\frac{1}{4}\pi r^2=r^2\times 0.7854$

moment on A of " " $=r^3\left(\frac{\pi}{4}-\frac{1}{3}\right)=r^3\times 0.452065$

Hence

$$n=\tfrac{1}{2}r(E+E')-r^2\times 0.7854$$

$$m=r^2(\tfrac{1}{3}E+\tfrac{1}{6}E')-r^3\times 0.452065$$

E and E' are always given by the conditions of the problem. They stand in this relation, $E'=E-r$ cot. I.

If the roof of the arch be inclined 45° we have $E'=E-r$.

If the roof is horizontal, we have $E'=E$; and, introducing the ratio $K=\frac{R}{r}$,

$$n=r^2(K-0.7854)$$

$$m=r^3(\tfrac{1}{2}K-0.452065)$$

$$\frac{m}{n}=r\left(\frac{\tfrac{1}{2}K-0.452065}{K-0.7854}\right)$$

THE ROOF GREATLY INCLINED, AND WITH LITTLE OR NO SURCHARGE.

66. When the roof of the arch is so steep and the arch so thin that we can regard the triangle $D\,E\,P$, fig. 13, as forming a part of the semi-arch or pier, we can give to m and n, in the equations of art. 64, a meaning which, without changing the form or purport of any of those formulæ, shall render their application somewhat easier.

Let n'=the surface of the whole semi-arch and its reduced load, and of that part of the pier which lies above the springing line.

m'=the moment of that surface in relation to the interior edge of the joint of the springing line.

h'=the height of the pier from its base *to the springing line.* Let E, l, F, r, x, δ, e be the same as in art. 64.

We have $n'=\frac{1}{2}$ tang. $I\times E^2-r^2\times 0.7854$;

$$m'=\tfrac{1}{2}\text{ tang. }I\times E^2(r-\tfrac{1}{3}\text{ tang. }I\times E)-r^3\times 0.452065$$

If the roof be inclined 45°, we have

$$n'=r^2(K^2-0.7854);$$

$$m'=r^3(K^2-K^3\times 0.4714-0.452065).$$

To determine the thickness of pier, we have

$$\tfrac{1}{2}h'e^2+n'e+m'=\delta Fl \qquad (30)'$$

$$e=-\frac{n'}{h'}+\sqrt{\frac{n'^2}{h'^2}-\frac{2m'}{h'}+\frac{2\delta Fl}{h'}} \qquad (31)'$$

in which δ is ordinarily taken at 1.90 or 2, and the resultant of the thrust thus increased, and of the weight of the semi-arch and pier, passes through the exterior edge of the base.

The point where the resultant of the true thrust and of the weights just alluded to cuts the base, is given as follows:

$$x=\frac{\tfrac{1}{2}h'e^2+n'e+m'-Fl}{eh'+n'} \qquad (32)'$$

in which we substitute for e the value determined by (31), or other values according to circumstances.

If we wish to determine the thickness of pier on the condition that the resultant of the true thrust and of the weight of the semi-arch and pier shall intersect the base of the pier at a distance equal to one-third its thickness from the exterior edge ($x=\frac{1}{3}e$), we have

$$\tfrac{1}{6}e^2h'+\tfrac{2}{3}n'e+m'=Fl. \qquad (30\tfrac{1}{3})'$$

$$e=-2\frac{n'}{h'}+\sqrt{4\frac{n'^2}{h'^2}-6\frac{m'}{h'}+6\frac{Fl}{h'}}. \qquad (31\tfrac{1}{3})'$$

If $x=\frac{2}{5}e$ we have,

$$\tfrac{1}{10}e^2h'+\tfrac{6}{10}n'e+m'=Fl. \qquad (30\tfrac{2}{5})'$$

$$e=-3\frac{n'}{h'}+\sqrt{9\frac{n'^2}{h'^2}-10\frac{m'}{h'}+10\frac{Fl}{h'}}. \qquad (31\tfrac{2}{5})'$$

If $x=pe$, p being any fraction whatever, we have

$$(\tfrac{1}{2}-p)e^2h'+(1-p)n'e+m'=Fl; \qquad (30p)'$$

$$e=-\left(\frac{1-p}{1-2p}\right)\times\frac{n'}{h'}+\sqrt{\left(\frac{1-p}{1-2p}\right)^2\times\frac{n'^2}{h'^2}-\frac{2}{1-2p}\times\frac{m'}{h'}+\frac{2}{1-2p}\frac{Fl}{h'}}. \qquad (31p)'$$

Finally, if the resultant pass through the middle of the base, $x=\frac{1}{2}e$, we have

$$\tfrac{1}{2}n'e+m'=Fl. \qquad (30\tfrac{1}{2})'$$

$$e=2\left(\frac{Fl}{n'}-\frac{m'}{n'}\right). \qquad (31\tfrac{1}{2})'$$

When we have determined e, (30)′, (31)′, for any particular value of δ, we can give to (32)′ the following more simple form :—

$$x=(\delta-1)\frac{Fl}{eh'+n'}. \qquad (32\delta)'$$

which, when $\delta=2$, becomes $\chi=\frac{Fl}{eh'+n'}$.

67. Example 1. The magazine-arch, with the roof inclined 45°, without surcharge.

$r=10'$; $R=12'$; $K=\frac{R}{r}=1.20$; $I=45°$; n', art. 66, = 65.46 ; m', art. 66, = 173.356 ; $h'=10'$; $l=h'+R=$ 22′. ; F, table C, $=r^2\times 0.25806=25.806$; from these data we have, by calculation,

$$\frac{n'}{h'}=6.546\,;\ \left(\frac{n'}{h'}\right)^2=42.85\,;\ \frac{m'}{h'}=17.3356\,;\ \frac{Fl}{h'}=56.7732\,;$$

hence, by the formulæ of art. 66, for strict equilibrium,

$\delta=1$, (31)′, $e=-6.546+\sqrt{42.85-2\times 17.3356+2\times 56.7732}=4'.487$.

for $\delta=2$, (31)′, $e=-6.546+\sqrt{42.85-2\times 17.3356+4\times 56.7732}=8'.792$.

" $x=\frac{1}{3}e$, $(31\frac{1}{3})'$, $e=-2\times 6.546+\sqrt{4\times 42.85-6\times 17.3356+6\times 56.7732}$ $=7'.107$.

" $x=\frac{2}{5}e$, $(31\frac{2}{5})'$, $e=-3\times 6.545+\sqrt{9\times 42.85-10\times 17.3356+10\times 56.7732}$ $=8'.29$.

" $x=\frac{1}{2}e$, $(31\frac{1}{2})'$, $e=12'.05$.

We may infer without further calculation that the rule of Audoy, which consists in doubling the horizontal thrust, or assuming $\delta=2$ in (31)′, is in this case perfectly safe; for it gives a greater thickness than $(31\frac{2}{5})'$, which requires the resultant to pass $\frac{2}{5}e$ from the exterior edge.

For $e=8'.792$ we find, by $(32)'$, $x=3'.7=e\times 0.421$. Making $h'=0$ in $(30)'$, we have, for strict equilibrium, or $\delta=1$, $e=2'.08$; for $\delta=2$, $e=6'.81$.

By comparing $(30)'$ with $(31\frac{1}{2})'$, we see that the thickness required for strict equilibrium at the springing line is precisely half the thickness required for the resultant to pass through the middle of the base.

Example 2. The magazine at Fort Jefferson, of which we gave the thrust in art. 63, fig. 12: $r=14'$; $R=17'.50$; $K=1.25$; $I=56°\ 3'\ 23''$; $t=$ depth of surcharge above the tangent planes $=5'.90$; $h=16'.5$ below the springing line$+13'.5$ above, $=30$; $l=16'.5+17'.5=34'$; $F=74.86$;

$E=\dfrac{R}{\sin. I}+t=27'$; $E'=E-r\cot. I=17'.58$ (arts. 64, 65);

$n=158.12$; $m=1097.82$; $\dfrac{m}{n}=6.943$; $\dfrac{n}{h}=5.27$; $\dfrac{n^2}{h^2}=27.78$;

$\dfrac{m}{h}=36.594$; $\dfrac{Fl}{h}=84.841$.

With these data, the formulæ of art. 64 give us, for strict equilibrium, or

$\delta=1$, (31), $e=-5.27+\sqrt{27.78-2\times 36.594+2\times 84.841}=5'.88$.

For $\delta=2$, (31), $e=-5.27+\sqrt{27.78-2\times 36.594+4\times 84.841}=11'.88$.

" $x=\frac{1}{3}e$, $(31\frac{1}{3})$, $e=-2\times 5.27+\sqrt{4\times 27.78-6\times 36.594+6\times 84.841}$ $=9'.48$.

" $x=\frac{2}{5}e$, $(31\frac{2}{5})$, $e=-3\times 5.27+\sqrt{9\times 27.78-10\times 36.594+10\times 84.841}$ $=11'.26$.

We see that the thickness required by the rule of Audoy, 11'.88, is amply sufficient, as it is greater than 11'.26, corresponding to $x=\frac{2}{5}e$.

But the pier of this magazine has a running gallery 3' wide, 18' high, with a 4' solid wall outside, and with its floor nearly on the level of the base.

As this case may occur again, we subjoin the necessary modification of (30), (31). It is evident that the pier will not go over in a solid mass, but that the divisions each side of the gallery will revolve separately.

Let e' represent the thickness of the solid wall outside the gallery; e'' this same thickness increased by the width of the gallery; e, as usual, the unknown whole thickness of the pier; h' the height of the gallery, supposed to have its floor on the level of the base.

The equation of moments corresponding to (30) is

$$\tfrac{1}{2}he^2+ne+m-\tfrac{1}{2}h'(e^2-e'^2)+\tfrac{1}{2}h'(e-e'')^2=\delta Fl,$$

giving

$$e=-\left(\frac{n-h'e''}{h}\right)+\sqrt{\left(\frac{n-h'e''}{h}\right)^2-2\left(\frac{m+\frac{1}{2}h'(e'^2+e''^2)}{h}\right)+\frac{2\delta Fl}{h}}. \tag{33}$$

In the present case we have $e'=4'$; $e''=e'+3'=7'$; $h'=18'$. Substituting these values, we have, for strict equilibrium, or $\delta=1$, $e=6'.59$; for $\delta=2$, $e=14'.04$.

Let us still further take into consideration, the effect of mortar upon the thrust. The arch is covered with concrete so as to make the vertical joint, extended through this concrete, 9′ long, and the joint at the reins over 5′ long. We suppose c, art 16, to be 25, and take only $\frac{1}{3}$ of that effective force. We must subtract from the thrust, art. 49, ($d=9'$, $d'=5'$, $y=R-\frac{1}{2}r=10'.50$), $\frac{1}{3}\times\frac{1}{6}\times c\left(\frac{d^2+d'^2}{y}\right)=$ 14.02, which reduces F to 60.84.

Substituting this value for F in the last term under the radical, we have, for $\delta=2$, $e=11'.77$. The actual thickness adopted for this magazine is 12′.

We take no account of the effect of adhesion upon the base of the pier; for, in consequence of the division of this pier into two parts, and of the great length of the lever arm of the thrust, this effect is almost nothing.

Example 3.—An arch at Fort Porter, fig. 11. The thrust of this arch has been given in art. 63, example 3. $r=6'$; $R=7'.668$; $K=1.278$; $F=22.63$; $l=18'$ below the springing line$+7'.668$ above$=25'.668$; $h=18'+12'=30'$; $E=CR'=14'.28$; E', on the side least loaded, $=Aa'=12'.59$; n, arts. 64, 65, $=52.3356$; m, arts. 64, 65, $=149.254$; hence, by calculation,

$$\frac{m}{n}=2.852\,;\ \frac{n}{h}=1.7445\,;\ \frac{n^2}{h^2}=3.0435\,;\ \frac{m}{h}=4.975\,;\ \frac{Fl}{h}=19.3625.$$

With these data, the formulæ of art. 64 give us,

For strict equilibrium, $\delta=1$, (31),		$e=3'.90.$
For $\delta=2$ (rule of Audoy),	"	$e=6'.65.$
For $x=\frac{1}{3}e$, $(31\frac{1}{3})$,		$e=6'.44.$
For $x=\frac{2}{5}e$, $(31\frac{2}{5})$,		$e=7'.86.$

The thickness given by the rule of Audoy, $6'.65$, is barely sufficient, as it exceeds but little the value of e corresponding to $x=\frac{1}{3}e$.

But the pier of this arch is not solid. It has counterforts on the inside, $3'$ wide and $6'.50$ apart, united by arches at top starting from the level of the springing line of the main arch. The pier outside, $4'$ in thickness, is continuous and solid.

Let e'=the known thickness of the solid wall on the outside; p=the proportion of the vacant space between two counterforts to the same distance increased by the width of one of the counterforts; h'=the mean height of the vacant spaces between the counterforts.

The equation of moments corresponding to (30) is

$$\tfrac{1}{2}he^2+ne+m-\tfrac{1}{2}ph'(e^2-e'^2)=\delta Fl, \text{ giving}$$

$$e=-\frac{n}{h-ph'}+\sqrt{\left(\frac{n}{h-ph'}\right)^2-\frac{2m+ph'e'^2}{h-ph'}+\frac{2\delta Fl}{h-ph'}} \qquad (34)$$

In the present case we have $p=\dfrac{6.5}{9.5}=\dfrac{13}{19}$; $h'=19'$ nearly; $e'=4'$. We have, therefore, for strict equilibrium, or $\delta=1$, $e=3'.85$; and by the rule of Audoy, $\delta=2$, $e=7'.71$. In (34) e is supposed to exceed e'.

Example 4.—The magazine of Vauban, fig. 13.

$r=12'.50$; $R=15'.50$; $K=1.24$; $E=$altitude of ridge above the springing line$=20'.50$; $I=49° 7' 17''$; $h'=8'$; $l'=h'+R=23'.50$; the thrust, already given for this arch, arts. 48, 63, is $F=r^2\times 0.229381=35.84$. From these data, referring to art. 66, we have by calculation, $n'=120.039$; $m'=235.06$; $Fl'=842.26$.

$$\frac{n'}{h'}=15.005;\ \frac{n'^2}{h'^2}=225.1463;\ \frac{m'}{h'}=29.3825;\ \frac{Fl'}{h'}=105.2823.$$

With these values, the formulæ of art. 66 give us,

for strict equilibrium, $\delta=1$, (31)', $e=4'.410$.

For $\delta=2$, rule of Audoy, (31)', $e=9'.234$.

For $x=\frac{1}{3}e$, $\delta=1$, $(31\frac{1}{3})'$, $e=6'.814$.

For $x=\frac{2}{5}e$, $\delta=1$, $(31\frac{2}{5})'$, $e=7'.761$.

For $x=\frac{1}{2}e$, $\delta=1$, $(31\frac{1}{2})'$, $e=10'.117$.

When $e=9'.234$, rule of Audoy, $(32\delta)'$, $x=4'.34=e\times 0.47$.

We shall give a discussion of this arch hereafter.

SECTION IV.

ARCHES IN SEGMENTS OR PARTS OF A CIRCLE, USUALLY CALLED SEGMENTAL ARCHES.

68. These arches are very common in fortifications, and still more common in bridges of large span.

Indeed, the semi-circular arch of large span, and of the usual thickness at the key, which is about $\frac{1}{26}$ of the span, has a great tendency, after the removal of the centering, to settle down at the key and spread out at the reins about 60° from the key, so that such arches can only be safely used when their thickness is greatly increased below the reins, or when their piers are continued above the springing line, in solid and almost incompressible masonry, as high as the reins.

Such arrangements in effect reduce semi-circular to segmental arches.

Segmental arches are fully given when we know the span$=s$, the rise of the intrados above the springing line $=f$, and the thickness at the key$=d$.

Let r, as usual, represent the radius of the intrados, v' the half-angle at the center. We have

$$r=\tfrac{1}{2}f+\frac{s^2}{8f}\,;\ \sin.v'=\frac{s}{2r}\,;\ \cos.v'=1-\frac{f}{r}.$$

As the thickness of the arch at the key is given, we know the value of the ratio of the two radii,

$$K=\frac{R}{r}=1+\frac{d}{r}.$$

When not otherwise mentioned, we shall suppose the thickness of the arch to be the same throughout. Should the thickness increase towards the reins, the formulæ and the tables to be explained hereafter will give a slight excess of thrust.

SEGMENTAL ARCHES WITHOUT SURCHARGE,—INTRADOS AND EXTRADOS PARALLEL FIG. 14.

69. Look in table A for the angle of rupture corresponding to the given value of K. If that angle be less than v', the thrust is evidently given at once by the table. But if the angle v' be less than the angle of rupture in table A, it is easy to see that the prism of maximum thrust extends to the springing line. The thrust (rotation) will in this case be given at once by (11) art. 28, when we have substituted for v in that formula the known value of v'.

In like manner the sliding thrust will be given by table A when v' exceeds 26°.

If v' be less than 26°, this thrust will be given by (17), art. 36, when we have substituted for v in that formula the known value of v'.

Table E, calculated by M. Petit, gives, for all the values of K between 1.01 and 1.40 inclusive, the actual thrust in seven systems of segmental arch, being the varieties in most common use. These varieties are as follows: $s=4$, 5, 6, 7, 8, 10, and 16 times f.

Above the horizontal line in each column, the sliding exceed the rotation thrusts, and the former only are given. Below the horizontal line the rotation thrusts only are given.

If the angle of rupture in table A, corresponding to systems not given in table E, that is, to segmental arches of which the half span is less than four times the rise, exceed v' by only six or eight degrees, the thrust may still be taken from table A without sensible error.

Illustration.—Second column of table E, $s=4f$, $v'=53° 7' 30''$.

For $K=1.18$ table E gives $F=r^2\times 0.10313$
" " " A " $v=58° 40'$, $F=r^2\times 0.10417$
Difference in the angles, $v-v'=5° 32' 30''$; error in the thrust, always in favor of stability, $r^2\times 0.00104$

70. *The rotation thrust, diminished by mortar*, is

$$F=r^2C-\tfrac{1}{6}c\left(\frac{d^2+d'^2}{f+d}\right), \qquad (35)$$

in which d'=the thickness of the arch at the springing line, r^2C= the thrust, without adhesion, obtained from table E or by direct calculation.

But if the thrust has been taken from table A, that is, if v' be nearly equal to v or exceed v, the effect of mortar and of surcharge has already been given in the discussion of the semicircular arch, art. 31 and following.

71. The sliding thrust diminished by the adhesion of mortar is, art. 37,

$$F=r^2\times C-\frac{cd'\cos. 30°}{\sin. (v'+30°)} \qquad (36)$$

r^2C being the thrust obtained, directly or by proportional parts, from table E, or by an independent calculation.

This last formula is, of course, to be used only when the dimensions of the given arch point to a decimal above the horizontal line in one of the columns.

If v' exceed 26°, the sliding thrust as affected by mortar and surcharge has already been given: art. 37 and following.

THICKNESS OF PIER.

72. Let n=surface of semi-arch $a\ b\ m\ n\ a$, fig. 14;
" m=moment of that surface in relation to m;
" l=the lever arm of the thrust, or elevation of a above the base of the pier;

Let h=the mean known or estimated height of the pier from its base to the upper surface of its surcharge;
" F=the horizontal thrust however determined;
" x=the distance between the exterior edge of the base of the pier and the point where that base is crossed by the curve of pressure;
" δ=the coefficient of stability;
" e=the unknown thickness of pier.

We suppose the small triangle $m\ n\ a'$ to belong both to the semi-arch and pier; thereby greatly simplifying the formulæ, while the very slight resulting error is always in favor of stability. We have,

$$n=r^2\frac{v'}{2}(K^2-1)^*;\ m=\frac{ns}{2}-\tfrac{1}{3}r^3(K^3-1)(1-\cos.\ v');\quad (37)$$

When the angle of rupture extends to the springing line, m and F stand in this relation,

$$m=F(f+d);$$

---

* arc of 1°=0.01745⅓; log. of ditto=—2.241877; r=1.

It will be most convenient, in calculating the value of n, to express v' in degrees and decimals of a degree.

so that, knowing one of those quantities, we can obtain the other without a separate calculation.

The subjoined formulæ are identical in form with those of art. 64, and only differ in the values of n and m, which we have given above.

$$x=o,\left\{\begin{array}{l}\frac{1}{2}he^2+ne+m=\delta Fl \qquad (30)S\\ e=-\frac{n}{h}+\sqrt{\frac{n^2}{h^2}-\frac{2m}{h}+\frac{2\delta Fl}{h}}; \qquad (31)S\end{array}\right.$$

$$x=\frac{\frac{1}{2}he^2+ne+m-Fl}{eh+n} \qquad (32)S$$

When e has been obtained from (31)S, for any particular value of δ, we have

$$x=(\delta-1)\frac{Fl}{eh+n} \qquad (32\delta)S$$

When $\delta=2$, $\qquad x=\frac{Fl}{eh+n}$.

Let the resultant pass through the base so as to make $x=\frac{1}{3}e$, we have

$$x=\tfrac{1}{3}e,\left\{\begin{array}{l}\frac{1}{6}e^2h+\frac{2}{3}ne+m=Fl; \qquad (30\tfrac{1}{3})S\\ e=-2\frac{n}{h}+\sqrt{4\frac{n^2}{h^2}-6\frac{m}{h}+6\frac{Fl}{h}}; \qquad (31\tfrac{1}{3})S\end{array}\right.$$

$$\text{If } x=\tfrac{2}{5}e,\left\{\begin{array}{l}\frac{1}{10}e^2h+\frac{6}{10}ne+m=Fl \qquad (30\tfrac{2}{5})S\\ e=-3\frac{n}{h}+\sqrt{9\frac{n^2}{h^2}-10\frac{m}{h}+10\frac{Fl}{h}}; \qquad (31\tfrac{2}{5})S\end{array}\right.$$

$$\text{If } x=\tfrac{1}{2}e,\left\{\begin{array}{l}\frac{1}{2}ne+m=Fl \qquad (30\tfrac{1}{2})S\\ e=2\left(\frac{Fl}{n}-\frac{m}{n}\right) \qquad (31\tfrac{1}{2})S\end{array}\right.$$

The discussion of these equations given in articles 64, 65, 66, need not be here repeated.

It is necessary to determine, once for all, in every arch, the values of F, m, and n. That done, the above equations are solved with great ease.

73. Example. We will take the case reported by Mr. Haupt, in his very excellent work on Bridge Construction, page 130. "The Monocacy, a very violent stream, is crossed by a beautiful stone bridge (aqueduct), of nine arches, each 54 feet span, and 9 feet rise; arches $2\frac{1}{2}$ feet thick, abutments 10 feet thick and 10 feet high, on a foundation 3 feet high and 13 feet wide.

"Some arches and piers had been built up and backed in; but, before the whole could be completed, a great flood swept the last center from under the arch just turned and not backed in, except partially on one side. The rise of this arch being only one sixth part of the span, must have pressed with tremendous effect upon its last pier, especially as the supports were very suddenly knocked from beneath it, and it was brought to bear very suddenly upon the pier. This had been well built with hydraulic cement of tolerably good quality, only eight or ten months before. The arch stood triumphantly, contrary to the expectation of all that witnessed it, who looked for nothing but the destruction of every arch then built, one after another." The pier had "lost much of its specific gravity by immersion."

We have in this case $s=54'$; $f=9'$; $d=2'.50$; $r=45'$; $R=47'.50$; $v'=36° 52' 10''$; $K=1+\frac{d}{r}=1.05555$; $h=10'$; $l=21'.50$; $s=6f$.

This arch belongs to one of the systems of table E (see column 4).

The thrust given in that column, is,

for $K=1.06$, $F=r^2\times0.04280$

" $K=1.05$, $F=r^2\times0.03709$

$$r^2\times0.00571\times\tfrac{5}{9} \qquad r^2\times0.03709$$
$$=r^2\times0.00317$$

Hence for $K=1.05\frac{5}{9}$ $\qquad F=r^2\times0.04026$

$=81.5265$ $\qquad n=74.41$; $m=F(9+2.5)=937.5547$

The exact values of m and F are a very little larger than those obtained above by interpolation, but the differences would produce no sensible effect upon the results.

We have, by calculation from the above data,

$$\frac{n}{h}=7.441\,;\ \frac{n^2}{h^2}=55.37\,;\ \frac{m}{h}=93.7555\,;\ \frac{Fl}{h}=175.2820$$

Substituting these values in the formulæ of 72, we have, for strict equilibrium, or

For :—

$\delta=1$, (31)S, $e=-7.44+\sqrt{55.37-2\times 93.7555+2\times 175.282}=7'.34.$

$\delta=2$, " $e=-7.44+\sqrt{55.37-2\times 93.7555+4\times 175.282}=16'.41.$

$\delta=1.25$, " $e=-7.44+\sqrt{55.37-2\times 93.7555+2\frac{1}{2}\times 175.282}=10'.05.$

$x=\frac{1}{3}e$ (31$\frac{1}{3}$)S, $e=-2\times 7.44+\sqrt{4\times 55.37-6\times 93.7555+6\times 175.282}=11'.78.$

$x=\frac{2}{5}e$ (31$\frac{2}{5}$)S, $e=-3\times 7.44+\sqrt{9\times 55.37-10\times 93.7555+10\times 175.282}=13'.92.$

$x=\frac{1}{2}e$ (31$\frac{1}{2}$)S, $e=2\left(\frac{Fl}{n}-\frac{m}{n}\right)=21'.91.$

Had the pier lost one half its weight by immersion, we find, substituting $\frac{1}{4}he^2$ for $\frac{1}{2}he^2$ in (30)S, the thickness necessary for strict equilibrium to be only 8′52.

We learn from (32)S, that the resultant of the thrust and of the weight of the semi-arch and pier crossed the base at the distance $x=2'.46=e\times 0.246$ from the exterior edge. Consequently, the foundation-joint of the pier was open on the inside as far as $(10'-3\times 2.'46)=2'.62$ from the inner edge.

We have, in fact, overrated the stability of this pier; for the thrust given in our tables is the horizontal pressure acting at the crown of the arch at the moment of rupture, and is not so great as the existing pressure where the thickness of pier is such as to prevent rupture. It is interesting to remark that, had the opposite half of this arch been loaded in masonry up to the horizontal tangent to the extrados at the crown, the thrust, table E′, would have been increased fifty per cent., while the elements of resistance would have remained the same. Consequently, the pier would have been overturned, for we have found that an increase of twenty-five per cent., $\delta=1.25$, required a thickness $e=10'.05$. Had the surcharge been only one half as heavy as masonry, the pier would have been, $\delta=1.25$, almost exactly in equilibrium.

SEGMENTAL ARCHES SURCHARGED HORIZONTALLY.

Figure 15.

74. This is the most common form of the river arch.

The surcharge of masonry and earth usually rises to a horizontal plane passing a little above the extrados of the key.

For the present we shall suppose this horizontal upper surface to be tangent to the extrados at the key; and we shall continue to suppose that the load between this plane and the extrados is of equal density with the masonry of the arch.

For notation, see art. 68.

Look in table D for the angle of rupture, v, corresponding to the given value of K. If that angle be less than v', the thrust is given at once by the table; and the effect of mortar and of surcharge will be the same as in semi-circular arches, arts. 14, 49, 50.

But if v' be less than v, the prism of maximum thrust extends evidently to the springing line; and, F as usual denoting the rotation thrust, we shall have, after substituting the known value of v' for v in (28)

$$F=\frac{r^2 \sin.^2 v'}{6(K-\cos. v')}\left\{ K^2 \left(6-3K-(3-2K)\cos. v'\right)- \frac{3v'}{\sin. v'}+\frac{1}{\cos.^2 \tfrac{1}{2}v'}\right\}$$

In like manner the sliding thrust will be given by

table D, if v' exceed 29°; and the effect of mortar and of surcharge will be the same as in semi-circular arches.

But if v' be less than 29°, the sliding thrust will be given by (25) when we have substituted for I, in that formula, 90°, and for v the known value of v'.

Table E', calculated for this paper, gives, either directly or by proportional parts, for all values of K between 1.01 and 1.40, and for all relations of the rise to the span between $s=4f$ and $s=16f$, the horizontal thrust at the extrados of the key.

Table E' is altogether analogous to table E.

Above the horizontal line in each column, the sliding exceed the rotation thrusts, and the former only are given. Below the horizontal lines, the rotation thrusts only are given.

Should the angle of rupture in table D exceed v' by only five or six degrees, the thrust may still be taken from that table without any sensible error; and the effect of mortar and of surcharge will be the same as in semi-circular arches.

75. The rotation thrust diminished by mortar, is

$$F=r^2C-\tfrac{1}{6}c\left(\frac{d^2+d'^2}{y}\right);$$

r^2C being the thrust obtained from table E' or by direct calculation, d and d' respectively the length of the upper and lower joint, both extended, if we please, beyond the true extrados of the arch, through a cover of masonry or concrete. If there be no such cover at the vertical joint, we have $y=f+d$. In all cases $y=f+$the thickness of the arch proper at the key.

The rotation thrust increased by a surcharge of the constant vertical depth t, is

$$F=r^2C+\frac{ts^2}{8r^2}\times\frac{r^2-d'^2}{f+d}; \qquad (38)$$

or, according to convenience,—

$$F = r^2C + \tfrac{1}{2}t \sin.^2 v' \times \frac{r^2 - d'^2}{f + d} \qquad (38)'$$

in which r^2C is the thrust given by table E′, or obtained by direct calculation, t the constant depth of the surcharge above the horizontal drawn tangent to the extrados at the key, d the length of the vertical joint, d' the length of the joint at the springing line.

76. *The sliding thrust increased by surcharge and diminished by mortar*, is

$$P = r^2C + t(r + d') \sin. v' \cot. (30° + v') - \frac{cd' \cos. 30°}{\sin.(v' + 30°)}; \qquad (39)$$

r^2C being the thrust obtained from table E′ or by direct calculation. This formula is, of course, to be used only when the dimensions of the given arch point to a decimal above the horizontal line in table E′.

If v' be nearly equal to 25°, or exceed 25°, the sliding thrust and the effect of surcharge are given in table F; the effect of mortar becoming at the same time, art. 37, $rc(K-1)$, or rather, cd'.

77. It generally happens that segmental arches of large span *increase in thickness* from the summit to the springing line. In such cases our formulæ, and the tables founded upon them, give thrusts a little in excess, for we neglect the small trapezoid $n\ n'\ r'\ r$, fig. 15, whose weight is in favor of stability.

Table E′ will give the thrust of such arches, very slightly in excess; but, in estimating the value of K for the horizontal column, we no longer make $K = \frac{R}{r}$, for these radii may be drawn from different centers; but we have

$$K = 1 + \frac{d}{r}$$

The effect of surcharge and mortar may be obtained

from the formulæ of arts. 75, 76, which apply accurately to the cases under consideration.

Those who wish to attain entire accuracy have only to subtract, from the thrust r^2C, as given by table E′, the following expression:

$$\tfrac{1}{2}\sin.^2 v'(d'^2-d^2)-\tfrac{1}{3}\sin.^2 v'\cos. v'\left(\frac{d'^3-d^3}{f+d}\right)$$

78. Example. Casemate arch of Fort Jefferson, supporting the second tier of guns. Figure 16.

The data are, $s=15'$; $f=2'$; $d=1'.50$; $d'=1'.50$; from which we deduce, $r=15.06$; $v'=30°$ nearly; $K=1.10$, nearly; and $s=7\tfrac{1}{2}f$. Table E′ gives

for $K=1.10$ and $s=7f$, $F=r^2\times 0.06784$
" $K=1.10$ and $s=8f$, $F=r^2\times 0.05967$
hence " $K=1.10$ and $s=7\tfrac{1}{2}f$, $F=r^2\times 0.06375=14.4635$
A direct calculation gave $F=r^2\times 0.06390$
the difference, $r^2\times 0.00015$, is, in effect, nothing.

But the arch has a surcharge, 6 inches deep throughout, which adds to the thrust, art. 75, if we suppose $v'=30°$, 4.00987.

By way of illustration, let us attribute to the mortar of the arch and of the concrete which covers it, an adhesive force of 3000 pounds per square foot. The masonry weighs, say 120 pounds per cubic foot; hence, art. 16, $c=\frac{3000}{120}=25$. We have d, the depth of the arch at the key, $1'.50$; and d', the depth of the arch and concrete at the springing line, a little over $4'$, say $4'$. Substituting these values, we have as the effect of mortar $\tfrac{1}{6}c\left(\frac{d'^2+d^2}{f+d}\right)=$ 21.72; and the final thrust $F=14.4635+4.00987-21.72=-3.25$. That is, the arch has no thrust. If we disregard the effect of mortar upon the vertical joint, we have $F=-.57$; still no thrust.

THICKNESS OF PIER.

79. Let s=the span; f=the rise; d=the thickness of the arch at the key; t=the depth of the surcharge above the key, the upper surface being horizontal.

n=the surface of that part of the arch and its load which lies directly over the half-span;

m=the moment of that surface in relation to the vertical passing through the interior edge of the joint of the springing line;

l=the lever-arm of the thrust, or elevation of the point a above the base of the pier.

h=the entire height of the pier from its base to the top of the surcharge over it=$E'D'$ fig. 15.

F, x, δ, e, the same as in art. 72.

We have

$$n=\tfrac{1}{2}s(f+d+t)-\tfrac{1}{4}r^2(2v'-\sin. 2v') \qquad (40)$$

$$m=\tfrac{1}{8}s^2(f+d+t)-r^3\left(\tfrac{1}{2}v' \sin. v'+\frac{\cos.^3 v'}{3}-\tfrac{1}{3}\right) \qquad (41)$$

The formulæ which give the thickness of pier under various circumstances, are precisely the same as in art. 72, and need not be here repeated.

Example. The lower casemate arch of Fort Jefferson, regarding the floor, eight and one half feet below the springing line, as the base of the pier. The data are, $h=12'.50$; $s=15'$; $f=2'$; $d=1'.50$; $t=0'.50$; $r=15'.06$; $v'=30°$; $K=1.10$; $l=12'$.

This is the arch of which we obtained the thrust, $F=14.46$ in art. 78. The above data give us

$n=30.-r^2\times 0.04529=19.73$; $m=112.50-r^3\times 0.0141=64.34$.

$$\frac{n}{h}=1.58;\ \frac{n^2}{h^2}=2.49;\ \frac{m}{h}=5.15;\ \frac{Fl}{h}=13.88$$

Hence, for strict equilibrium, $\delta=1$, in (31)S, $e=2'.89$

for $\delta=1.40$, in (31)S, ... $e=3'.99$

" $x=\tfrac{1}{3}e$, $(31\tfrac{1}{3})S$, ... $e=4'.74$

We see that, disregarding the effect of mortar, the pier should be at least 4'.74 thick.

SEGMENTAL ARCHES WITH A SURCHARGE ON EACH SIDE OF THE CENTRAL RIDGE, RISING TO A PLANE OR ROOF AS IN THE MAGAZINE ARCH, FIGURE 19.

80. Let s=the span; f=the rise; t=the depth of the surcharge, if any, above the two planes parallel to the roof and tangent to the extrados; v'=the semi-angle at the center; r=the radius of the intrados; d=the thickness at the crown; d'=the thickness at the springing line; I= the angle between the roof and a vertical. We have

$$K=1+\frac{d}{r};\ r=\tfrac{1}{2}f+\frac{s^2}{8f};\ \sin. v'=\frac{s}{2r};\ \cos. v'=1-\frac{f}{r}.$$

Look on table F for the angle of rupture, v, corresponding to the given values of K and I. This angle is given in three columns only, viz., under I=90°, 60°, and 45°. Its value for other values of I may be estimated with sufficient accuracy by inspection, as it will be sufficient for our present purpose if we know that angle within six or eight degrees. If that angle be less than v', or exceed v' by only six or eight degrees, the thrust and the effect of surcharge are given at once by that table, precisely as if the intrados were a semicircle. The effect of mortar will also be the same as in semicircular arches.

But if v' be less than v, the angle of greatest thrust extends evidently to the springing line, and the thrust itself will be given by (24), when we have substituted for v and I, in that formula, the known value of v' and I in the given arch.

In like manner, if v' exceed say 25°, the sliding thrust, if greater than the rotation thrust, will be given by table F; and the effect of surcharge will also be given by that table.

But if v' be less than 25°, the sliding thrust will be given by (25), when we have substituted for v and I in that equation, the known values of v' and I in the given arch.

The rotation thrust, diminished by the effect of mortar, is

$$F = r^2 C - \tfrac{1}{6} c \frac{d^2 + d'^2}{y}$$

$r^2 C$ being the thrust obtained from table F, or by direct calculation, and the last term being the effect of mortar; d and d' may be the whole length of the vertical and lower joints extended through any cover of masonry or concrete. When there is no such cover at the vertical joint, we have $y = f + d$. At all times we have $y = r(K - \cos. v')$.

The rotation thrust, increased by a surcharge of uniform depth, t, above the roof of the arch, which last we suppose to be tangent to the extrados, is

$$F = r^2 C + \tfrac{1}{2} t \sin.^2 v' \times \frac{r^2 - d'^2}{f + d}$$

$r^2 C$ being the thrust independently of surcharge.

The sliding thrust, increased by surcharge and diminished by the effect of mortar, is

$$P = r^2 C + t(r + d') \sin. v' \cot. (30° + v') - \frac{cd' \cot. 30°}{\sin. (v' + 30°)}$$

$r^2 C$ being the sliding thrust without regard to surcharge or mortar. In this formula we suppose v' to be less than 25°; if greater than 25°, the sliding thrust is the same as in semicircular arches, and is given at once by table F, whenever the sliding is greater than the rotation thrust.

81. Example. The upper casemate arch of Fort Jefferson, figure 17, upper part; surcharged with concrete up to the roof, $A\ O$, and above that roof with earth up to a horizontal line $8\frac{1}{2}$ feet above the springing line. The data are, $s = 15'$; $f = 3'$; $v = 43° 36'$; $r = 10'.875$; $d = R - r = 2'.28$;

$K=1.21$; relative weights of equal volumes of earth and masonry as 3 to 4.

Reducing the elevation of the surcharge of earth in the proportion of 3 to 4, we may regard all below the reduced surface D' R' O' as having the density of masonry.

Drawing the line R D parallel to R' D' and tangent to the extrados of the arch, we divide the figure of the semi-arch into two parts; the one including all below this tangent; the other a surcharge of uniform depth above that line.

The angle, I, between R D or R' D' and a vertical, we find to be 82° 24′ 20″. As the angle of rupture in table F corresponding to $K=1.21$ and $I=90$, is 63°, and the angle corresponding to $K=1.21$ and $I=60$ is 54°, we know that the prism of maximum thrust extends to the springing line.

Substituting for K, v', and I, in (24), the values above indicated, we obtain $F=r^2\times.10727=12.687$. Table F gives, for the same values of K and I, $F=r^2\times 0.12141$.

The addition to the thrust caused by a surcharge of uniform depth, $t=2'.725$, is, art. 80, $=13.886$; giving as the entire thrust $F=26.573$.

The effect of the adhesion of mortar upon the thrust is ($d=4'$; $d'=4'$; $y=5.28$; $c=25$.),

$$\tfrac{1}{6}c\frac{d^2+d'^2}{y}=25.25\,;$$

leaving, as the final thrust,

$$F=26.573-25.25=1.32.$$

In assuming $c=25$, we have not over-estimated the effect of good mortar, and may regard the arch in question as without thrust, provided there be no cracks in any of the joints. Unfortunately such cracks are very apt to occur, even during the construction of the arch. We have supposed the vertical and lower joints to extend into the concrete covering, making d and d' each 4 feet.

THICKNESS OF PIER.

82. Let s=the span; f=the rise; d=the thickness of the arch at the crown.

E=the elevation of the reduced ridge above the springing line=$m' R'$, fig. 19.

E'=the elevation of the reduced roof above the springing line, measured on the inner face of the pier, prolonged, $=m\,a'$, fig. 19.

n=the surface of that part of the semi-arch and its load which lies directly over the half-span.

m=the moment of that surface in relation to the inner face of the pier.

l=the lever arm of the thrust=$a\,q$, fig 19.

h=the mean height of the pier from its base to the top of the reduced surcharge upon it, to be estimated if not known.

δ=the coefficient of stability. F=the thrust.

e=the unknown thickness of pier.

E and E' are always known.

We have

$$n=\tfrac{1}{4}s(E+E')-\tfrac{1}{4}r^2(2v'-\sin.2v'). \qquad (42)$$

$$m=\tfrac{1}{12}s^2(E+\tfrac{1}{2}E')-r^3\left(\tfrac{1}{2}v'\sin.v'+\frac{\cos.^3 v'}{3}-\tfrac{1}{3}\right). \qquad (43)$$

The formulæ which give the thickness of pier under various suppositions, are precisely the same as in articles 64, 72, and need not be repeated. The formulæ of 64, we have already said, are universal. The reader is referred to that article for a discussion of the formulæ, and for the equation of the curve of pressure or resistance in the pier.

Example. The upper casemate arch of Fort Jefferson, of which we obtained the thrust in art. 81. Let the floor 10 feet below the springing line, be the base of the pier, fig. 17.

We have $E=m'\,R'=8'.125$; $E'=m\,a'=7'.125$; $r=10'.875$; $v'=43°\,36'\,10''$; $s=15'$; $h=17'$; $l=15'.28$; $f=3'$;

$n=57.19-r^2\times0.1308=41.73$; $m=219.14-r^3\times0.05566=147.55$; $F=26.573$.

$$\frac{n}{h}=2.455;\ \frac{n^2}{h^2}=6.026;\ \frac{m}{h}=8.68;\ \frac{Fl}{h}=23.882.$$

With these data, the formulæ of art. 64 give us,

For strict equilibrium, $\delta=1$, (31), . . $e=3'.58$
For $\delta=2$, rule of Audoy for large arches, (31), $e=6'.72$
For $\delta=1.50$, (31), ... $e=5'.31$
For $x=\frac{1}{3}e$, $(31\frac{1}{3})$, ... $e=5'.83$
For $x=\frac{2}{5}e$, $(31\frac{2}{5})$, ... $e=7'.00$
For $x=\frac{1}{2}e$, $(31\frac{1}{2})$, ... $e=12'.40$

The thickness given by the rule of Audoy would seem, in this case, to be about right; as it is nearly equal to that which corresponds to $x=\frac{2}{5}e$.

Were we to take into consideration the adhesion of mortar, and give to that force one half the value assigned in art. 81, we should find the actual thickness, 4′, to be amply sufficient.

THRUST OF THE COMMUNICATION ARCHES OF A FORT UPON THE SCARP WALL, AND THE CURVE OF PRESSURE IN THE LATTER.

83. This is one of the most important applications of the theory of the arch. The scarp should be able to resist the thrust of the communication arches without any lateral motion whatever; and to this end the curve of pressure in the scarp should pass through the middle of the foundations, or very near that point.

Each communication arch, besides its own proper load, supports through its entire span the weight of one half of each of the adjacent casemate arches, with all the surcharge of earth and masonry which may belong to the latter.

The thrust, therefore, of the communication arches, and particularly of the upper one, is very great; and the effect of the latter is still further increased by the great leverage with which it acts, that is, by its great elevation above the base of the scarp.

These arches, on the outside, rest upon small piers carried up in contact with the scarp wall, but nowhere bonded in with it.

84. Example. Communication arches and scarp of Fort Jefferson, figs. 17, 18.

Lower arch. Span $=s=12'.25$; rise $=f=1'.75$; thickness at the key $=d=1'.88$; depth of surcharge above the key $=t=2'.87$; radius of the intrados $=r=11'.59$; $K=1+\frac{d}{r}=1.16\frac{1}{5}$; $s=7f$; elevation of the extrados of the crown above the base of the scarp $=l=11'.63$; surface $m\ b\ m$ of the segment of the adjacent casemate arch $=a=\frac{1}{2}r^2(2v'-\sin. 2v')=20.54$.

But we advise the reader, in all problems of this kind, to regard the segment of a circle as the segment of a parabola standing on the same span, and tangent to the circle at the summit. This greatly diminishes the labor of the calculation, without leading to any sensible error in the results. According to this supposition we have $a=\frac{2}{3}$ span $\times$ rise $=$ (in the case presented above) $\frac{2}{3}\times15\times2=20$.

The center of gravity of the semiparabolic segment standing on a horizontal base, is at the distance of $\frac{3}{8}$ of this base from the altitude or axis of the whole segment.

Let F as usual represent the thrust, we have

$F=4r^2\times0.0832$..table E′, the thrust without surcharge, ... $=43.16$

$+4\times\frac{1}{8}\times\frac{ts^2}{f+d}$..effect of surcharge from ref. (17′.13) to ref. (20′), ... $=59.34$

$+\frac{4\times15-a}{f+d}\times\frac{s^2}{8}$..effect of the adjacent casemate arch from (16′) to (20′), . . $=206.70$

$F=309.20$

We have computed the thrust upon the whole length of one pier, which is 4′.

In computing the surcharge we suppose the load to be limited to the inner face of the pier, and not as usual, to extend over the skewback.

Upper arch. $s=12'.25$; $f=3'$; $d=1'.88$; $t=12'$; $r=7'.7527$; $K=1.24\frac{1}{4}$; $s=4.08\frac{1}{3}f$; $l'=25'.63$; $a=\frac{2}{3}15\times 3=30$.

$F'=4r^2\times 0.13233$..table E′, thrust without surcharge, ... $=31.81$

$+4\times\frac{1}{8}\times\frac{ts^2}{f+d}$..effect of surcharge from (31′.13) to, say, (43′.13), ... $=184.50$

$+\frac{15\times 13-a}{f+d}\times\frac{s^2}{8}$..effect of adjacent casemate arch, (30′) to (43′), ... $=634.23$

$F'=850.54$

Let N=the volume of all the solids between the interior face of the scarp and the parallel vertical plane passing through the crown of the communication arches and above the floor of the lower casemates, which is at the reference (7′.50).

M=the sum of the moments of these solids in reference to the interior face of the scarp.

$N=4\times 2\times 37.50$..the pier proper from (5.50) to (43), ... $=300.00$

$+4\left(6.50\times\frac{12.25}{2}-\frac{2}{3}\times\frac{12.25}{2}\times 1.75\right)$ the lower arch from (13′.50) to (20′), . $=130.67$

$+4\left(16.75\times\frac{12.25}{2}-\frac{2}{3}\times\frac{12.25}{2}\times 3\right)$ the upper arch and load, (26′25) to (43′), $=361.36$

Carried to page 283, . . . 792.03

Brot. forward, ... 792.03

$+(15\times4-\frac{2}{3}15\times2)\left(2+\frac{12.25}{2}\right)$ lower casemate arch and load, (16′) to (20′), $=325.00$ (IV)

$+(13\times15-\frac{2}{3}15\times3)\left(2+\frac{12.25}{2}\right)$ upper casemate arch and load, (30′) to (43′), $=1340.63$ (V)

$N=2457.66$

$M=2\times4\times\frac{2}{2}\times37.50$, the pier from (5′.5) to (43′), $=300.00$

$$+\left\{\begin{array}{l}4(6.50\times\frac{12.25}{2}\left(2+\frac{12.25}{4}\right))\\ -4\times\frac{12.25}{2}\times1.75\times\frac{2}{3}\left(2+\frac{5}{8}\times\frac{12.25}{2}\right)\end{array}\right\}$$ lower communication arch and load from (13′.50) to (20′), ... $=639.64$

$$+\left\{\begin{array}{l}4\times(16.75)\times\frac{12.25}{2}\left(2+\frac{12.25}{4}\right)\\ -4\times\frac{2}{3}\times\frac{12.25}{2}\times3\left(2+\frac{5}{8}\times\frac{12.25}{2}\right)\end{array}\right\}$$ upper com. arch from (26′.25) to (43′), . . $=1791.97$

$+$ (IV) $325\times\frac{1}{2}\left(2+\frac{12.25}{2}\right)$ lower casemate arch from (16′) to (20′), ... $=1320.31$

$+$ (V) $1340.63\times\frac{1}{2}\left(2+\frac{12.25}{2}\right)$ upper casemate arch from (30′) to (43′), ... $=5446.31$

$M=9498.23$

We have calculated the values of F, F', N, and M for 19′ in length of the scarp. Dividing each by 19 we have their mean values corresponding to one foot in length of scarp. Let

$$\frac{N}{19}=129.35=n;\quad \frac{M}{19}=499.91=m;\quad \frac{F}{19}=16.274=F;\quad \frac{F'}{19}=44.765=F';$$

the known height of scarp from (5′.50) to (43′)$=37'.5=h$; the known thickness of scarp$=8'=e$.

x=the distance between the exterior face of the scarp and the point where the curve of pressure cuts the base.

Let us first suppose the pier 2′ by 4′, which supports one half the weight of the communication arches and their respective loads, to form an integral part of the scarp.

We have, art. 64,

$$x=\frac{\frac{1}{2}he^2+ne+m-Fl-F'l'}{he+n}=3'.256. \qquad (44)$$

This is the equation of the curve of pressure in the pier (scarp), in which e, n, m, F, and F' are constant, and h, l, and l' vary by equal differences.

Giving to h, l, and l', the values which correspond to the bottom of the foundations, viz., $h=48$; $l=22'.13$; $l'=36'.13$, we find $x=2'.13$.

As the foundations extend 4′ in front of the scarp, we see that the curve of pressure passes very nearly through the middle of the lowest course of masonry, its best possible situation. Consequently, the scarp is in no danger of rotary motion.

Let us now suppose the piers $2'\times 4'$ to be entirely separate from the scarp, as in fact they are. We have

$$x=\frac{\frac{1}{2}he^2+m-Fl-F'l'}{he} \qquad (45)$$

Giving, when $h=37'.50$; $l=11'.63$; $l'=25'.63$, $x=1'.21$
" $h=48'.00$; $l=22'13$; $l'=36'.13$, $x=0'.15$
" $h=32'.00$; $l=6'.13$; $l'=20'.13$, $x=2'.04$

The lower portions of both of these curves are sketched on fig. 18; the outer curve, $c'\,c'$, corresponding with these last results, the inner curve, $c\,c$, corresponding to the first supposition. The distance of this curve from the surface, at the point where it approaches the surface most nearly, is the best measure of the stability of the sustaining wall. At t' the distance $c'\,t'$ is $1'.21=e(8')\times 0.151$. There is no danger of the pier or scarp overturning; but there are two other points to which we must direct our attention.

(I). The horizontal joint $t\,t'$, reference $(5'.50)$, may open on the inside and allow the scarp to move laterally through a certain angle around c', near t', as center.

(II). The bricks at t', the part most compressed, may be crushed by the superincumbent weight.

As to the first, we can make no estimate of the extent of angular motion, not knowing the rate of compression of brick and concrete masonry under a given pressure.

As to the second, the entire weight supported by the joint $t\,t'$ is, $he=300$ cubic feet of masonry.

The pressure is greatest at t'; it is 0 at the distance $3x=3'.63$ from t'; the mean pressure is he divided by three times x; the pressure, per unit of surface, at t', is double the mean pressure. Calling this pressure per unit of surface at t', p, we have $p=2\times\frac{he}{3x}=165.29=18{,}182.$ pounds, supposing one cubic foot of the mixed masonry to weigh 110 pounds.

This pressure, about 126 pounds per square inch, is rather too great, but probably does not exceed the allowed limit, one tenth the crushing force.

There are, however, some elements of stability which we have not taken into consideration.

We are warned by the cracks often seen in old works, not to rely, in any degree, upon adhesion of mortar in the communication and casemate arches. But there is another force which can hardly fail; viz., adhesion in the joints of the scarp. This force is

$$\tfrac{1}{6}c\times e^2=\tfrac{1}{6}\times 25\times(8)^2=266.67,$$

and the value of x becomes, at the joint $t\,t'$, where $h=37'.50$,

$$x=\frac{\frac{1}{2}he^2+m+\frac{1}{6}ce^2-Fl-F'l'}{he}=2'.10 \qquad (46)$$

which reduces the pressure, per square inch, at t', to 72.75 pounds. To this last pressure we ought to add the reaction of adhesion.

PRESSURE UPON THE OUTER PIERS OF THE COMMUNICATION ARCHES.

These piers have an area in the horizontal section of $2' \times 4' = 8$, and each one of them has to sustain the whole value of N computed above.

They are subject, therefore, to a pressure of 307.21 per square foot; that is, each square foot bears a weight equal to that of a column of the same material one foot square and 307′.21 high; a pressure of 33,793 pounds per square foot, or 234.67 pounds per square inch.

SEGMENTAL ARCHES—APPROXIMATE FORMULÆ.

85. Tables E and E' give, in most cases with sufficient accuracy, either directly or by proportional parts, the thrust of the segmental ring of equal thickness throughout, table E, and of the same ring loaded in masonry up to the level of the extrados at the crown, table E′.

But those tables have not been extended to very flat arches, the last column in both corresponding to $s = 16f$, and $v' = 14° \; 15'$; nor do they apply very well to cases in which s exceeds $10f$, or v' is less than $22° \; 37' \; 10''$.

When it becomes necessary to make an independent calculation, and to ascertain the thrust without the aid of these tables, the exact methods already given are, it must be confessed, rather complex and tedious.

We shall now give a much shorter method, sufficiently exact for all those cases in which v', the semi-angle at the center, does not exceed 30°; and applicable, with little error, to much larger values of v', particularly when the span is small, as it usually is in fortifications.

The circular arc $m\,b$, fig. 15, departs but little from the parabola having its vertex at b, and passing through the point m. The equation of moments which determines the thrust, is—

$F \times a\,m' =$ moment $a\,m'\,m\,n\,r\,a$* $-$ moment $m\,b\,m'\,m$; m being the center of moments. Now the moment of the parabolic surface $m\,b\,m'\,m$, in relation to m, is $\frac{2}{3}\,m\,m' \times b\,m' \times \frac{5}{8} \times m\,m' = \frac{5}{48} s^2 f$, $(s = 2\,mm')$; and the parabolic surface $m\,b\,m'\,m$, is $\frac{2}{3}\,m\,m' \times m'\,b = \frac{1}{3} sf$.

As the parabola is wholly below the circular arc at all points between b and m, we in effect suppose the arch to be a little heavier than it really is; and shall neutralize the error in part, or more than neutralize it, by adding the small triangle $m\,n\,t$, to that part of the arch which is on the left of the center of rotation.

Let $a\,m' = y$; $r =$ radius of the intrados; $R =$ radius of the extrados; $K = \frac{R}{r}$; if the arch increase in thickness towards the pier or springing line, $K = \frac{d}{r}$, d being the thickness of the arch at the crown; $v' =$ the semi-angle at the center. We have, in relation to m as center, moment $a\,m'\,m\,t\,n\,r\,a = y \times R$ sin. $v'(r$ sin. $v' - \frac{1}{2} R$ sin. $v') = \frac{1}{4} y \times K \times s^2 (1 - \frac{1}{2} K) = \frac{1}{4} y s^2 (K - \frac{1}{2} K^2)$. We have, therefore, as the thrust of the segmental arch loaded up to the level of the extrados at the crown,

$$F = \tfrac{1}{4} s^2 \left(K - \tfrac{1}{2} K^2 - \frac{5f}{12y}\right). \qquad (47)$$

Illustrations. Suppose $s = 10f$; giving $r = 13f$; $v' = 22° \; 37' \; 10''$; and let $K = 1.10$.

The above formula gives, $F = s^2 \times 0.07845$	$= r^2 \times 0.04642$
Table E′ gives for the same case, . .	$F = r^2 \times 0.04655$
Error,	$= r^2 \times 0.00013$

Suppose $s = 6f$; $r = 5f$; $v' = 36° \; 52' \; 10''$; $K = 1.10$.

The above equation gives, . .	$F = r^2 \times 0.07820$
Table E′ gives for the same case, .	$F = r^2 \times 0.07724$
Error,	$= r^2 \times 0.00096$

* The point r, omitted on the left side of fig. 15, is vertically over n on the horizontal through a.

This approximate formula, (47), gives with all desirable accuracy the thrust of the casemate arches of Fort Jefferson, art. 78.

86. The thrust of the segmental arch loaded horizontally up to a plane passing at the distance t above the crown of the arch, is

$$F=\tfrac{1}{4}s^2(K-\tfrac{1}{2}K^2-\tfrac{5}{12}\frac{f}{y})+\tfrac{1}{4}s^2(K-\tfrac{1}{2}K^2)\frac{t}{y} \qquad (48)$$

In all cases $y=f+d$.

87. The thrust of the segmental arch loaded up to any plane $D'\ R'$, fig. 19.

Let $m'\ R'=E;\ m\ a'=E';\ n\ r=E''$; the known distance $m\ t=m\ n\times\sin.\ v'=D$. We have

$$F=\frac{s^2}{12y}(E+\tfrac{1}{2}E'-\tfrac{5}{4}f)-\frac{D^2}{3y}(E''+\tfrac{1}{2}E') \qquad (49)$$

The last term is usually small, and in very light arches may be omitted altogether. D and E'' can always be taken with sufficient accuracy from a drawing of the arch. Equation (49) of course includes (48), but is more general in its character. It does not contain the ratio K, and is not founded upon the supposition that the arch is of equal thickness throughout. Moreover, it is strictly accurate as to the moment of that part of the arch and its load which overlies the skewback; the little triangle $n\ t\ m$ no longer forming any part of this moment.

Applied to the case in which the surcharge is horizontal, we have $E'=E;\ E''=E-m\ n\times\cos.\ v'$; in all cases $y=f+d=a\ m'$.

Illustration. Let us apply (49) to the upper casemate arch of Fort Jefferson (see arts. 81, 82).

The thrust given by (49) is .	$F=26.81$
The exact thrust, art. 81, is . .	$F=26.57$
The difference,	$=$ 0 24, always

in favor of stability, is, we see, very small, notwithstanding the great extent of the semi-angle at the center, $v'=43° 36' 10''$.

We are therefore disposed to recommend formula (49) for exclusive use in calculating the thrust of the segmental arches of fortifications, when the thrust can not be obtained from the tables of circular or other arches contained in this paper.

88. The sliding thrust of segmental arches, when the angle of rupture extends to the springing line, is, using the notation of the preceding article,

$$P=\left(\tfrac{1}{4}s(E+E'-\tfrac{4}{3}f)+\frac{D}{2}(E'+E'')\right)\times \text{cotang.}(v'+30°) \qquad (50)$$

We can generally tell in advance, whether the true thrust is due to rotation or sliding; if not, it will be necessary to calculate both.

THICKNESS OF PIER—APPROXIMATE FORMULÆ.

89. For notation, see art. 82. Still regarding the intrados $m\,b$, fig. 19, as a parabola, we have

$$n=\tfrac{1}{4}s(E+E'-\tfrac{4}{3}f) \qquad (51)$$

$$m=\tfrac{1}{12}s^2(E+\tfrac{1}{2}E'-\tfrac{5}{4}f) \qquad (52)$$

s is in all cases the span, f the rise.

Applying formulæ (49), (51), (52) to the upper casemate arch of Fort Jefferson,

We find, when $\delta=1$, equation (31), . $e=3'.59$
The exact formulæ, art. 82, gave us, . . $e=3'.58$
When $\delta=2$, equation (31). . . $e=6'.74$
The exact formulæ, art. 82, gave . . $e=6'.72$

It thus appears that while the approximate methods require far less labor than the exact, they lead to almost identical results. The error committed in obtaining the thrust, is balanced in part, or more than balanced, when we apply (51), (52) to the determination of the thickness of pier. Equations (51), (52) may be used when the thrust has been obtained by exact methods; but the error in the thickness of pier will be somewhat increased.

The formulæ given for the thickness of pier in art. 64 are, as we have repeatedly stated, universal.

The principle of these approximate methods has already been applied in calculating the stability of the scarp wall of Fort Jefferson; and we have gone over the same ground by the more laborious, exact modes of computation. The results were almost identical; but we could not always look for such close approximation.

SECTION V.

ELLIPTICAL ARCHES.

90. Elliptical arches are but little used on fortifications, where economy and stability are more regarded than architectural effect. They are, however, sometimes used in stone and brick bridges on great thoroughfares, and particularly in the neighborhood of large cities.

The rise of the arch of almost all long bridges, is less than the half-span.

There are three principal varieties of the intrados:

1st. The ellipse;

2d. The segment of a circle;

3d. The 3, 5, 7, &c., centered arch.

The 2d, or segmental arch, is the strongest, the most economical, and, in general, the best. It is more easily built, less liable to change its form after the removal of the center, on receiving its final load, or any variable and occasional load, and has less horizontal thrust at the key than any other arch of the same span and rise; and its appearance, when the rise is small in relation to the span, is more agreeable to the eye than that of the flat ellipse. This variety has already been disposed of. We will here add the remark, that the segmental arch or ring should increase in thickness, from the key to the springing line, at such a rate as to become, if continued to 60° from the key, about one half greater than it is at the key. Such increase will, in general, not only insure the requisite stiffness or stability of form in the arch itself, but will nearly equalize the pressure, per unit of surface, upon the joints of the key and springing line.

Should the intrados of the segmental arch extend more than 60° from the key, the augmentation of thickness must continue.

Arches of the 3d class are all approximations, more or less close, to the ellipse having the same rise and span. With five or more centers, the approximation becomes almost an identity; and we may regard the ellipse as representing all these arches, that is, as having the same thrust and requiring the same thickness at the key and the same thickness of pier.

THRUST OF THE ELLIPTICAL ARCH WITHOUT LOAD.

Figure 20.

91. Let $A\ C$, the half-span and semi-transverse axis, $=r$; $C\ b$, the rise and semi-conjugate axis, $=f$; $a\ b$, the thickness at the key, $=d$. Let us compare this arch with a circular arch of the same span, and of a thickness, $a'b'=d'$, at the key, as much greater than the corresponding thickness of the elliptical ring, as the half-span is greater than the rise.

And let us further suppose the vertical depth of the elliptical ring to bear a constant ratio to the depth of the auxiliary circular arch, both measured on the same vertical line; so that, on any vertical line $m\,r'$, we shall have,

$$m\,r : m'\,r' :: ab : a'\,b' :: f : r.$$

This requires the extrados of the elliptical arch to be another ellipse, having, for its axes, $C\,a=f+d$, and $C\,B=C\,a'=r+\frac{r}{f}\times d$. This arrangement gives a continual augmentation, not too great, to the thickness of the elliptical arch. Comparing together the segments $m\,r\,a\,b$, $m'\,r'\,a'\,b'$, included between the vertical of the key and any other vertical $m'\,r'$, we see that their horizontal dimensions are the same, while their vertical dimensions bear the constant ratio of f to r. Consequently, the surfaces of those segments sustain the same constant ratio, and their centers of gravity are in the same vertical line. Projecting m and m' horizontally on $C\,a'$ at t and t', and disregarding, for the present, the negative influence upon the thrust of the surfaces, nearly triangular, $m\,n\,r$ and $m'\,n'\,r'$; designating by S, the surface $m\,r\,a\,b$; by p, the distance of the center of gravity of this surface from the vertical through m; by y, the lever arm $a\,t$; by S', p', y' the corresponding surface, distance, and lever-arm, $a'\,t'$, of the circular arch,—we have for the thrust, F, of the elliptical arch, corresponding to any position of the vertical line $m\,r'$,

$$F=\frac{Sp}{y}, \text{ and, for the circular arch, } F'=\frac{S'p'}{y'}.$$

But we have already found $p=p'$, $S=\frac{f}{r}S'$, and we have $f : r : C\,b : C\,b' :: C\,a : C\,a' :: C\,t : C\,t' : C\,a-C\,t\ (=y) : C\,a'-C\,t'\ (=y')$. Consequently, $y=\frac{f}{r}\times y'$; and $F=F'$.

This relation exists for all positions of the joint of rupture; hence, the maximum or true thrust of the two arches will be the same, and we are able to announce this principle:—

The thrust of a semicircular arch, of equal thickness throughout, and without load, is nearly equal to the thrust of an elliptical arch of the same span, and of a vertical depth at the key and at every other point as much less than the depth of the circular arch, on the same vertical lines, as the rise of the elliptical arch is less than the half-span.

We shall therefore be able, with little error, to obtain the thrust of unloaded elliptical arches, from table A.

92. The result, however, thus obtained, requires a slight addition. We have neglected the difference in effect of the small surfaces $m\ n\ r$, $m'\ n'\ r'$, which tend to diminish the thrust of the arches to which they respectively belong. If the moments of these two surfaces in relation to the vertical through m, like the moments of the segments $m\ r\ a\ b$, $m'\ r'\ a'\ b'$, stood in the proportion of f to r, no correction would be necessary. But such is not the case.

Draw the tangents $m\ o$, $m'\ o$, to the intrados of the elliptical and of the auxiliary circular arch, meeting on the transverse axis or horizontal of the springing line at o; draw the normal $m\ p'$ to the ellipse intersecting $A\ C$ at p'; prolong the line $p'\ m$ to n, the extrados of the elliptical arch: and the line $p'\ m'$ to n'' the extrados of the circular arch. n and n'' are evidently on the same vertical line. Let v represent the angle between any joint $m\ n$—supposed to be normal to the intrados—and a vertical; v' the corresponding angle $n'\ m'\ r'$, or $m'\ C\ a'$, of the circle; and V the angle $n''\ m'\ r'$. We have v=angle $p\ o\ m$; v'=angle $p\ o\ m'$; V=angle $p\ m'\ p'$; tang. $v=\frac{f}{r}$tang.v'; tang. $V=\frac{f}{r}$tang.$v=\frac{f^2}{r^2}$tang.v'. From these relations v and V are easily calculated when v' is given.

The triangles $m\ n\ r$, $m'\ n''\ r'$, have the same altitudes, and bases $m\ r$, $m'\ r'$, in the proportion of f to r. Consequently, they have the same effect upon the thrust; and the required correction consists in adding to the thrust, as given by table A, the effect of the triangle $m' n' n''$. Let A represent the required addition. We have

$$A = \frac{m'r'}{a't'}\left(\frac{(m'n')^2 \sin.^2 v' - (m'n'')^2 \sin.^2 V}{6}\right) \qquad (53)$$

Now, in all the cases likely to occur in practice, the angle of rupture corresponding to the maximum thrust, is in the neighborhood of 60°; and we shall calculate the value of A on that supposition. K representing the ratio of the two radii of the circular arch, we have, when $v'=60°$, $m'r'=r(\sqrt{K^2-0.75}-0.50)$; $a't'=r(K-0.50)$; $m'n'=r(K-1)$; $m'n''=r(\sqrt{K^2-\sin.^2(60°-V)}-\cos.(60°-V))$; tang. $V=\frac{f^2}{r^2}\sqrt{3}$.

We subjoin the values of A corresponding to $f=\frac{1}{2}r$, and to all values of K between 1 and 1.60.

TABLE A'.

VALUES OF $\frac{A}{r^2}$ TO BE ADDED TO THE COEFFICIENTS OF r^2 GIVEN BY THE 4TH COLUMN OF TABLE A, CALCULATED ON THE SUPPOSITION THAT $\frac{f}{r}=\frac{1}{2}$.

Value of $K=1+\frac{d}{f}$	Value of $\frac{A}{r^2}$.	$K=1+\frac{d}{f}$.	$\frac{A}{r^2}$.	$K=1+\frac{d}{f}$.	$\frac{A}{r^2}$.	$K=1+\frac{d}{f}$.	$\frac{A}{r^2}$.
1.01	0.00000	1.16	0.00092	1.31	0.00510	1.46	0.01343
1.02	0.00000	1.17	0.00108	1.32	0.00552	1.47	0.01414
1.03	0.00000	1.18	0.00126	1.33	0.00596	1.48	0.01487
1.04	0.00002	1.19	0.00144	1.34	0.00642	1.49	0.01562
1.05	0.00004	1.20	0.00165	1.35	0.00690	1.50	0.01639
1.06	0.00006	1.21	0.00188	1.36	0.00740	1.51	0.01718
1.07	0.00009	1.22	0.00212	1.37	0.00792	1.52	0.01799
1.08	0.00014	1.23	0.00238	1.38	0.00845	1.53	0.01882
1.09	0.00019	1.24	0.00266	1.39	0.00900	1.54	0.01967
1.10	0.00025	1.25	0.00295	1.40	0.00957	1.55	0.02054
1.11	0.00033	1.26	0.00326	1.41	0.01016	1.56	0.02143
1.12	0.00042	1.27	0.00358	1.42	0.01077	1.57	0.02234
1.13	0.00052	1.28	0.00393	1.43	0.01140	1.58	0.02328
1.14	0.00064	1.29	0.00430	1.44	0.01206	1.59	0.02423
1.15	0.00078	1.30	0.00469	1.45	0.01274	1.60	0.02519

The value, A', of A corresponding to any other relation of f to r, will be given, with sufficient accuracy, by the following formula:

$$A'=2A(1-\frac{f}{r}).$$

This last formula will give thrusts slightly in excess for values of $\frac{f}{r}$ between 1 and $\frac{1}{2}$, and thrusts a little too small for values of $\frac{f}{r}$ less than $\frac{1}{2}$.

93. Recapitulation. To find the thrust of the unloaded elliptical arch, the extrados being an ellipse similar to the intrados; r=the half span; f=the rise; d=the thickness at the key:

Look in table A, 4th column, for the coefficient, C, of r^2, opposite $K=1+\frac{d}{f}$; to this, add the product $C'=2(1-\frac{f}{r})\times\frac{A}{r^2}$, $\frac{A}{r^2}$ being taken from the above table A′ opposite the same value of K. Then $F=r^2(C+C')$.

Example. $r=10'$; $f=6'\,8''$; $d=1'.50$; hence $K=1+\frac{d}{f}=1.225$.

Value of C, 4th column of table A, mean between $K=1.22$ and $K=1.23$ $=0.12044$

Value of $C'=2(1-\frac{2}{3})\times 0.00225$; $\frac{A}{r^2}$ being the mean between $K=1.22$ and 1.23, table A′ $=0.00150$

Total thrust $F=r^2\times 0.12194$

M. Audoy gives as the thrust of a three-center arch of the same span and rise and thickness, the intrados being described with three arcs of 60° each, $F=r^2\times 0.12569$

Difference, $=r^2\times 0.00375$

=about three per cent. of the true thrust.

Example 2. $r=10'$; $f=5'$; $d=2'$, hence $K=1+\frac{2}{5}=1.40$.

Value of C, 4th column of table A, opposite $K=1.40$ $=0.16167$

Value of $C'=2(1-\frac{1}{2})\times 0.00957$ table A′ opposite $K=1.40$ $=0.00957$

$$F=r^2\times 0.17124$$

M. Audoy gives as the thrust of a five-center arch of the same span, rise, and thickness,

$$F=r^2\times 0.17914$$

$$\text{Difference}=F=r^2\times 0.00790$$

=about $4\frac{1}{2}$ per cent. of the true thrust.

The rule stated above gives immediately, and with all desirable accuracy, the thrust of elliptical arches, unloaded. Table H contains, all calculated, the rotation thrusts in two systems of elliptical arches, corresponding respectively to $\frac{f}{r}=\frac{1}{2}$ and $\frac{f}{r}=\frac{2}{3}$. The first column gives the quotient of the span divided by the thickness at the key, this quotient being the proper measure of the lightness of the arch. That table seems to require no explanation.

SLIDING THRUST OF UNLOADED ELLIPTICAL ARCHES.

Figure 20.

94. It appears from table A, that the rotation thrust of the unloaded circular arch exceeds the sliding thrust for all values of K less than 1.45. It appears from table A′, art. 92, that the rotation thrust of the elliptical ring, bounded by similar ellipses, is greater than the rotation thrust of the circular arch resting upon the same span and having a thickness at the key as much greater than the thickness of the elliptical arch as the half-span is greater than the rise; and that the difference increases as K increases.

Without stopping to demonstrate it, we here state the fact that the sliding thrust of the elliptical arch is always *less* than that of the auxiliary circular arch above described. Putting these facts together, we can give the following rule as perfectly safe, though liable to give a thrust too great:

Find the rotation thrust, art. 93. Should this thrust be less than the sliding thrust found in table A, opposite $K=1+\frac{d}{f}$, adopt the latter as the true thrust.

THICKNESS OF PIER—ELLIPTICAL ARCHES—UNLOADED.

Figure 20.

95. Let F=the thrust; h=the height of pier from the base to the springing line; l=the lever-arm of the thrust or elevation of a above the base of the pier; n=the surface of the semi-arch $A\ B\ a\ b$; m=the moment of that surface in relation to A; δ=the coefficient of stability; e=the unknown thickness of pier.

$$n=\frac{\pi}{4}rd\left(2+\frac{d}{f}\right);\quad m=r^2d\left(.5708-.2146\times\frac{d}{f}-\tfrac{1}{3}\times\frac{d^2}{f^2}\right);\quad (54)$$

$$\tfrac{1}{2}he^2+ne+m=\delta Fl$$

$$e=-\frac{n}{h}+\sqrt{\frac{n^2}{h^2}-2\frac{m}{h}+2\frac{\delta Fl}{h}}$$

THRUST OF ELLIPTICAL ARCHES SUSTAINING A LOAD OF MASONRY, OR OF EQUAL WEIGHT WITH MASONRY, RISING ON EACH SIDE OF THE CENTRAL RIDGE, TO A ROOF TANGENT TO THE EXTRADOS. *Figure* 21.

96. Let us compare the given arch with a circular arch of the same span, and of a thickness at the key as much greater than the thickness of the elliptical arch as the half-span is greater than the rise; and let us suppose the

loads of the two arches to sustain this same relation in their vertical depths. We suppose the thickness of the two arches at the springing line to be the same, which requires the extrados of the elliptical arch to be an ellipse similar to the intrados. $R\,P$, the roof of the given arch intersecting the horizontal of the springing line at P; draw $P\,R'$ tangent to the extrados of the circular arch. The two arches thus constructed, sustain to each other the relation described above. We have, by supposition, $a\,b : a'\,b' :: f : r$. Draw the vertical $d\,D'$ passing through the points of tangency D and D'.

Draw any other vertical line, $p\,u'$ cutting at m the intrados, at r the extrados, and at u the roof of the elliptical arch; at m', r', u' the corresponding parts of the circular arch. We have

$$p\,u : p\,u' :: d\,D : d\,D' :: p\,r : p\,r' :: C\,a : C\,a' :: C\,b : C\,b' :: f : r :: p\,m : p\,m'. \text{ Hence } m\,u : m'\,u' :: f : r.$$

Moreover projecting m and m' horizontally on the vertical through C, at t and t', we have, as in art. 91, $a\,t : a'\,t' :: f : r$.

Pursuing precisely the same course of reasoning as in art. 91, we see that the thrusts due to the segments $m\,u\,R\,b$, $m'\,u'\,R'\,b'$ are the same in the two arches, wherever the vertical $m\,m'$ be drawn. Consequently, the maximum thrust of the two arches is the same, and we can announce this principle:

The thrust of an elliptical arch loaded in masonry up to a plane tangent to the extrados, supposed to be similar to the intrados, is nearly equal to the thrust of a circular arch of the same span, and of a thickness of ring and of load at the key as much greater than the corresponding depths of the elliptical arch, as the half-span is greater than the rise; the load of the circular arch also rising to a plane tangent to its extrados.

We can, therefore, in most cases, obtain the required

thrust from table F. The result, however, thus obtained, will require a slight addition, viz:

$$\frac{\text{moment on } m' \text{ of the surface } m'\,n'\,i'\,i''\,n''\,m'}{\text{lever arm } a'\,t'} = A. \quad (55)$$

which may be calculated on the supposition that the angle of rupture of the circular arch is 60°.

It will be best to construct the diagram and obtain the elements of this calculation by protraction.

For obvious reasons the addition required will generally exceed but little the values given in table A′, art. 92.

Rule.—Suppose the angle $CRP=I'$ to be given by its tangent. Let angle $CR'P=I$; half-span$=r$; rise$=f$; thickness at the key$=ab=d$. We have tang. $I=\frac{f}{r}$tang. I', which gives I.

Obtain from table F the coefficient C of r^2 corresponding to this value of I and to $K=1+\frac{d}{f}$; to this add the product $2\left(1-\frac{f}{r}\right)\times\frac{A}{r^2}=C'$, $\frac{A}{r^2}$ being taken from table A′, art 92, opposite the same value of K.

Then the thrust $F=r^2(C+C')$.

To this we ought to add, when $n'\,i'$, $n''\,i''$, 60° from the key, have any considerable magnitude, the effect upon the thrust due to the trapezoid $n'\,i'\,i''\,n''$.

97. Example: $r=10$ feet; $f=6\frac{2}{3}$ feet; $I'=60°$; $d=1'.30$; $K=1+\frac{d}{f}=1.195$; $I=49°\ 6'\ 24''=49°.10\frac{2}{3}$; $50°-I=0°.89\frac{1}{3}$.

Coefficient of r^2, table F, for $K=1.195$,	$I=45°=C=$	0.25676
" " " "	$I=50°$ "	0.20942
	Difference,	0.04734

$5° : 0°.89\frac{1}{3} :: 0.04734 : x$	$=0.00846$
Add C, as above, for $K=1.195$; $I=50°$,	0.20942
Add from table A′, art 92, $2(1-\frac{2}{3})\times 0.00155$,	0.00103
Total thrust,	$F=r^2\times 0.21891$
M. Audoy gives as the thrust of a three-center arch of the same rise, span, and load,	$r^2\times 0.22075$
Difference$=\frac{5}{6}$ of 1 per cent., . . .	$=r^2\times 0.00184$

The rule given above can only be used when the angle I is greater than 45°, or but little less than that limit.

In other cases it will be best to investigate the thrust geometrically.

The effect of a surcharge of uniform vertical depth may be obtained from the table in art. 104; but the addition thus found will be a little too large.

Let t represent the depth of the surcharge. Look in that table opposite $K=1+\frac{d}{f}$ for the value of C; the required addition will be $A=r^2\times\frac{t}{f}C$.

THICKNESS OF PIER. *Figure* 21.

98. The general formulæ of art. 64 are all applicable to the elliptical arch. E, E', l, &c., must be taken from the given elliptical arch. The values of n and m will be as follows:

$$\left.\begin{aligned} n&=\tfrac{1}{2}r(E+E')-fr\times 0.7854 \\ m&=r^2(\tfrac{1}{3}E+\tfrac{1}{6}E')-fr^2\times 0.452065 \end{aligned}\right\} \qquad (56)$$

ELLIPTICAL ARCHES LOADED HORIZONTALLY UP TO THE LEVEL OF THE EXTRADOS AT THE KEY. *Figure* 22.

99. This is the most common form of the elliptical arch, almost the only form in practical use.

Let $r = A\ C$ = the half-span and semi-transverse axis of the ellipse; $f = Cb$ = the rise, and semi-conjugate axis; $d = ab$ = the thickness at the key. This thickness we suppose to be constant. The calculated thrust will be a little larger than it would have been had the extrados been another ellipse similar to the intrados.

Let us compare the given arch with a circular arch, surcharged in like manner horizontally, having the same span, and a thickness at the key as much greater than the thickness of the elliptical arch as the half-span is greater than the rise.

All the vertical dimensions of the auxiliary circular arch bear a constant proportion to the corresponding dimensions of the elliptical arch; so that, drawing any vertical, $p\ m\ m'\ u'$, we have

$$\frac{f}{r} = \frac{ab}{a'b'} = \frac{Cb}{Cb'} = \frac{Ca}{Ca'} = \frac{pu}{pu'} = \frac{pm}{pm'} = \frac{mu}{m'u'}.$$

Consequently the surfaces $m\ u\ a\ b$, $m'\ u'\ a'\ b'$, are also in the proportion of f to r; their centers of gravity are on the same vertical line; their lever arms, $a\ t$, $a'\ t'$, or $m\ u$, $m'\ u'$, are in the proportion of f to r.

These surfaces, therefore, have the same thrust wherever the vertical line be drawn. Their maximum thrusts will be the same; and we come to this conclusion:

The thrust of an elliptical arch sustaining a load of masonry, or of equal weight with masonry, rising to the horizontal line tangent to the extrados at the key, is nearly equal to the thrust of the semicircular arch, loaded in like manner, having the same span and a thickness at the key as much greater than the thickness of the elliptical arch as the half-span is greater than the rise.

We shall therefore be able to obtain from table D, with little labor, the thrust of elliptical arches.

The thrust thus obtained would be perfectly correct if the moments, in relation to the vertical through m, of the two surfaces $m\ n\ i\ u$, $m'\ n'\ i'\ u'$, stood like the segments on the right of that vertical, in the relation of f to r.

But this is not the case; and it is necessary to correct the result. In calculating table D, we have, in effect, subtracted, from the thrust due to the segment $m'\ u'\ a'\ b'$, the negative influence of $m'\ n'\ i'\ u'$, both taken at the angle of maximum thrust.

For our present purpose we should have subtracted only the effect of $m'\ n''\ i''\ u'$, which stands very nearly in the required relation to the surface $m\ n\ i\ u$. The joint $m\ n = a\ b = d$ is supposed to be normal to the intrados; $m'\ n''$ parallel and equal to $m\ n$. It is evidently necessary to add to the results of table D the difference of the effects of the two surfaces, $m'\ n'\ i'\ u'$, $m'\ n''\ i''\ u'$; or, increasing this difference slightly, the effect of the surface $s\ s'\ i'\ i''$, of which the altitude, $m'\ u'$, is also the lever arm of the thrust. Naming v the angle between $m\ n$ and a vertical, v' the angle between $m'\ n'$ and a vertical, we have, tang. $v = \frac{f}{r}$ tang. v'; and for the thrust,

$$F = r^2\left(C + \frac{\frac{1}{2}\left(\frac{r}{f}d\right)^2 \sin.^2 v' - \frac{1}{2}\,d^2 \sin.^2 v}{r^2}\right) \qquad (57)$$

in which C is taken from table D, and v' is supposed to be the angle of maximum thrust. This angle never differs much from 60°. We are at liberty, therefore, in all cases, to suppose $v' = 60°$; which gives

$$\sin.^2 v' = \tfrac{3}{4};\ \sin.^2 v = \frac{3\frac{f^2}{r^2}}{1 + 3\frac{f^2}{r^2}}$$

Table G, calculated from the above formula, gives, either directly or by proportional parts, the thrusts of all elliptical arches in practicable use.

The first column is the quotient of the span divided by the thickness of the arch at the key, this quotient being the proper measure of the massiveness or lightness of the arch.

100. The table on the following page gives the horizontal thrusts of elliptical and segmental arches of the same span, rise, and thickness, in four systems, all the arches being surcharged horizontally.

The reader will perhaps be surprised to see that there is but little difference in the thrusts of the two kinds of arches, and that, in very light arches, the difference is in favor of the elliptical intrados. When the rise is one fourth or one fifth of the span and the thickness about one twenty-fifth of the span, the thrust is nearly the same in elliptical and segmental arches.

To explain briefly the manner of comparing these thrusts: In tables E′ and D, r is the radius of the intrados; in the following table, r is the half-span. Let r=the half-span; f=the rise; d=the thickness at key; r'=the radius of the intrados of the segmental arch of the same span, rise, and thickness; K=the ratio of the two radii of the segmental arch; $K'=\frac{2r}{d}$. We have

$$r'=\tfrac{1}{2}r\left(\frac{f}{r}+\frac{r}{f}\right);\quad K=1+\frac{d}{r'}=1+\frac{4}{K'\times\left(\frac{f}{r}+\frac{r}{f}\right)};\qquad (58)$$

$$F=r'^2\times C=r^2\times\tfrac{1}{4}\left(\frac{f}{r}+\frac{r}{f}\right)^2\times C.$$

From this last formula the coefficients of r^2 in the following table have been computed from the coefficients of r'^2, (r^2), in tables E′ and D.

101. *Table of horizontal thrusts of elliptical and segmental arches of the same span, rise, and thickness at the key, in four systems; surcharged horizontally to the horizontal plane tangent to the extrados at the key; each arch of the same thickness throughout; r=the half-span; d=the thickness at the key; F'=thrust of elliptical arches; F=thrust of segmental arches.*

$\frac{2r}{d}=K'$.	Rise $=\frac{1}{5}$ the span.				Rise $=\frac{1}{4}$ the span.			
	$1+\frac{d}{r'}=K$.	Thrust in the elliptical arch $=F'$ $=r^2\times C$.	Thrust in the segmental arch $=F$ $=r^2\times C$.	$\frac{F'}{F}$.	$1+\frac{d}{r'}=K$.	Thrust in the elliptical arch $=F'$ $=r^2\times C$.	Thrust in the segmental arch $=F$ $=r^2\times C$.	$\frac{F'}{F}$.
60	1.02300	0.09874	0.10747	0.920	1.02⅔	0.09075	0.09840	0.920
50	1.02760	0.10628	0.11334	0.940	1.0320	0.09703	0.10322	0.940
40	1.03448	0.11687	0.12169	0.960	1.0400	0.10600	0.11021	0.960
30	1.04600	0.13308	0.13479	0.990	1.05⅓	0.11977	0.12101	0.990
25	1.05520	0.14469	0.14450	1.000	1.0640	0.13005	0.12911	1.010
20	1.06900	0.16054	0.15798	1.020	1.0800	0.14359	0.14040	1.020
15	1.09000	0.18355	0.17610	1.040	1.10⅔	0.16349	0.15692	1.040
10	1.13800	0.22374	0.20880	1.070	1.1600	0.19564	0.18300	1.070
8					1.2000	0.21684	0.19737	1.100
	Rise $=\frac{1}{3}$ the span.				Rise $=\frac{3}{8}$ the span.			
60	1.03077	0.08238	0.08478	0.970	1.0320	0.07943	0.07905	1.000
50	1.03690	0.08727	0.08837	0.990	1.0384	0.08386	0.08250	1.016
40	1.04615	0.09448	0.09373	1.010	1.0480	0.09047	0.08764	1.030
30	1.06150	0.10527	0.10222	1.030	1.0640	0.10011	0.09580	1.045
25	1.07380	0.11336	0.10869	1.043	1.0768	0.10747	0.10174	1.056
20	1.09230	0.12453	0.11719	1.060	1.0960	0.11758	0.10988	1.070
15	1.12300	0.14065	0.12999	1.080	1.1280	0.13225	0.12194	1.085
10	1.18460	0.16564	0.14965	1.110	1.1920	0.15474	0.14008	1.100
8	1.23077	0.17977	0.15966	1.130	1.2400	0.16680	0.14906	1.120
6	1.30770	0.19848	0.16872	1.170	1.3200	0.18082	0.15690	1.150

102. In the preceding table we have supposed every arch to have a constant thickness throughout.

In practice, all light arches should increase in thickness from the key to the springing line, as already explained. Such increase, applied to the arches of the preceding table will diminish the thrusts of elliptical and segmental arches, without sensibly changing their relative magnitudes.

EFFECT OF SURCHARGE UPON THE ROTATION THRUST.

Figure 22.

103. Suppose a surcharge of the density of the arch and of the uniform vertical depth $t=ad$. On the auxiliary circular arch lay off $a'\,d'=\frac{r}{f}\times t$. Let us take into account in reference to any joints $m\,n$, $m'\,n'$, only that part of the surcharge which overlies the segments upon the right of the vertical, $m\,m'$. The effect of the surcharge will be precisely the same in the two arches. But the addition to the thrust caused by this surcharge in the circular arch will be $A=\frac{r}{f}tr\frac{\sin.^2 v'}{K-\cos.v'}$; of which the maximum value is

$$A=r^2\times\frac{t}{f}\times(K-\sqrt{K^2-1}). \qquad (59)$$

The following table gives the values of the factor $(K-\sqrt{K^2-1})$ for values of K ranging from 1 to 1.40.

104. *Table of* additions *to the rotation thrust caused by a surcharge of constant vertical depth; d=the thickness of the elliptical arch at the key; r=the half-span; f= the rise; t=the depth of the surcharge on the elliptical arch; A=the addition to the thrust of the elliptical arch; C=the decimal in any column; K=the ratio of the two radii of the auxiliary semicircular arch. We have* $K=1+\frac{d}{f}$; $A=r^2\times\frac{t}{f}\times C$.

The results of this table are always slightly in excess.

$1+\frac{d}{f}=\frac{R}{r}$ $=K.$	$A=r^2\times\frac{t}{f}\times C.$ C.	$1+\frac{d}{f}=\frac{R}{r}$ $=K.$	$A=r^2\times\frac{t}{f}\times C.$ C.	K.	$A=r^2\times\frac{t}{f}\times C.$ C.	K.	$A=r^2\times\frac{t}{f}\times C.$ C.
1.00	1.00000	1.11	0.62823	1.22	0.52114	1.33	0.45313
1.01	0.86823	1.12	0.61562	1.23	0.51383	1.34	0.44804
1.02	0.81900	1.13	0.60379	1.24	0.50679	1.35	0.44308
1.03	0.78322	1.14	0.59264	1.25	0.50000	1.36	0.43826
1.04	0.75434	1.15	0.58211	1.26	0.49345	1.37	0.43357
1.05	0.72984	1.16	0.57212	1.27	0.48712	1.38	0.42900
1.06	0.70843	1.17	0.56263	1.28	0.48100	1.39	0.42455
1.07	0.68934	1.18	0.55358	1.29	0.47508	1.40	0.42020
1.08	0.67208	1.19	0.54494	1.30	0.46934		
1.09	0.65630	1.20	0.53668	1.31	0.46378		
1.10	0.64174	1.21	0.52875	1.32	0.45837		

105. Example. The Waterloo Bridge: span=120 feet $=2r$; rise=32 feet$=f$; thickness at the key=4.50 feet$=d$. These dimensions give, the number in the first column of table G, $K'=\frac{2r}{d}=26\frac{2}{3}$; $f=r\times 0.53\frac{1}{3}$.

Thrust, 3d column table G, for $K'=26$,

$f=r\times 0.50$, ... $F=r^2\times 0.12767$

Ditto for $K'=28$, $f=r\times 0.50$, . . $F=r^2\times 0.12347$

Subtracting one third of the difference from the former, we have, for $K'=26\frac{2}{3}$,
$f=r\times.50$, ... $F=r^2\times0.12627$

In like manner we find for $K'=26\frac{2}{3}, f=$
$\frac{27\frac{1}{2}}{50}r=r\times0.55$, ... $F=r^2\times0.12068$

Adding one third of the difference to the latter we have the required thrust, corresponding to $K'=26\frac{2}{3}, f=r\times0.53\frac{1}{3}$, $F=r^2\times0.12254$

Suppose a surcharge 4 feet deep throughout, we find, art. 104, opposite $K=1+\frac{d}{f}=1+\frac{4.50}{32}=1.14$, $A=r^2\times\frac{t}{f}\times C=r^2$
$\times\frac{4}{32}\times0.59264$, ... $=r^2\times0.07408$

Total thrust, $F=r^2\times0.19662$

$=707.83$; that is, the thrust upon one foot in width of the bridge at the key, is equivalent to the weight of a column, of the material of the bridge, one foot square and 707.83 feet high. Dividing this by the thickness of the arch, $4\frac{1}{2}$ feet, we have, as the mean pressure upon each square foot of surface at the key, 157.30. This mean pressure, according to the best authorities, should never exceed one twentieth of the ultimate strength of the material.

Example II. $r=10'$; $f=6\frac{2}{3}$ feet; $d=1'$; giving $K'=20$; $f=\frac{2}{3}r$;

Thrust, 6th column table G, opposite $K'=20$, ... $F=r^2\times0.12453$

Three-center arch of the same rise, span, and thickness, M. Audoy, . . $F=r^2\times0.13089$

Difference, about 5 per cent. of the thrust, $=r^2\times0.00636$

SLIDING THRUST OF ELLIPTICAL ARCHES SURCHARGED HORIZONTALLY.

106. This thrust will always be less than the rotation thrust, unless the arch have an enormous thickness at the key.

For reasons substantially the same with those given in art. 94, we are justified in offering the following rule as perfectly safe, but liable to give a thrust somewhat too large.

Rule. Find the rotation thrust as above explained. Should this thrust be less than the sliding thrust in table D, opposite $K=1+\frac{d}{f}$, adopt the latter as the true thrust.

THICKNESS OF PIER.

107. The formulæ of art. 64 are applicable to all cases. Applied to elliptical arches surcharged horizontally, we have

$$E=E'=f+d+t;\ n=r\times E-rf\times 0.7854;\ m=\tfrac{1}{2}r^2E-r^2f\times 0.452065; \tag{60}$$

in all cases $l=$the elevation of the extrados at the crown above the base of the pier.

Example. Waterloo Bridge, dimensions and load given in art. 105. Depth of the pier below the springing line$=$ $19'.50$; $h=60'$; $E=32'+4'.50+4'=40'.50$; $n=60\times 40.50-60\times 32\times 0.7854=922.03$; $m=\frac{1}{2}(60)^2\times 40.50-(60)^2\times 32\times 0.452065=20822$. $l=56'$; $\frac{n}{h}=15.367$; $\frac{n^2}{h^2}=236.15$; $\frac{m}{h}=347.03$; $\frac{Fl}{h}=660.64$; F, art. 105, $=707.83$.

These values substituted in (31), art. 64, give, for strict equilibrium, $\delta=1$, ... $e=14'.02$
(31), art. 64, give, for $\delta=2$, ... $e=31'.37$
($31\frac{1}{3}$), " " $x=\frac{1}{3}e$, ... $e=22'.43$
($31\frac{2}{5}$), " " $x=\frac{2}{5}e$, ... $e=26'.43$

The thickness of the existing piers is, at the bottom 30′, at the springing line 20′, and the piers extend above and below the bridge about one-fourth the width of the bridge, each way. Every pier, therefore, of this celebrated bridge, is an abutment pier, with very nearly the excess of stability prescribed by the French engineers. Comparing the moment of the thrust with the sum of the moments of all the elements of resistance, we find δ, the coefficient of stability, to be very nearly 1.79.

CIRCULAR ARCHES OF 180°, WITH PARALLEL EXTRADOS.

(A) *Table giving the angle of rupture, the thrust, and the limit thickness of piers.*

Value of the ratio $K=\frac{R}{r}$.	Ratio of the diameter to the thickness.	Value of the Angle of Rupture.	Ratio C, of the thrust to the square of the radius r. of the intrados.		Ratio $\sqrt{2.C.}$ of the limit thickness of Pier to the radius of the intrados.	
		Rotation.	Rotation.	Sliding.	Strict Equilibrium.	Co-efficient of stability, 1.90
2.732	1.154	0° 00′	0.00000	0.98923		
2.70	1.176	13 42	0.00211	0.96262		
2.65	1.212	22 00	0.00319	0.02168		
2.60	1.250	27 30	0.00808	0.88151		
2.50	1.333	35 52	0.02283	0.80346		
2.40	1.428	42 06	0.04109	0.72847		
2.30	1.538	46 47	0.06835	0.65654		
2.20	1.666	51 04	0.08648	0.58767		
2.10	1.810	54 27	0.10926	0.52186		
2.00	2.000	57 17	0.13017	0.45912	0.9582	1.3223
1.90	2.282	59 37	0.14813	0.39943	0.8938	1.2320
1.80	2.500	61 24	0.16373	0.34281	0.8280	1.1414
1.70	2.857	62 53	0.17180	0.28924	0.7606	1.0484
1.60	3.333	63 49	0.17517	0.23874	0.6910	0.9525
1.59	3.389	63 52	0.17533	0.23386	0.6839	0.9427
1.58	3.448	63 55	0.17535	0.22901	0.6768	0.9329
1.57	3.508	63 58	0.17524	0.22434	0.6698	0.9233
1.56	3.571	64 01	0.17499	0.21940	0.6624	0.9131
1.55	3.636	64 03	0.17478	0.21464	0.6552	0.9031
1.54	3.703	64 05	0.17445	0.20991	0.6479	0.8931
1.53	3.773	64 07	0.17397	0.20521	0.6406	0.8831
1.52	3.846	64 08	0.17352	0.20054	0.6333	0.8730
1.51	3.920	64 08	0.17310	0.19590	0.6259	0.8628
1.50	4.000	64 09	0.17254	0.19130	0.6185	0.8527
1.49	4.081	64 08	0.17180	0.18673	0.6111	0.8424
1.48	4.166	64 08	0.17095	0.18218	0.6036	0.8320
1.47	4.255	64 07	0.17008	0.17766	0.5961	0.8216
1.46	4.347	64 06	0.16915	0.17318	0.5885	0.8112
1.45	4.444	64 05	0.16798	0.16872	0.5809	0.8007
1.44	4.545	64 03	0.16683	0.16430	0.5776	0.7962
1.43	4.651	64 00	0.16568	0.15991	0.5756	0.7934
1.42	4.761	63 56	0.16448	0.15555	0.5735	0.7906
1.41	4.878	63 52	0.16317	0.15122	0.5713	0.7874
1.40	5.000	63 48	0.16167	0.14691	0.5686	0.7838
1.39	5.128	63 43	0.16014	0.14264	0.5659	0.7801
1.38	5.263	63 38	0.15845	0.13841	0.5629	0.7760
1.37	5.406	63 32	0.15672	0.13420	0.5598	0.7717

Circular Arches of 180°, with Parallel Extrados.

(A) *Table giving the angle of rupture, the thrust, and the limit thickness of piers.*

Value of the ratio $K=\frac{R}{r}$	Ratio of the diameter to the thickness.	Value of the angle of rupture.	Ratio, C. of the thrust to the square of the radius, r, of the intrados.		Ratio $\sqrt{2}.\ C$. of the limit thickness of pier to the radius of the intrados.	
		Rotation.	Rotation.	Sliding	Strict Equilibrium.	Co-efficient of stability 1.90.
1.36	5.555	63° 26′	0.15482	0.13002	0.5564	0.7670
1.35	5.714	63 19	0.15287	0.12587	0.5529	0.7622
1.34	5.882	63 10	0.15096	0.12176	0.5495	0.7574
1.33	6.060	63 00	0.14896	0.11767	0.5458	0.7524
1.32	6.264	62 50	0.14678	0.11362	0.5418	0.7468
1.31	6.451	62 33	0.14510	0.10959	0.5387	0.7425
1.30	6.666	62 14	0.14330	0.10559	0.5353	0.7379
1.29	6.896	62 09	0.14013	0.10163	0.5294	0.7297
1.28	7.142	62 03	0.13691	0.09770	0.5233	0.7213
1.27	7.407	61 47	0.13430	0.09379	0.5183	0.7144
1.26	7.692	61 30	0.13157	0.08992	0.5130	0.7071
1.25	8.000	61 15	0.12847	0.08608	0.5069	0.6987
1.24	8.333	61 01	0.12516	0.08227	0.5003	0.6896
1.23	8.695	60 40	0.12201	9.07849	0.4940	0.6809
1.22	9.090	60 19	0.11887	0.07474	0.4876	0.6721
1.21	9.523	60 00	0.11516	0.07102	0.4799	0.6615
1.20	10.000	59 41	0.11140	0.06733	0.4720	0.6504
1.19	10.526	59 10	0.10791	0.06368	0.4646	0.6404
1.18	11.111	58 40	0.10417	0.06005	0.4564	0.6292
1.17	11.764	58 09	0.10021	0.05646	0.4472	0.6171
1.16	12.500	57 40	0.09593	0.05289	0.4380	0.6038
1.15	13.333	57 01	0.09176	0.04935	0.4284	0.5905
1.14	14.285	56 23	0.08729	0.04585	0.4178	0.5759
1.13	15.384	55 45	0.08254	0.04237	0.4063	0.5601
1.12	16.666	54 48	0.07789	0.03984	0.3947	0.5444
1.11	18.181	54 10	0.07273	0.03552	0.3814	0.5259
1.10	20.000	53 15	0.06754	0.03213	0.3675	0.5066
1.09	22.222	52 14	0.06177	0.02879		
1.08	25.000	51 07	0.05649	0.02546		
1.07	28.571	49 48	0.05065	0.02217		
1.06	33.333	48 18	0.04455	0.01891		
1.05	40.000	46 32	0.03813	0.01568		
1.04	50.000	44 04	0.03139	0.01249		
1.03	66.666	41 04	0.02459	0.00932		
1.02	100.000	38 12	0.01691	0.00618		
1.01	200.000	32 36	0.00889	0.00308		
1.00	Infini.	0 00	0.00000	0.00000		

Circular Arches of 180°—Extrados and Intrados Parallel.

(B) *Table of Thickness of Piers.*

Value of the ratio $K=\frac{R}{r}$	Ratio of the diameter to the thickness	Ratio $\frac{e}{r}$ of the thickness of piers to the radius of the intrados, in function of the ratio $\frac{r}{h}$, of this radius, to the height of the piers. CASE OF STRICT EQUILIBRIUM.
2.00	2.000	$-2.3562\frac{r}{h}+\sqrt{(5.5517\frac{r^2}{h^2}+1.7907\frac{r}{h}+0.9182)}$
1.90	2.222	$-2.0449\frac{r}{h}+\sqrt{(4.2021\frac{r^2}{h^2}+1.3240\frac{r}{h}+0.7988)}$
1.80	2.500	$-1.7593\frac{r}{h}+\sqrt{(3.0951\frac{r^2}{h^2}+0.9368\frac{r}{h}+0.6856)}$
1.70	2.857	$-1.4844\frac{r}{h}+\sqrt{(2.2034\frac{r^2}{h^2}+0.6933\frac{r}{h}+0.5785)}$
1.60	3.333	$-1.2252\frac{r}{h}+\sqrt{(1.5012\frac{r^2}{h^2}+0.3775\frac{r}{h}+0.4775)}$
1.59	3.389	$-1.2001\frac{r}{h}+\sqrt{(1.4404\frac{r^2}{h^2}+0.3566\frac{r}{h}+0.4677)}$
1.58	3.448	$-1.1752\frac{r}{h}+\sqrt{(1.3812\frac{r^2}{h^2}+0.3361\frac{r}{h}+0.4580)}$
1.57	3.508	$-1.1513\frac{r}{h}+\sqrt{(1.3255\frac{r^2}{h^2}+0.3151\frac{r}{h}+0.4487)}$
1.56	3.571	$-1.1261\frac{r}{h}+\sqrt{(1.2677\frac{r^2}{h^2}+0.2966\frac{r}{h}+0.4388)}$
1.55	3.636	$-1.1015\frac{r}{h}+\sqrt{(1.2133\frac{r^2}{h^2}+0.2783\frac{r}{h}+0.4293)}$
1.54	3.703	$-1.0772\frac{r}{h}+\sqrt{(1.1605\frac{r^2}{h^2}+0.2603\frac{r}{h}+0.4198)}$
1.53	3.773	$-1.0531\frac{r}{h}+\sqrt{(1.1091\frac{r^2}{h^2}+0.2428\frac{r}{h}+0.4104)}$
1.52	3.846	$-1.0292\frac{r}{h}+\sqrt{(1.0592\frac{r^2}{h^2}+0.2224\frac{r}{h}+0.4011)}$
1.51	3.920	$-1.0073\frac{r}{h}+\sqrt{(1.0146\frac{r^2}{h^2}+0.2056\frac{r}{h}+0.3918)}$
1.50	4.000	$-0.9817\frac{r}{h}+\sqrt{(0.9638\frac{r^2}{h^2}+0.1937\frac{r}{h}+0.3826)}$
1.49	4.081	$-0.9583\frac{r}{h}+\sqrt{(0.9184\frac{r^2}{h^2}+0.1684\frac{r}{h}+0.3735)}$
1.48	4.166	$-0.9349\frac{r}{h}+\sqrt{(0.8741\frac{r^2}{h^2}+0.1659\frac{r}{h}+0.3644)}$
1.47	4.255	$-0.9125\frac{r}{h}+\sqrt{(0.8328\frac{r^2}{h^2}+0.1482\frac{r}{h}+0.3553)}$
1.46	4.347	$-0.8887\frac{r}{h}+\sqrt{(0.7899\frac{r^2}{h^2}+0.1362\frac{r}{h}+0.3464)}$
1.45	4.444	$-0.8659\frac{r}{h}+\sqrt{(0.7498\frac{r^2}{h^2}+0.1232\frac{r}{h}+0.3374)}$
1.44	4.545	$-0.8432\frac{r}{h}+\sqrt{(0.7110\frac{r^2}{h^2}+0.1181\frac{r}{h}+0.3337)}$
1.43	4.651	$-0.8206\frac{r}{h}+\sqrt{(0.6735\frac{r^2}{h^2}+0.1153\frac{r}{h}+0.3314)}$
1.42	4.761	$-0.7983\frac{r}{h}+\sqrt{(0.6372\frac{r^2}{h^2}+0.1143\frac{r}{h}+0.3290)}$
1.41	4.878	$-0.7760\frac{r}{h}+\sqrt{(0.6023\frac{r^2}{h^2}+0.1102\frac{r}{h}+0.3263)}$
1.40	5.000	$-0.7540\frac{r}{h}+\sqrt{(0.5685\frac{r^2}{h^2}+0.1074\frac{r}{h}+0.3233)}$
1.39	5.128	$-0.7321\frac{r}{h}+\sqrt{(0.5359\frac{r^2}{h^2}+0.1048\frac{r}{h}+0.3203)}$
1.38	5.263	$-0.7103\frac{r}{h}+\sqrt{(0.5045\frac{r^2}{h^2}+0.1021\frac{r}{h}+0.3169)}$

CIRCULAR ARCHES OF 180°—EXTRADOS AND INTRADOS PARALLEL.

Continuation of Table (B). *Thickness of Piers.*

Value of the ratio $K=\frac{R}{r}$	Ratio of the diameter to the thickness	Ratio $\frac{e}{r}$ of the thickness of piers to the radius of the intrados, in function of the ratio $\frac{r}{h}$, of this radius, to the height of the piers. CASE OF STRICT EQUILIBRIUM.
1.37	5.406	$-0.6887\frac{r}{h}+\sqrt{(0.4743\frac{r^2}{h^2}+0.0995\frac{r}{h}+0.3134)}$
1.36	5.555	$-0.6673\frac{r}{h}+\sqrt{(0.4452\frac{r^2}{h^2}+0.0969\frac{r}{h}+0.3096)}$
1.35	5.714	$-0.6460\frac{r}{h}+\sqrt{(0.4173\frac{r^2}{h^2}+0.0944\frac{r}{h}+0.3057)}$
1.34	5.882	$-0.6249\frac{r}{h}+\sqrt{(0.3904\frac{r^2}{h^2}+0.0926\frac{r}{h}+0.3019)}$
1.33	6.060	$-0.6050\frac{r}{h}+\sqrt{(0.3660\frac{r^2}{h^2}+0.0903\frac{r}{h}+0.2979)}$
1.32	6.264	$-0.5831\frac{r}{h}+\sqrt{(0.3400\frac{r^2}{h^2}+0.0880\frac{r}{h}+0.2936)}$
1.31	6.451	$-0.5624\frac{r}{h}+\sqrt{(0.3163\frac{r^2}{h^2}+0.0875\frac{r}{h}+0.2902)}$
1.30	6.666	$-0.5419\frac{r}{h}+\sqrt{(0.2937\frac{r^2}{h^2}+0.0867\frac{r}{h}+0.2866)}$
1.29	6.896	$-0.5216\frac{r}{h}+\sqrt{(0.2720\frac{r^2}{h^2}+0.0828\frac{r}{h}+0.2803)}$
1.28	7.142	$-0.5014\frac{r}{h}+\sqrt{(0.2520\frac{r^2}{h^2}+0.0801\frac{r}{h}+0.2738)}$
1.27	7.407	$-0.4926\frac{r}{h}+\sqrt{(0.2426\frac{r^2}{h^2}+0.0778\frac{r}{h}+0.2686)}$
1.26	7.692	$-0.4615\frac{r}{h}+\sqrt{(0.2130\frac{r^2}{h^2}+0.0755\frac{r}{h}+0.2631)}$
1.25	8.000	$-0.4418\frac{r}{h}+\sqrt{(0.1952\frac{r^2}{h^2}+0.0730\frac{r}{h}+0.2569)}$
1.24	8.333	$-0.4222\frac{r}{h}+\sqrt{(0.1783\frac{r^2}{h^2}+0.0713\frac{r}{h}+0.2503)}$
1.23	8.695	$-0.4028\frac{r}{h}+\sqrt{(0.1623\frac{r^2}{h^2}+0.0684\frac{r}{h}+0.2440)}$
1.22	9.090	$-0.3836\frac{r}{h}+\sqrt{(0.1471\frac{r^2}{h^2}+0.0674\frac{r}{h}+0.2377)}$
1.21	9.523	$-0.3645\frac{r}{h}+\sqrt{(0.1329\frac{r^2}{h^2}+0.0641\frac{r}{h}+0.2303)}$
1.20	10.000	$-0.3456\frac{r}{h}+\sqrt{(0.1194\frac{r^2}{h^2}+0.0614\frac{r}{h}+0.2228)}$
1.19	10.526	$-0.3268\frac{r}{h}+\sqrt{(0.1068\frac{r^2}{h^2}+0.0600\frac{r}{h}+0.2158)}$
1.18	11.111	$-0.3082\frac{r}{h}+\sqrt{(0.0950\frac{r^2}{h^2}+0.0581\frac{r}{h}+0.2083)}$
1.17	11.764	$-0.2897\frac{r}{h}+\sqrt{(0.0840\frac{r^2}{h^2}+0.0561\frac{r}{h}+0.2004)}$
1.16	12.500	$-0.2714\frac{r}{h}+\sqrt{(0.0734\frac{r^2}{h^2}+0.0559\frac{r}{h}+0.1919)}$
1.15	13.333	$-0.2533\frac{r}{h}+\sqrt{(0.0642\frac{r^2}{h^2}+0.0536\frac{r}{h}+0.1835)}$
1.14	14.285	$-0.2353\frac{r}{h}+\sqrt{(0.0554\frac{r^2}{h^2}+0.0513\frac{r}{h}+0.1745)}$
1.13	15.384	$-0.2175\frac{r}{h}+\sqrt{(0.0473\frac{r^2}{h^2}+0.0490\frac{r}{h}+0.1651)}$
1.12	16.666	$-0.1998\frac{r}{h}+\sqrt{(0.0399\frac{r^2}{h^2}+0.0467\frac{r}{h}+0.1557)}$
1.11	18.181	$-0.1823\frac{r}{h}+\sqrt{(0.0332\frac{r^2}{h^2}+0.0426\frac{r}{h}+0.1455)}$
1.10	20.000	$-0.1649\frac{r}{h}+\sqrt{(0.0272\frac{r^2}{h^2}+0.0394\frac{r}{h}+0.1351)}$

Circular Arches of 180°, with a Surcharge in Masonry inclined 45° on each side of the Central Ridge.

(C) *Table giving the angle of rupture, the thrust, and the limit thickness of piers.*

Value of the ratio $K=\frac{R}{r}$	Ratio of the diameter to the thickness.	Value of the angle of rupture.	Ratio, C, of the thrust to the square of the radius, r, of the intrados.		Ratio $\sqrt{2}.C.$ of the limit thickness of pier to the radius of the intrados.	
		Rotat'n.	Rotation.	Sliding.	Strict Equilibrium.	Coefficient of stability 2.
2.00	2.000	60°	0.26424	0.74361	1.2212	1.7246
1.90	2.222	60	0.28416	0.65648	1.1458	1.6204
1.80	2.500	60	0.29907	0.57383	1.0759	1.5147
1.70	2.857	60	0.30867	0.49564	0.9956	1.4081
1.60	3.333	60	0.31245	0.42191	0.9186	1.2990
1.59	3.389	60	0.31249	0.41478	0.9108	1.2880
1.58	3.448	60	0.31257	0.40841	0.9038	1.2781
1.57	3.508	61	0.31264	0.40067	0.8952	1.2660
1.56	3.571	61	0.31246	0.39367	0.8864	1.2548
1.55	3.636	61	0.31222	0.38673	0.8795	1.2437
1.54	3.703	61	0.31191	0.37983	0.8716	1.2318
1.53	3.773	61	0.31153	0.37297	0.8637	1.2214
1.52	3.846	61	0.31108	0.36615	0.8557	1.2102
1.51	3.920	61	0.31056	0.35938	0.8478	1.1989
1.50	4.000	61	0.30996	0.35266	0.8398	1.1877
1.49	4.081	61	0.30928	0.34598	0.8318	1.1764
1.48	4.166	61	0.30855	0.33934	0.8238	1.1650
1.47	4.255	61	0.30772	0.33275	0.8158	1.1537
1.46	4.347	60	0.30685	0.32621	0.8077	1.1422
1.45	4.444	60	0.30587	0.31971	0.7996	1.1308
1.44	4.545	60	0.30485	0.31325	0.7915	1.1193
1.43	4.651	60	0.30408	0.30684	0.7834	1.1078
1.42	4.761	60	0.30296	0.30047	0.7784	1.1008
1.41	4.878	60	0.30173		0.7768	1.0986
1.40	5.000	59	0.30001	0.28787	0.7746	1.0954
1.39	5.128	59	0.29712		0.7709	1.0914
1.38	5.263	59	0.29706		0.7690	1.0914
1.37	5.406	59	0.29550		0.7688	1.0872

Circular Arches of 180°, with a Surcharge in Masonry inclined 45° on each side of the Central Ridge.

(C) *Table giving the angle of rupture, the thrust, and the limit thickness of piers.*

Value of the ratio $K=\frac{R}{r}$.	Ratio of the diameter to the thickness.	Value of the angle of rupture. Rotat'n.	Ratio, C, of the thrust to the square of the radius, r, of the intrados. Rotation.	Sliding.	Ratio $\sqrt{2.C}$ of the limit thickness of pier to the radius of the intrados. Strict Equilibrium.	Coefficient of stability 2.
1.36	5.555	59°	0.29386		0.7665	1.0841
1.35	5.714	58	0.29285		0.7653	1.0823
1.34	5.882	58	0.29037		0.7621	1.0777
1.33	6.060	58	0.28850		0.7596	1.0742
1.32	6.264	58	0.28654		0.7570	1.0705
1.31	6.451	57	0.28456		0.7544	1.0668
1.30	6.666	57	0.28231	0.22756	0.7514	1.0626
1.29	6.896	57	0.28027		0.7487	1.0588
1.28	7.142	56	0.27810		0.7458	1.0547
1.27	7.407	56	0.27578		0.7427	1.0503
1.26	7.692	55	0.27343		0.7395	1.0458
1.25	8.000	54	0.27102		0.7362	1.0412
1.24	8.333	53	0.26850		0.7328	1.0363
1.23	8.695	53	0.26608		0.7274	1.0316
1.22	9.090	52	0.26377		0.7263	1.0272
1.21	9.523	51	0.26074		0.7221	1.0217
1.20	10.000	50	0.25806	0.17172	0.7184	1.0160
1.19	10.526	50	0.25546		0.7148	1.0109
1.18	11.111	49	0.25277		0.7111	1.0045
1.17	11.764	49	0.25010		0.7072	1.0002
1.16	12.500	48	0.24742		0.7034	0.9948
1.15	13.333	47	0.24477		0.6997	0.9894
1.14	14.285	46	0.24218		0.6960	0.9842
1.13	15.384	44	0.23967		0.6923	0.9791
1.12	16.666	43	0.23732		0.6889	0.9743
1.11	18.181	43	0.23502		0.6856	0.9695
1.10	20.000	42	0.23292	0.12032	0.6825	0.9652
1.05	40.000	36	0.22902		0.6768	0.9571

Circular Arches of 180°, Loaded up to the Level of the Top of the Key.

(D) *Table giving the angle of rupture, the thrust, and the limit thickness of piers.*

Value of the Ratio. $K=\frac{R}{r}$.	Ratio of the diameter to the thickness.	Value of the angle of rupture.	Ratio, C, of the thrust to the square of the radius, r, of the intrados.		Ratio of the limit thickness of pier to the radius of the intrados.	
		Rotat'n.	Rotation.	Sliding.	Strict Equilibrium.	Coefficient of stability 1.90.
2.00	2.000	36°	0.05486	0.50358	1.0036	1.3834
1.90	2.222	39	0.07101	0.43966	0.9377	1.2925
1.80	2.500	44	0.08850	0.37901	0.8706	1.2001
1.70	2.857	48	0.10631	0.32164	0.8020	1.1055
1.60	3.333	52	0.12300	0.26755	0.7315	1.0082
1.59	3.389	52	0.12453	0.26232	0.7243	0.9984
1.58	3.448	53	0.12602	0.25712	0.7171	0.9885
1.57	3.508	53	0.12747	0.25196	0.7099	0.9784
1.56	3.571	54	0.12837	0.24683	0.7026	0.9684
1.55	3.636	54	0.13027	0.24173	0.6953	0.9584
1.54	3.703	55	0.13153	0.23667	0.6880	0.9483
1.53	3.773	55	0.13289	0.23163	0.6806	0.9381
1.52	3.846	55	0.13414	0.22664	0.6732	0.9280
1.51	3.920	55	0.13531	0.22167	0.6658	0.9177
1.50	4.000	56	0.13648	0.21673	0.6583	0.9075
1.49	4.081	56	0.13756	0.21183	0.6509	0.8972
1.48	4.166	56	0.13856	0.20696	0.6433	0.8868
1.47	4.255	57	0.13952	0.20213	0.6358	0.8764
1.46	4.347	57	0.14041	0.19733	0.6282	0.8659
1.45	4.444	57	0.14122	0.19256	0.6206	0.8554
1.44	4.545	58	0.14195	0.18782	0.6129	0.8448
1.43	4.651	58	0.14268	0.18312	0.6052	0.8341
1.42	4.761	58	0.14311	0.17845	0.5974	0.8234
1.41	4.878	59	0.14376	0.17381	0.5896	0.8126
1.40	5.000	59	0.14421	0.16920	0.5817	0.8018
1.39	5.128	59	0.14456	0.16463	0.5738	0.7909
1.38	5.263	59	0.14481	0.16009	0.5658	0.7799
1.37	5.406	60	0.14498	0.15558	0.5578	0.7689
1.36	5.555	60	0.14506	0.15111	0.5497	0.7577
1.35	5.714	60	0.14504	0.14666	0.5416	0.7465
1.34	5.882	60	0.14491	0.14225	0.5383	0.7420
1.33	6.060	61	0.14467		0.5379	0.7414
1.32	6.264	61	0.14460		0.5377	0.7412

CIRCULAR ARCHES OF 180, LOADED UP TO THE LEVEL OF THE TOP OF THE KEY.

(D) *Table giving the angle of rupture, the thrust, and the limit thickness of piers.*

Value of the Ratio $K=\frac{R}{r}$.	Ratio of the diameter to the thickness.	Value of the angle of rupture.	Ratio, C, of the thrust to the square of the radius, r, of the intrados.		Ratio of the limit thickness of pier to the radius of the intrados	
		Rotat'n.	Rotation.	Sliding.	Strict Equilibrium	Coefficient of stability 1.90.
1.31	6.451	61°	0.143900		0.5358	0.7394
1.30	6.666	61	0.143320	0.12495	0.5354	0.7379
1.29	6.896	61	0.142640		0.5341	0.7362
1.28	7.142	62	0.141860		0.5326	0.7342
1.27	7.407	62	0.141010		0.5310	0.7320
1.26	7.692	62	0.139880		0.5289	0.7290
1.25	8.000	62	0.138720	0.10405	0.5267	0.7260
1.24	8.333	62	0.137370		0.5235	0.7225
1.23	8.695	63	0.135930		0.5214	0.7187
1.22	9.090	63	0.134370		0.5184	0.7145
1.21	9.523	63	0.132630		0.5150	0.7090
1.20	10.000	63	0.130730	0.08397	0.5113	0.7048
1.19	10.526	63	0.128700		0.5073	0.6993
1.18	11.111	63	0.126500		0.5030	0.6933
1.17	11.764	64	0.124150		0.4983	0.6868
1.16	12.500	64	0.121820		0.4936	0.6803
1.15	13.333	64	0.118950	0.06471	0.4877	0.6723
1.14	14.285	64	0.116080		0.4818	0.6641
1.13	15.384	64	0.113030		0.4755	0.6553
1.12	16.666	64	0.109790		0.4686	0.6459
1.11	18.181	65	0.106410		0.4613	0.6358
1.10	20.000	65	0.102790	0.04627	0.4535	0.6249
1.09	22.222	66	0.098992		0.4449	0.6133
1.08	25.000	66	0.094967		0.4358	0.6007
1.07	28.571	67	0.091189		0.4270	0.5886
1.06	33.333	68	0.086376		0.4156	0.5729
1.05	40.000	69	0.081755	0.02865	0.4044	0.5573
1.04	50.000	70	0.076857			
1.03	66.666	71	0.071853			
1.02	100.000	73	0.066469			
1.01	200.000	74	0.061324			
1.00		75	0.055472	0.01185		

SEGMENTAL ARCHES—EXTRADOS AND INTRADOS PARALLEL.

(E) *Table of thrusts in seven systems; s=the span; f=the rise; C=the decimal in any column; F=the thrust $=r^2C$.*

Value of the ratio $K=\frac{R}{r}$.	The thrust = the decimal × the square of the radius of the intrados.						
	$s=4f$. $r=\frac{5}{2}f$. $v=53°\ 7'\ 30''$.	$s=5f$. $r=\frac{29}{8}f$. $v=43°36'10''$	$s=6f$. $r=5f$. $v=36°52'\ 10''$	$s=7f$. $r=\frac{53}{8}f$. $v=31°53'26''$	$s=8f$. $r=\frac{17}{2}f$. $v=28°\ 4'\ 20''$.	$s=10f$. $r=13f$. $v=22°37'10''$	$s=16f$. $r=32.5f$. $v=14°\ 15'$.
1.40	0.15445	0.14691	0.14691	0.14691	0.14691	0.14478	
1.35	0.14717	0.13030	0.12587	0.12587	0.12587	0.12405	
1.34	0.14543	0.12987	0.12171	0.12171	0.12171	0.11999	
1.33	0.14364	0.12781	0.11767	0.11767	0.11767	0.11596	
1.32	0.14173	0.12634	0.11362	0.11362	0.11362	0.11196	
1.31	0.13975	0.12486	0.10959	0.10959	0.10959	0.10800	
1.30	0.13764	0.12331	0.10682	0.10559	0.10559	0.10406	
1.29	0.13543	0.12164	0.10563	0.10163	0.10163	0.10016	
1.28	0.13311	0.11988	0.10437	0.09770	0.09770	0.09628	
1.27	0.13068	0.11803	0.10304	0.09379	0.09379	0.09244	
1.26	0.12815	0.11609	0.10160	0.08992	0.08992	0.08862	
1.25	0.12547	0.11402	0.10009	0.08668	0.08608	0.08483	0.07180
1.24	0.12270	0.11251	0.09850	0.08549	0.08227	0.08108	0.06862
1.23	0.12031	0.10958	0.09679	0.08423	0.07849	0.07735	0.06547
1.22	0.11675	0.10725	0.09499	0.08291	0.07474	0.07366	0.06234
1.21	0.11354	0.10460	0.09305	0.08148	0.07102	0.06999	0.05924
1.20	0.11023	0.10196	0.09102	0.07999	0.06981	0.06636	0.05616
1.19	0.10676	0.09915	0.08885	0.07834	0.06859	0.06275	0.05311
1.18	0.10313	0.09617	0.08653	0.07651	0.06727	0.05918	0.05008
1.17	0.09934	0.09303	0.08408	0.07468	0.06583	0.05212	0.04709
1.16	0.09537	0.08975	0.08144	0.07264	0.06420	0.05004	0.04411
1.15	0.09123	0.08634	0.07866	0.07050	0.06259	0.04904	0.04116
1.14	0.08690	0.08257	0.07568	0.06812	0.06077	0.04803	0.03824
1.13	0.08238	0.07869	0.07251	0.06558	0.05890	0.04671	0.03534
1.12	0.07764	0.07459	0.06911	0.06297	0.05659	0.04451	0.03247
1.11	0.07269	0.07042	0.06548	0.06026	0.05421	0.04384	0.02962
1.10	0.06737	0.06563	0.06158	0.05666	0.05160	0.04214	0.02681
1.09	0.06211	0.06077	0.05739	0.05345	0.04871	0.04023	0.02401
1.08	0.05636	0.05652	0.05288	0.04934	0.04552	0.03806	0.02192
1.07	0.05052	0.05011	0.04804	0.04426	0.04200	0.03560	0.02111
1.06	0.04431	0.04428	0.04280	0.04058	0.03861	0.03276	0.02002
1.05	0.03776	0.03804	0.03709	0.03550	0.03357	0.02944	0.01882
1.04	0.03096	0.03144	0.03095	0.02992	0.02862	0.02561	0.01720
1.03	0.02378	0.02437	0.02424	0.02369	0.02293	0.02131	0.01524
1.02	0.01625	0.01681	0.01690	0.01673	0.01640	0.01546	0.01199
1.01	0.00834	0.00871	0.00886	0.00889	0.00885	0.00862	0.00747

TABLE E′.

SEGMENTAL ARCHES LOADED UP TO THE LEVEL OF THE SUMMIT OF THE KEY.

Table of thrusts in seven systems.

Value of the ratio $K=\frac{R}{r}$.	Multiply the decimal by the square of the radius of the intrados; $F=r^2 \times C$.						
	$s=4f$. $r=5\frac{1}{2}f$. $v=53° 7' 30''$.	$s=5f$. $r=\frac{29}{8}f$. $v=43° 36' 10''$	$s=6f$. $r=5f$. $v=36° 52' 10''$	$s=7f$. $r=\frac{53}{8}f$. $v=31° 53' 26''$	$s=8f$. $r=\frac{17}{2}f$. $v=28° 4' 20''$.	$s=10f$. $r=13f$. $v=22° 37' 10''$	$s=16f$. $r=32.5f$ $v=14° 15'$.
1.40	0.16920	0.16920	0.16920	0.16920	0.16920	0.15932	0.12760
1.39	0.16463	0.16462	0.16463	0.16463	0.16463	0.15490	0.12397
1.38	0.16009	0.16009	0.16009	0.16009	0.16009	0.15052	0.12035
1.37	0.15558	0.15558	0.15558	0.15558	0.15558	0.14617	0.11677
1.36	0.15111	0.15111	0.15111	0.15111	0.15111	0.14185	0.11322
1.35	0.14666	0.14666	0.14666	0.14666	0.14666	0.13756	0.10969
1.34	0.14225	0.14225	0.14225	0.14225	0.14225	0.13330	0.10619
1.33	0.14138	0.13787	0.13787	0.13787	0.13787	0.12908	0.10271
1.32	0.14090	0.13353	0.13353	0.13353	0.13353	0.12488	0.09926
1.31	0.14032	0.12922	0.12922	0.12922	0.12922	0.12073	0.09583
1.30	0.13964	0.12499	0.12495	0.12495	0.12495	0.11659	0.09243
1.29	0.13885	0.12425	0.12071	0.12071	0.12071	0.11250	0.08906
1.28	0.13794	0.12342	0.11650	0.11650	0.11650	0.10843	0.08572
1.27	0.13693	0.12250	0.11232	0.11232	0.11232	0.10439	0.08240
1.26	0.13579	0.12148	0.10817	0.10817	0.10817	0.10039	0.07910
1.25	0.13454	0.12036	0.10456	0.10405	0.10405	0.09643	0.07583
1.24	0.13316	0.11914	0.10359	0.09997	0.09997	0.09249	0.07259
1.23	0.13166	0.11780	0.10254	0.09592	0.09592	0.08858	0.06937
1.22	0.13002	0.11635	0.10138	0.09190	0.09190	0.08469	0.06618
1.21	0.12824	0.11478	0.10012	0.08792	0.08792	0.08085	0.06302
1.20	0.12632	0.11309	0.09876	0.08527	0.08397	0.07704	0.05988
1.19	0.12426	0.11127	0.09728	0.08412	0.08005	0.07325	0.05677
1.18	0.12204	0.10930	0.09569	0.08287	0.07617	0.06950	0.05368
1.17	0.11966	0.10719	0.09396	0.08150	0.07232	0.06579	0.05062
1.16	0.11712	0.10492	0.09209	0.08002	0.06947	0.06210	0.04758
1.15	0.11440	0.10248	0.09007	0.07840	0.06819	0.05845	0.04457
1.14	0.11151	0.09987	0.08788	0.07664	0.06680	0.05483	0.04159
1.13	0.10842	0.09707	0.08553	0.07473	0.06527	0.05124	0.03864
1.12	0.10514	0.09408	0.08298	0.07263	0.06359	0.04911	0.03571
1.11	0.10166	0.09087	0.08022	0.07034	0.06173	0.04791	0.03281
1.10	0.09796	0.08744	0.07724	0.06784	0.05967	0.04655	0.02993
1.09	0.09403	0.08376	0.07401	0.06510	0.05738	0.04503	0.02708
1.08	0.08986	0.07982	0.07051	0.06209	0.05485	0.04329	0.02425
1.07	0.08544	0.07559	0.06671	0.05878	0.05202	0.04129	0.02251
1.06	0.08076	0.07106	0.06257	0.05511	0.04884	0.03897	0.02168
1.05	0.07579	0.06620	0.05806	0.05106	0.04526	0.03629	0.02064
1.04	0.07053	0.06098	0.05314	0.04654	0.04120	0.03313	0.01929
1.03	0.06495	0.05536	0.04775	0.04149	0.03656	0.02935	0.01756
1.02	0.05904	0.04931	0.04182	0.03583	0.03123	0.02479	0.01499
1.01	0.05277	0.04279	0.03530	0.02942	0.02505	0.01915	0.01125

TABLE F.—CIRCULAR ARCHES OF 180°, WITH A LOAD OF ON EACH SIDE OF THE CENTRAL RIDGE, TO A ROOF

[I=the angle between the roof and a vertical; r=the extrados; C=the decimal in any column; F= the springing line. The last two columns give the addition with masonry, and of the uniform depth t above the

Value of $K=\frac{R}{r}$. (1)	Ratio of the diameter to the thickness. (2)	$I=90°$ $E=R$ Angle of rupture	$I=90°$ $E=R$ $F=r^2 \times C$ (3)	$I=85°$ $E=R \times 1.00382$ $F=r^2 C$. (4)	$I=80°$ $E=R \times 1.01543$ $F=r^2 C$. (5)	$I=75°$ $E=R \times 1.03528$ $F=r^2 C$. (6)	$I=70°$ $E=R \times 1.06418$ $F=r^2 C$. (7)	$I=65°$ $E=R \times 1.10338$ $F=r^2 C$. (8)	$I=60°$ $E=R \times 1.15470$ Angle of rupture.	$I=60°$ $E=R \times 1.15470$ $F=r^2 C$. (9)
1.50	4.000	29°	0.21673	0.20535	0.19883	0.19787	0.20289	0.21470	23°	0.23408
1.48	4.166	29	0.20696	0.19588	0.18952	0.18858	0.19346	0.20498	23	0.22388
1.46	4.347	29	0.19733	0.18654	0.18033	0.17941	0.18416	0.19539	23	0.21381
1.44	4.545	29	0.18782	0.17733	0.17127	0.17036	0.17498	0.18594	23	0.20387
1.42	4.761	29	0.17845	0.16824	0.16234	0.16144	0.16594	0.17661	58	0.19510
1.40	5.000	29	0.16920	0.15928	0.15353	0.15265	0.15877	0.17307	58	0.19291
1.39	5.128	29	0.16463	0.15485	0.14917	0.14840	0.15783	0.17201	58	0.19170
1.38	5.263	29	0.16009	0.15045	0.14484	0.14768	0.15688	0.17086	58	0.19041
1.37	5.406	29	0.15558	0.14608	0.14221	0.14685	0.15583	0.16962	58	0.18903
1.36	5.555	29	0.15111	0.14174	0.14157	0.14593	0.15468	0.16829	58	0.18755
1.35	5.714	29	0.14666	0.14094	0.14083	0.14492	0.15344	0.16686	58	0.18599
1.34	5.882	60	0.14491	0.14044	0.14002	0.14380	0.15210	0.16534	58	0.18433
1.33	6.060	61	0.14467	0.13984	0.13908	0.14258	0.15066	0.16372	58	0.18257
1.32	6.264	61	0.14460	0.13913	0.13805	0.14126	0.14914	0.16200	58	0.18070
1.31	6.451	61	0.14390	0.13830	0.13691	0.13984	0.14750	0.16017	57	0.17877
1.30	6.666	61	0.14332	0.13736	0.13567	0.13832	0.14571	0.15824	57	0.17674
1.29	6.896	61	0.14264	0.13631	0.13431	0.13666	0.14385	0.15620	57	0.17458
1.28	7.142	62	0.14186	0.13512	0.13282	0.13490	0.14188	0.15405	57	0.17232
1.27	7.407	62	0.14101	0.13381	0.13121	0.13303	0.13979	0.15178	56	0.16996
1.26	7.692	62	0.13988	0.13242	0.12948	0.13103	0.13761	0.14940	56	0.16750
1.25	8.000	62	0.13872	0.13089	0.12762	0.12891	0.13525	0.14693	56	0.16492
1.24	8.333	62	0.13737	0.12923	0.12563	0.12666	0.13277	0.14434	55	0.16224
1.23	8.695	63	0.13593	0.12743	0.12350	0.12427	0.13018	0.14163	55	0.15946
1.22	9.090	63	0.13437	0.12550	0.12124	0.12175	0.12745	0.13878	55	0.15654
1.21	9.523	63	0.13263	0.12339	0.11883	0.11909	0.12458	0.13578	54	0.15353
1.20	10.000	63	0.13073	0.12116	0.11628	0.11628	0.12155	0.13264	54	0.15038
1.19	10.526	63	0.12870	0.11877	0.11357	0.11332	0.11840	0.12938	53	0.14713
1.18	11.111	63	0.12650	0.11623	0.11071	0.11020	0.11515	0.12602	52	0.14375
1.17	11.764	64	0.12415	0.11352	0.10768	0.10693	0.11166	0.12249	51	0.14027
1.16	12.500	64	0.12182	0.11063	0.10450	0.10349	0.10804	0.11876	51	0.13669
1.15	13.333	64	0.11895	0.10759	0.10119	0.09989	0.10426	0.11498	50	0.13294
1.14	14.285	64	0.11608	0.10443	0.09768	0.09609	0.10028	0.11106	49	0.12913
1.13	15.384	64	0.11303	0.10105	0.09398	0.09212	0.09612	0.10685	48	0.12521
1.12	16.666	64	0.10979	0.09749	0.09009	0.08796	0.09178	0.10249	46	0.12119
1.11	18.181	65	0.10641	0.09373	0.08601	0.08360	0.08725	0.09792	45	0.11710
1.10	20.000	65	0.10279	0.08978	0.08175	0.07903	0.08250	0.09312	44	0.11290
1.08	25.000	66	0.09497	0.08140	0.07264	0.06925				
1.06	33.333	68	0.08638	0.07213	0.06281	0.05865				
1.04	50.000	70	0.07686	0.06186	0.05207	0.04707				
1.02	100.000	73	0.06647	0.05112	0.04034	0.03422				

MASONRY OR OF EQUAL WEIGHT WITH MASONRY, RISING TANGENT TO THE EXTRADOS.

radius of the intrados; $R=Kr$=the radius of the thrust; E=the elevation of the ridge above the to the thrust caused by a surcharge of equal weight roof, in the case of rotation and the case of sliding.]

$I=55°$ $E=R\times$ 1.22078 $F=r^2C$. (10)	$I=50°$ $E=R\times$ 1 30541 $F=r^2C$. (11)	$I=45°$ $E=R\times 1.41421$ Angle of rupture.	$F=r^2C$. (12)	Angle which renders the effect of the surcharge a maximum.	Add for a surch'ge of uniform depth t, the addition= $A=rtC$. Rotation. (13)	Add for a surcharge of uniform depth t, $A=rtC$. Sliding. (14)	$K=\frac{R}{r}$.
0.26225	0.30085	22°	0.35266	The addition to be taken from this column when the thrust comes below the horizontal line near the top of each column.		0.44388	1.50
0.25133	0.28891	22	0.33934			0.43796	1.48
0.24056	0.27712	22	0.32621			0.43204	1.46
0.22993	0.26551	22	0.31325			0.42612	1.44
0.22178	0.25665	60	0.30296	65°	0.33918	0.42020	1.42
0.21941	0.25418	59	0.30001	65	0.35297	0.41429	1.40
0.21810	0.25284	59	0.29712	64	0.35998	0.41133	1.39
0.21671	0.25138	59	0.29706	64	0.36705	0.40837	1.38
0.21522	0.24985	59	0.29550	64	0.37421	0.40541	1.37
0.21365	0.24826	59	0.29386	64	0.38146	0.40245	1.36
0.21199	0.24653	58	0.29285	63	0.38880	0.39949	1.35
0.21023	0.24473	58	0.29037	63	0.39625	The addition to be made from this column when the thrust comes above the horizontal line near the top of each column.	1.34
0.20838	0.24284	58	0.28850	63	0.40379		1.33
0.20643	0.24086	58	0.28654	62	0.41143		1.32
0.20437	0.23876	57	0.28456	62	0.41920		1.31
0.20227	0.23670	57	0.28231	62	0.42711		1.30
0.20009	0.23451	57	0.28027	61	0.43513		1.29
0.19780	0.23220	56	0.27810	61	0.44329		1.28
0.19540	0.22983	56	0.27578	60	0.45161		1.27
0.19289	0.22732	55	0.27343	60	0.46009		1.26
0.19027	0.22478	54	0.27102	60	0.46875		1.25
0.18757	0.22219	53	0.26850	59	0.47760		1.24
0.18481	0.21948	53	0.26608	59	0.48665		1.23
0.18192	0.21665	52	0.26377	58	0.49592		1.22
0.17890	0.21385	51	0.26074	58	0.50543		1.21
0.17588	0.21095	50	0.25806	57	0.51520		1.20
0.17273	0.20790	50	0.25546	56	0.52527		1.19
0.16944	0.20493	49	0.25277	56	0.53564		1.18
0.16617	0.20182	49	0.25010	55	0.54637	Angle of rupture 25°, which gives very nearly the maxi'm effect to the surcharge.	1.17
0.16273	0.19857	48	0.24742	55	0.55748		1.16
0.15913	0.19515	47	0.24477	54	0.56901		1.15
		46	0.24218	53	0.58102		1.14
		44	0.23967	52	0.59359		1.13
		43	0.23732	52	0.60676		1.12
		43	0.23502	51	0.62063		1.11
		42	0.23292	50	0.63532		1.10
				47	0.66778		1.08
				44	0.70588		1.06
				41	0.75313		1.04
				35	0.81867		1.02

TABLE G.

ELLIPTICAL ARCHES OF 180°, WITH A LOAD OF MASONRY, OR OF EQUAL WEIGHT WITH MASONRY, RISING TO THE LEVEL OF THE TOP OF THE KEY.

[r=the half span; f=the rise; C=the decimal in any column; F=the thrust$=r^2C$. The true thrust due, in every case, to rotation.]

Table of Thrusts in Eight Systems.

Ratio of the span to the thickness. (1)	$f=\frac{2}{5}r$ $=\frac{1}{5}$ the span. (2)	$f=\frac{1}{2}r$ $=\frac{1}{4}$ the span. (3)	$f=\frac{27\frac{1}{2}}{50}r$ $=\frac{27\frac{1}{2}}{100}$ the span. (4)	$f=\frac{3}{5}r$ $=\frac{3}{10}$ the span. (5)	$f=\frac{2}{3}r$ $=\frac{1}{3}$ the span. (6)	$f=\frac{3}{4}r$ $=\frac{3}{8}$ the span. (7)	$f=\frac{4}{5}r$ $=\frac{2}{5}$ the span. (8)	$f=\frac{9}{10}r$ $=\frac{9}{20}$ the span. (9)
6.00			0.23337	0.21612	0.19848	0.18082	0.17190	0.15706
6.50			0.22332	0.20903	0.19312	0.17714	0.16904	0.15523
7.00		0.23222	0.21598	0.20277	0.18830	0.17358	0.16605	0.15330
7.50		0.22387	0.20932	0.19725	0.18390	0.17014	0.16304	0.15081
8.00		0.21684	0.20347	0.19221	0.17977	0.16680	0.16015	0.14846
8.50		0.21064	0.19824	0.18779	0.17594	0.16369	0.15716	0.14606
9.00		0.20513	0.19351	0.18359	0.17231	0.16049	0.15436	0.14367
9.50		0.20005	0.18915	0.17971	0.16904	0.15755	0.15164	0.14132
10.00	0.22374	0.19564	0.18511	0.17604	0.16564	0.15474	0.14901	0.13907
10.50	0.21809	0.19143	0.18134	0.17283	0.16255	0.15199	0.14643	0.13686
11.00	0.21298	0.18756	0.17780	0.16939	0.15969	0.14936	0.14401	0.13451
12.00	0.20393	0.18050	0.17133	0.16340	0.15422	0.14452	0.13946	0.13066
13.00	0.19633	0.17420	0.16555	0.15798	0.14926	0.14006	0.13526	0.12695
14.00	0.18956	0.16855	0.16029	0.15306	0.14477	0.13599	0.13141	0.12368
15.00	0.18355	0.16349	0.15552	0.14863	0.14065	0.13225	0.12795	0.12035
16.00	0.17817	0.15881	0.15116	0.14455	0.13687	0.12889	0.12476	0.11745
17.00	0.17312	0.15449	0.14718	0.14076	0.13341	0.12581	0.12167	0.11472
18.00	0.16861	0.15060	0.14348	0.13730	0.13027	0.12278	0.11892	0.11226
19.00	0.16442	0.14696	0.14008	0.13410	0.12740	0.12009	0.11636	0.10997
20.00	0.16054	0.14359	0.13692	0.13120	0.12453	0.11758	0.11399	0.10788
21.00	0.15690	0.14046	0.13398	0.12854	0.12200	0.11527	0.11180	0.10589
22.00	0.15355	0.13753	0.13134	0.12584	0.11959	0.11310	0.10977	0.10405
23.00	0.15042	0.13480	0.12885	0.12341	0.11737	0.11109	0.10789	0.10233
24.00	0.14746	0.13231	0.12635	0.12118	0.11529	0.10924	0.10609	0.10073
25.00	0.14469	0.13005	0.12407	0.11906	0.11336	0.10747	0.10444	0.09924
26.00	0.14208	0.12767	0.12197	0.11708	0.11154	0.10581	0.10286	0.09781
28.00	0.13730	0.12347	0.11810	0.11346	0.10823	0.10278	0.10001	0.09528
30.00	0.13308	0.11977	0.11463	0.11026	0.10527	0.10011	0.09745	0.09321
33.00	0.12740	0.11491	0.11016	0.10604	0.10139	0.09659	0.09431	0.09031
36.00	0.12250	0.11076	0.10625	0.10240	0.09804	0.09382	0.09172	0.08755
40.00	0.11687	0.10600	0.10185	0.09827	0.09448	0.09047	0.08823	0.08460
45.00	0.11110	0.10108	0.09728	0.09428	0.09069	0.08673	0.08484	0.08169
50.00	0.10628	0.09703	0.09383	0.09089	0.08727	0.08386	0.08217	0.07922
55.00	0.10222	0.09392	0.09065	0.08770	0.08455	0.08148	0.07987	0.07720
60.00	0.09874	0.09075	0.08779	0.08520	0.08238	0.07943	0.07796	0.07550

TABLE H.

THRUST OF THE UNLOADED ELLIPTICAL RING BOUNDED BY SIMILAR ELLIPSES.

[r=the span; f=the rise; d=the thickness at the key; C=the decimal in any column; F=the thrust=r^2C; semi-axes of the intrados, f and r; semi-axes of the extrados $f+d$, and $r+\frac{r}{f}d$.]

Thrust in Two Systems.

Value of $\frac{2r}{d}$	Rise=$\frac{1}{4}$ the span. $f=\frac{1}{2}r$.	Rise=$\frac{1}{3}$ the span. $f=\frac{2}{3}r$.	Value of $\frac{2r}{d}$	Rise=$\frac{1}{4}$ the span. $f=\frac{1}{2}r$.	Rise=$\frac{1}{3}$ the span. $f=\frac{2}{3}r$.
	$F=r^2\times$	$F=r^2\times$		$F=r^2\times$	$F\times r^2\times$
6.00		0.18273	19.00	0.11725	0.09559
6.50		0.17772	20.00	0.11305	0.09222
7.00	0.19773	0.17255	21.00	0.10953	0.08904
7.50	0.19412	0.16761	22.00	0.10614	0.08592
8.00	0.18893	0.16265	23.00	0.10291	0.08304
8.50	0.18431	0.15782	24.00	0.09981	0.08050
9.00	0.17970	0.15341	25.00	0.09685	0.07815
9.50	0.17544	0.14938	26.00	0.09419	0.07575
10.00	0.17124	0.14621	28.00	0.08924	0.07144
10.50	0.16776	0.14132	30.00	0.08468	0.06770
11.00	0.16310	0.13730	33.00	0.07889	0.06241
12.00	0.15574	0.13030	36.00	0.07364	0.05835
13.00	0.14968	0.12376	40.00	0.06779	0.05364
14.00	0.14233	0.11799	45.00	0.06137	0.04867
15.00	0.13686	0.11242	50.00	0.05663	0.04459
16.00	0.13142	0.10783	55.00	0.05235	0.04172
17.00	0.12621	0.10352	60.00	0.04870	0.03815
18.00	0.12174	0.09941			

SECTION VI.

CURVE OF PRESSURE.

108. In the preceding part of this work, we have followed the theory of Coulomb, Audoy, and Poncelet, and calculated the thrust of arches at the moment of rupture. We have called this the maximum thrust of the arch.

At that imaginary moment, the horizontal thrust at the key, in the ordinary mode of rupture, acts upon a single point or line of the extrados; the resultant of this thrust, and of the weight of that part of the arch and its load which lies above the joint of rupture, comes upon the intrados of that joint; and the resultant of the same thrust, and of the weight of the whole semi-arch and pier, falls entirely upon the exterior edge of the base of the pier (see figures 2, 3).

No masonry could withstand this pressure exerted upon mere points or edges.

Not only must rupture be avoided, but we must take care not to approach that condition; that is, we must, if possible, so proportion and build the arch and its pier, as to keep the curve of pressure near the middle of the joints.

Let us suppose any arch to be on the point of falling in consequence of the insufficient thickness of its pier. The curve of pressure, touching the extrados at the key, and the intrados at the reins about 60° from the key, passes finally through the exterior edge of the base.

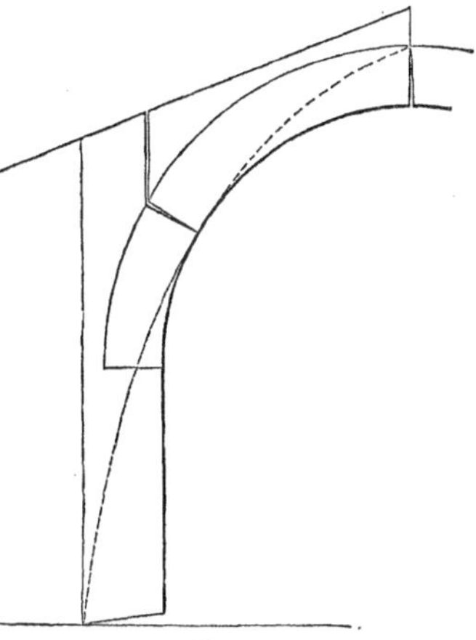
FIG. 23.

Before reaching this condition of rupture, the vertical joint has gradually opened on the lower side, the joint at the reins on the exterior side, the pier has slightly yielded to the pressure of the arch, the key has settled down, the reins have spread out.

These movements, from which the best of arches are not entirely free, are often developed, in badly proportioned works, so as to exhibit wide cracks at the key and reins, without any immediate danger to the structure. They are due to two principal causes: in single arches, to deficiency of mass in the pier; in continuous arches, to the absence of suitable arrangements for preventing lateral motion at the reins.

109. *In single or abutment arches, the magnitude of the horizontal thrust, and the place of the curve of pressure in the arch, depend largely upon the dimensions of the pier.*

Let us for a moment admit that the pier or abutment is absolutely immovable, and that the material of the arch is susceptible of but very little compression. And let us further admit, what has been abundantly proved in this paper, and confirmed by numerous observations, that the *joint of rupture*, about 60° from

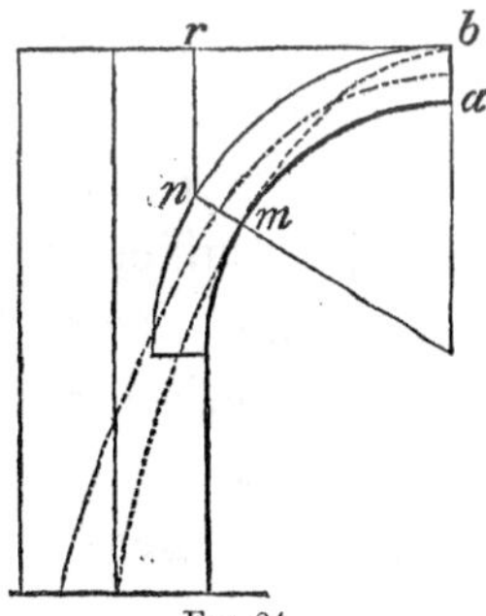

FIG. 24.

the key, is the weakest joint, or joint first to open at the extrados. As the arch below that joint, *m n*, being firmly attached to the pier, is immovable, and the masonry above that joint, by supposition, nearly incompressible, it is evident that the pressure at the key, *a b*, and at the *joint of rupture*, *m n*, will act all along those joints; in other words, those joints will be everywhere in contact. In the most perfect condition of stability, the resultant of the horizontal forces acting along the key, *a b*, will pass through the middle of that joint; in like manner the resultant of all the forces acting along *m n*, normal to that joint, will pass through its middle point.

Let us now suppose the thickness of the pier to be gradually diminished until its top begins to move away from the arch: the crown will begin to settle, the reins will spread out, the curve of pressure will approach the extrados at the key and the intrados at the reins; finally, when the pier has been sufficiently reduced, the curve of pressure will pass through the extremities of those joints.

Thus, by mere external changes in the pier, we have caused the curve of pressure in the arch to move by degrees, from the place of most perfect stability, to that of final rupture and fall.

In this final condition, the thrust of the arch is the horizontal force which, applied at the extrados of the key, is just sufficient to prevent the rotation of the segment above the joint of rupture around the intrados of that joint; this force acting with a lever arm equal to the vertical distance between these points. On the other hand, in the condition of most perfect stability, the acting thrust is the horizontal force which, applied to the middle of the key, is just sufficient to prevent the rotation of the same upper segment around the middle of the joint of rupture; this force acting with a lever-arm equal to the vertical distance between these middle points.

This real thrust, acting when the arch is firmly established upon its piers, is much greater than the final thrust exerted at the moment of rupture,—sometimes more than double.

We thus perceive that what has been called the maximum thrust in the former part of this work, is really the least thrust that can ever act at the crown of the arch, and that this minimum is attained at the moment of rupture.

The effective thrust is increased in the same arch as its lever-arm is diminished, or as the curve of pressure falls at the key and rises at the reins.

In ordinary circular, segmental, and elliptical arches, surcharged horizontally, or surcharged more at the key than at the reins, the curve of pressure can never fall below the middle of the key, or rise above the middle of the reins.

110. *The effective horizontal thrust, the place of the curve of pressure, and the stability of continuous arches, resting on intermediate piers, depend largely upon the material of the top of the pier between the arches.* If this filling be of earth, or of indifferent masonry, the reins of the arch will spread out, the curve of pressure will rise at the crown and fall at the reins, the key will settle down, cracks make their appearance, and the whole assume an appearance of instability, or even worse.

The remedy of this is simple and certain.

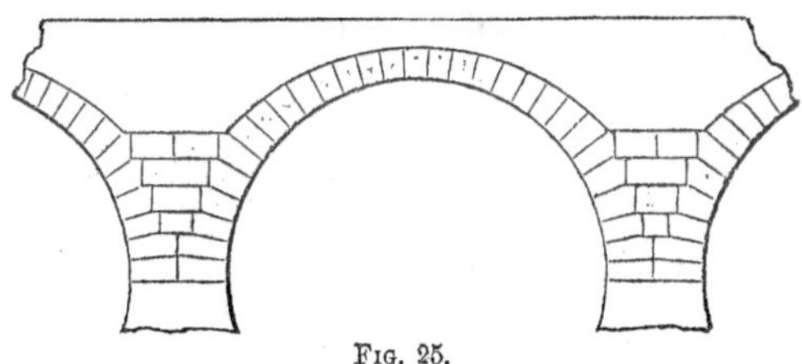

Fig. 25.

The arch, if light, should increase in thickness from the key towards the springing line, so as to add, 60° degrees from the key, at least fifty per cent. to the thickness at the key; and the spaces between the arches, over the piers, must be filled with closely jointed, solid masonry, in horizontal courses, abutting, in vertical joints, upon the adjacent voussoirs, and extending as high as, say, within 45° of the crown. These precautions are best illustrated in the London Bridge, the most remarkable structure of its kind, perhaps, in the world. A reversed arch, of equal thickness with the arch proper, is laid upon the top of each pier, abutting, in vertical joints, upon the voussoirs of the reins and lower parts of the adjacent arches. The joints are as thin as possible; and no other motion can occur in the arch than the little which arises from the compressibility of the granite. These precautions secure to the semicircular or elliptical arch, all the stiffness and stability of the segmental arch.

111. *The curve of pressure at any joint should not pass within one third of its length from either edge.*

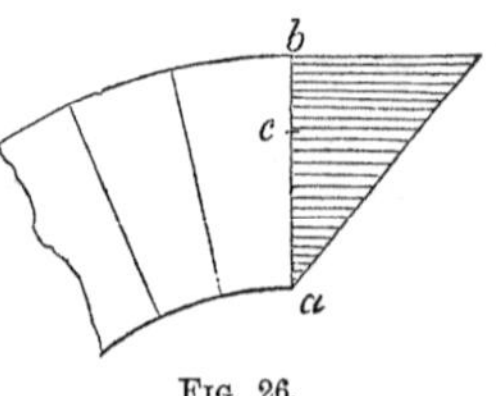

FIG. 26.

Suppose the pressure to be nothing at the intrados, a, and to increase uniformly from that point to the extrados, b. It is plain that the pressure at any point along $a\,b$, will be represented by the ordinate of a certain triangle. The whole pressure will be represented by the surface of that triangle; and the point of application of the resultant of all the pressures will be at c, opposite the center of gravity of that triangle. We then have $c\,b=\frac{1}{3}\,a\,b$. *Vice versa*, if the point of application be at c, $c\,b=\frac{1}{3}\,a\,b$, we know that the pressure is nothing at a.

If the point of application be at c, $c\,b$ being less than $\frac{1}{3}\,a\,b$, c being still opposite the center of gravity of the triangle whose ordinates represent the pressure, we know that the vertex of that triangle, and point of no pressure, are at e, $b\,e=3\times b\,c$.

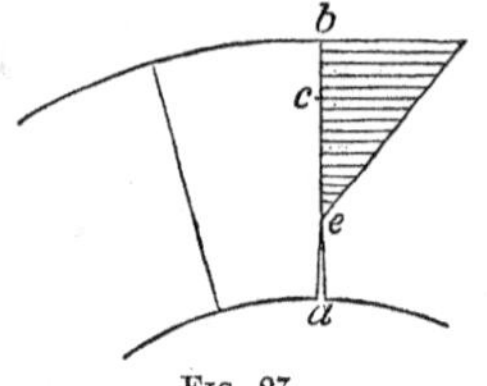

FIG. 27.

In this case, the joint $a\,b$ will open at a, as far as e; the adjacent joints will also open until we come to one where the curve of pressure passes within the prescribed limit.

This reasoning is, of course, applicable to all the joints; and we readily conclude that the curve of pressure should lie entirely between two other curves which divide the joints into three equal parts.

The foregoing reasoning is based on the principle, first applied, we believe, by Navier, that the material of the arch is perfectly elastic, and that the pressure upon any joint varies uniformly from the extremity most pressed to the point of no pressure. In fact, the last condition alone is sufficient, as it allows us to represent the pressure, upon the several points of any joint, by the ordinates of a triangle or trapezoid.

PRESSURE, PER UNIT OF SURFACE, UPON THE JOINTS.

112. Let F represent the total perpendicular pressure upon any joint; d, the length of the joint; l, the distance between the resultant or curve of pressure, and the nearest edge of that joint; P, the pressure per unit of surface at the edge most exposed.

If the curve of pressure pass through the middle of the joint, we have $P=\frac{F}{d}$.

If the curve of pressure pass at one third the length of the joint from either edge, as b, we have the pressure at b equal to twice the mean pressure along $a\,b$, or $P=\frac{2F}{d}$.

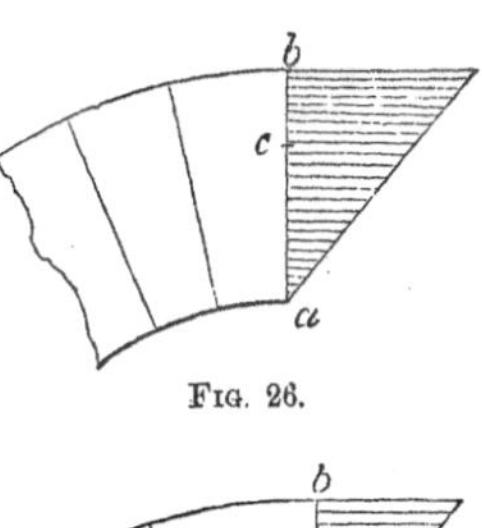

FIG. 26.

If l be less than $\frac{1}{3}\,d$, or $c\,b$ less than $\frac{1}{3}\,a\,b$, the whole pressure comes upon $e\,b$, and we have $P=\frac{2F}{eb}$.

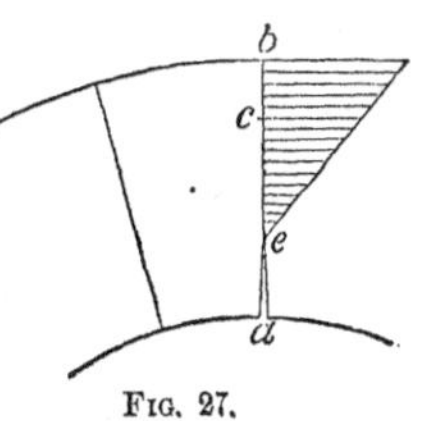

FIG. 27.

We have no good means of estimating the distance eb; but, what is more to the purpose, we can generally confine the curve of pressure within the two curves above mentioned, or even keep it still nearer the middle points of the joints.

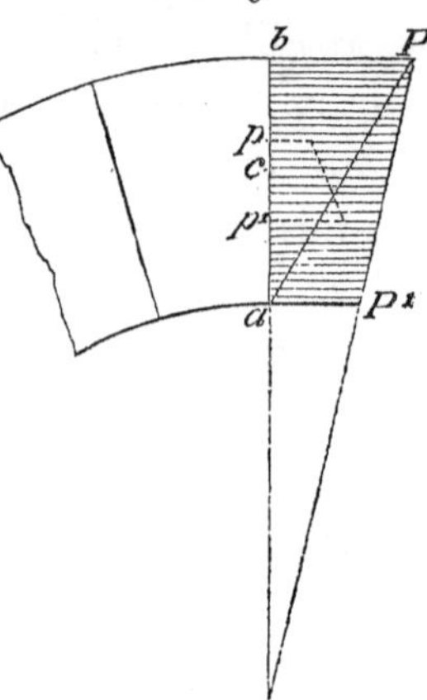

FIG. 28.

The pressure being nowhere nothing upon the joint itself, will be represented by the ordinates of some trapezoid $a\,b\,P\,P^1$. P, P^1, representing the pressures, per unit of surface, at b and a, respectively, we shall have, $P : P^1 :: b\,P : a\,P^1$;

moreover, $F = \dfrac{P+P^1}{2} \times d.$

The resultant of all the pressures will pass through the center of gravity of the trapezoid.

Let p, p^1, c, be the projections, upon $a\,b$, of the centers of gravity of the two triangles $a\,b\,P$, $a\,P\,P^1$, and the whole trapezoid $a\,b\,P\,P^1$, respectively. The point c is found by dividing $p^1\,p$ in the inverse ratio of $a\,P^1$ to $b\,P$. We have

$$p^1\,c : c\,p :: b\,P : a\,P^1 :: P : P^1;$$

$$p^1\,c : p^1 p :: P : P + P^1; \text{ giving } P = \frac{p^1 c(P+P^1)}{p_1 p};$$

but $p^1\,c = \frac{2}{3}d - l$; $P + P^1 = \dfrac{2F}{d}$; $p^1\,p = \frac{1}{3}d$.

$$\text{Hence } P = \frac{2F}{d} \times \frac{(\frac{2}{3}d - l)}{\frac{1}{3}d} \tag{59}$$

$\dfrac{F}{d}$ is the mean pressure per unit of surface.

From (59) the values of P already given, are readily deduced. The formula, however, is not applicable to the case in which the point of no pressure comes within the extremities of the joint.

THE TRUE THRUST OF THE ARCH.

113. We have reminded the reader that almost all arches, on the removal of the center, show a tendency to settle down at the key and spread out at the reins. This

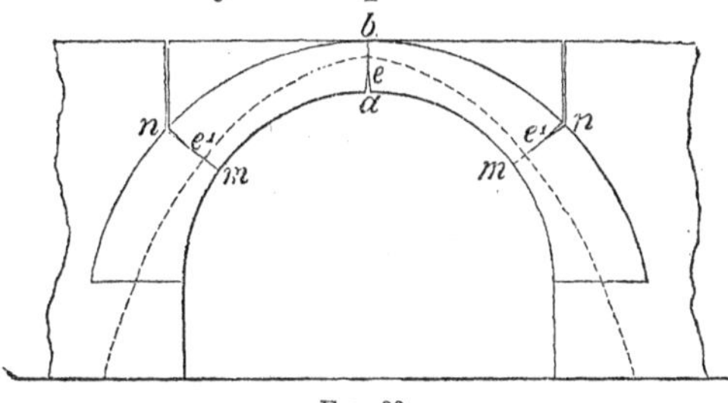

FIG. 29.

tendency often results in the production of cracks, at the intrados of the key, and at the extrados of the reins on each side of the key.

Suppose the crack at the key to extend from *a* to a certain point *e:* the whole pressure comes upon *e b*, the remaining part of the joint, and all that part of the arch near the key which lies below the joint *e*, is worse than useless; in like manner, supposing the joint at the reins to open from *n* to e', that part of the arch which is external to e' is useless. If mere weight be wanted at any point, it will be better to load the arch with some cheap material.

We have also reminded the reader of the self-evident truth, that the movements and cracks in question will always be developed unless the pier opposes a sufficient resistance. If the pier, though large enough to prevent actual rupture and fall, is still weak, the crown will continue to settle, *and the horizontal thrust to diminish*, until the pier is able to withstand the diminished thrust. The arch, in diminishing its thrust, tries, as it were, to accommodate itself to the weakness of the pier. Between the condition of most perfect stability, the curve of pressure passing near the middle of the joints, and the condition of final rupture and fall, the existing thrust becomes less and less, varying sometimes, as we shall hereafter see, in a ratio as great as 2 to 1, or larger still.

This condition of most perfect stability is highly favorable to the joints of the arch, the pressure being nearly equally distributed; but it is the condition which gives rise to the greatest thrust, and requires the greatest magnitude of pier.

We can not say that the pier ought, in all cases to be large enough to withstand so great a thrust; but it is very certain that the pier ought to withstand that diminished thrust which is developed when the curve of pressure at the crown and at the reins, passes through the limits already fixed; viz., at the key, $\frac{1}{3}$ the length of the joint from the extrados, and at the reins, $\frac{1}{3}$ the length of the joint from the intrados. If the pier cannot withstand this thrust, the joints of the arch will certainly open.

We have here a perfectly distinct point of departure for a new calculation of the thrust of arches.

Draw the curves a' m', b' n', dividing all the joints into three equal parts. Suppose the horizontal thrust to be applied at b' on the key, b' b $=\frac{1}{3} b\, a$.

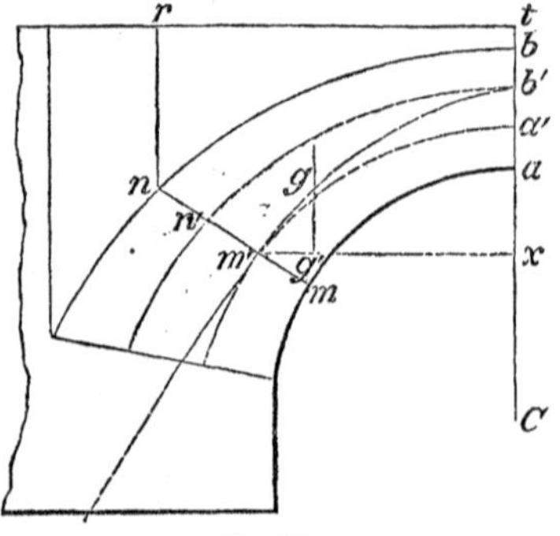

Fig. 30.

Draw any joint $m\, m'\, n'\, n$, the vertical $n\, r$ through the surcharge, and the line $r\, t$ representing the top of the surcharge; project m' horizontally at x on the vertical, $C b$, which divides the arch into two equal parts; and project g, the center of gravity of the segment $m\, n\, r\, t\, a$ on $m'\, x$ at g'. Let $y',=b'\, x$, represent the lever arm of the thrust, and $p',=m'\, g'$, the lever arm of the segment.

As the resultant of the thrust, applied at b', and the weight of the segment resting on $m\, n$, applied at g, its center of gravity, passes, by supposition, through m', $m\, m'=$

$\frac{1}{3}m\,n$, there must be, in case of equilibrium, an equality of moments in relation to that point. Hence, F' representing the force, and S' the surface $m\,n\,r\,t\,b\,a\,m$, we must have

$$F' \times y' = S' \times p' \text{ or } F' = \frac{S'p'}{y'}.$$

This force F' will be small when the joint $m\,n$ is near the key; it will increase as the joint departs from the key, and become a maximum at the reins, about 60° from the key.

Suppose $m\,n$, to be the joint of rupture corresponding to the maximum value of F'. The curve of pressure between the key and the joint of rupture will be situated entirely between the limit curves, $a'\,m'$, $b'\,n'$, which divide the joints into three equal parts. From b', where it is nearest to the extrados, it will gradually depart from the extrados, pass through the middle of some joint about midway between $a\,b$ and $m\,n$, continue to approach the intrados, and come nearest, relatively, to that curve at m', $m\,m' = \frac{1}{3}\,m\,n$; it will there be tangent to the inferior curve $a'\,m'$, and begin to recede from the intrados. In light arches, the curve of pressure after leaving b', may at first pass a little above the superior limit, $b'\,n'$; but it never can pass within the inferior limit, $a'\,m'$, either above or below the joint of maximum thrust. The reader, by a little reflection, will see the truth of this last remark, and will also see its importance.

THRUST OF THE UNLOADED CIRCULAR RING OF EQUAL THICKNESS THROUGHOUT, ON THE SUPPOSITION THAT NO JOINT SHALL OPEN, THE CURVE OF PRESSURE AT THE KEY BEING ONE THIRD THE LENGTH OF THE JOINT FROM THE EXTRADOS,—AT THE REINS, ONE THIRD THE LENGTH OF THE JOINT FROM THE INTRADOS.

114. The point of application of the thrust is at b', $b'\,b=\frac{1}{3}a\,b$. The arcs, $a'\,m'$, $b'\,n'$, dividing the joints into three equal parts, the segment $m\;n\;b\;a$, corresponding to any joint $m\;n$, is exactly equal to three times the central segment, $m'\,n'\,b'\,a'$; and the center of gravity of the whole is near the center of gravity of this central part. In the light arches of ordinary use these centers may be regarded as coinciding. Suppose them to coincide.

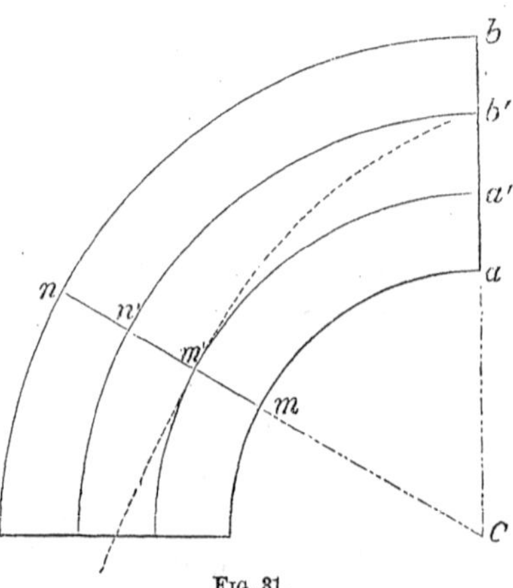

Fig. 31.

The thrust of the arch $m\;n\;b\;a$, on the condition expressed at the head of this article, is precisely equal to three times the thrust of the arch $m'\,n'\,b'\,a'$, calculated on the condition of actual rupture.

This last thrust for all proportions of the two radii is given by table A, from which the following has been deduced. We briefly explain the mode of computation.

Let K represent the ratio of the two radii of the given arch; K' the ratio of the radii of the central arch; F' the thrust of this last arch taken from table A; F the required thrust of the given arch. We have

$$K'=1+\frac{K-1}{K+2}\,;\; F=3\times F'\times(\tfrac{2}{3}+\tfrac{1}{3}K)^2=r^2\times 3\times(\tfrac{2}{3}+\tfrac{1}{3}K)^2\times C.$$

Table AA, at the end of this paper, gives the values of F, or the actual thrust of the circular ring, for all the values of K between 1.01 and 1.40 inclusive.

For explanation see the head of that table.

This table proves that the effective thrust acting when the arch is firmly established upon its piers, is much greater than the thrust at the moment of actual rupture. The ratio, δ, of these two thrusts, beginning at 1.065 for $K=1.01$, becomes 1.204 for $K=1.08$, 1.35 for $K=1.17$, 1.50 for $K=1.25$, 1.83 for $K=1.40$. It attains its greatest value, 1.94, when $K=1.45$.

The values of F corresponding to $K=1.01$, 1.02, have been calculated by the law of differences, table A not giving those values.

THRUST OF SEMICIRCULAR ARCHES SURCHARGED HORIZONTALLY.

115. This is by far the most common form of the arch. All arches carry loads, and these loads most frequently rise to a surface nearly horizontal.

It is plain that the pier should oppose to the thrust of the arch a resistance sufficient to prevent the formation of cracks or openings at the weakest joints, or joints which actually open in case of rupture and fall. Figs. 2, 3.

The actual thrust of the arch, when the joint at the key is about to open at the intrados, and the joint at the reins is about to open at the extrados, is evidently the very minimum which the pier is required to oppose. If the pier is unable, in the slightest degree, to meet this thrust, it is evident that the joints in question will open, and continue to open, until the pier is able to withstand the diminished thrust, or until the structure falls.

Let us assume that the pier is able to withstand that greater thrust which is developed in the condition of most perfect stability, when the curve of pressure, or resultant of all the pressures, passes through the middle of the key and the middle of the reins. By the latter we mean the weakest joint, generally about 60° from the key.

In the investigation of this thrust we shall suppose the thickness of the arch to be the same throughout; while in practice, as we have repeatedly stated, this thickness should gradually increase from the key, so as to become about fifty per cent. larger at the reins. This increase will slightly diminish the thrust, and slightly elevate the curve of pressure at the reins. The curve of pressure passing through the middle of the joint at the reins, supposed to be equal in length with the joint at the key, will pass through the inferior limit of the former joint when increased by fifty per cent.; viz., within one third of its length from the intrados. It will be a little below the superior limit at the key; that is, by the difference between $\frac{2}{3}$ and $\frac{1}{2}$, or by $\frac{1}{6}$ the depth of that joint.

Almost all large bridges are exceedingly light in their proportions; they are made generally of the most incompressible stone; and it is not too much to say that their piers should be able to withstand the thrust in question developed in the condition of most perfect stability. Applied to arches very heavy in their proportions, whether large or small in their actual dimensions, this would perhaps be an exaggerated thrust. Such arches have an excess of thickness throughout, and require no increase at the reins.

Assume the curve of pressure to pass through c, the middle of the key, and to touch the line drawn through the middle point of all the joints, supposed to be equal in length, at c_1, on some joint, $m\ n$, such as to give the greatest possible thrust on the condition imposed.

To illustrate this method in advance of more particular calculations, suppose the thickness of the arch to be $\frac{1}{20}$

the span, or $K=1.10$. Let us find the value of the horizontal force, F', which, applied at c, the middle of $a\,b$, shall hold in equilibrium any segment, $a\,m\,n\,r\,b\,a$, on c_1, the middle of the lower joint. Let $v=$the angle, $m\,C\,a$, between the joint $m\,n$ and a vertical; $r=$the radius of the intrados; $m\,n=a\,b$; in all cases $m\,c_1=\frac{1}{2}\,m\,n=$say $\frac{1}{3}m\,n_1$, the joint of the practical arch.

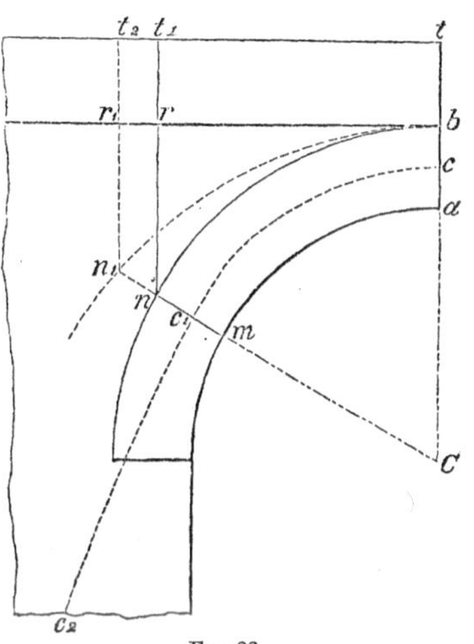

FIG. 32.

Values of v.	Values of F'.	Values of v.	Values of F'.
0°	$r^2\times0.10492$	50°	$r^2\times0.13563$
5	" 0.10544	55	" 0.13746
10	" 0.10698	58	" 0.13795
15	" 0.10945	59	" 0.13801$=F$, the max'm.
20	" 0.11270	60	" 0.13800
25	" 0.11654	65	" 0.13708
30	" 0.12073	70	" 0.13457
35	" 0.12504	75	" 0.13038
40	" 0.12914	80	
45	" 0.13277	90	" 0.10825

The angle of maximum thrust is in this case 59 or 60 degrees, and the curve of pressure corresponding to that maximum, passing through the middle of the key and the middle of the reins, 59° from the key, is traced, necessarily, outside or above the central point of every other joint. If it were inside of the middle of any joint, as at $v=20°$, it would immmediately follow that the value of F' corresponding to the middle of that joint, must be greater than F, the actual maximum thrust.

We may learn from the above table that the curve of pressure corresponding to the maximum F, passing through the middle of the key and of the reins, is, everywhere between those joints, very near the central points, since the maximum, F, so little exceeds the other values of F'.

In the upper parts of the arch, a very small change in the lever arm of F', or vertical distance between c and c_1, would make a large change in the value of F'.

These remarks are applicable, though in different degrees, to the curve of pressure corresponding to all values of K.

CALCULATION OF THE MAXIMUM THRUST OF SEMICIRCULAR ARCHES SURCHARGED HORIZONTALLY; THE CURVE OF PRESSURE PASSING THROUGH THE MIDDLE OF THE KEY AND OF THE JOINT OF GREATEST THRUST; THE JOINTS OF EQUAL LENGTH THROUGHOUT.

116. R=the radius of the extrados; r=the radius of the intrados; d=the thickness of the arch at the key; $K=\frac{R}{r}=1+\frac{d}{r}$; v=the angle between any joint and a vertical.

By a course of investigation similar to that explained in the note appended to equation (24), art. 48, we find, as the general expression of the horizontal force, F', which, applied at c, the middle of the key, shall hold in equilibrium any segment $a\,m\,n\,r\,b\,a$ on c_1, the middle of the lower joint,

$$F'=r^2\times\left(\frac{\cos.^2\tfrac{1}{2}v(2-\cos.v)K^2+\tfrac{1}{3}\cos.^2\tfrac{1}{2}v\cos.vK^3+\tfrac{2}{3}}{K+1}-\tfrac{1}{2}v\ \text{cotang.}\,\tfrac{1}{2}v\right). \qquad (60)$$

In like manner we find, under the same supposition as to the curve of pressure, as a general expression of A', the addition to the thrust caused by a surcharge of constant depth, t, above the extrados of the key,

$$A'=rt\left(\frac{K(1+\cos.v)}{K+1}\right). \qquad (61)$$

The maximum value of A' corresponds always to $v=0$; it then becomes,

$$A=2rt\frac{K}{K+1}. \qquad (61)m$$

The total thrust obtained in any given case by adding this value of A to the maximum value of F', in (60), would involve an error in excess, very proper in light arches, but not required perhaps in heavy ones. The words light and heavy, here used, refer to the proportions of the arch, not to its absolute dimensions.

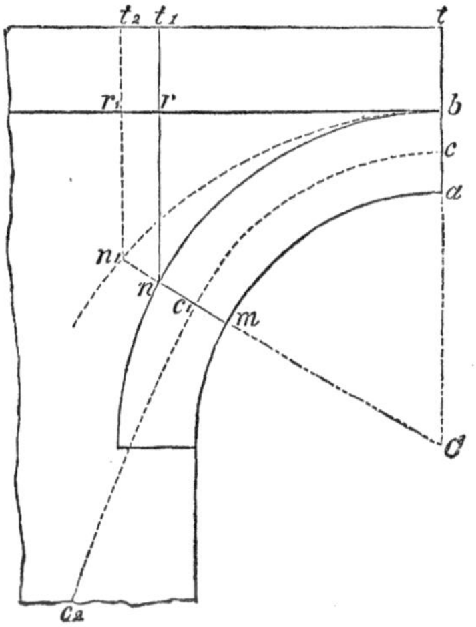

We give below the numerical forms of (60) and (61) corresponding to values of v beginning with zero and increasing by 5° to 75°, and to $v=90°$. By three or four substitutions the reader can obtain the maximum *sum* of F' and A' when r, K, and t are known. In practice, the thickness of the arch generally increases from the key to the reins or to the springing line. In this case, $K=1+\frac{d}{r}$. The results will be a little in excess.

Fig. 32.

The sum of F' and A' thus obtained will correspond to the angle of maximum thrust within $2\frac{1}{2}$ degrees; and this is quite near enough.

$$v=0;\ F'=r^2\left(\frac{K^2+\frac{1}{3}K^3+\frac{2}{3}}{K+1}-1.\right)$$

$$A'=rt\left(\frac{2K}{K+1}\right)$$

$$v=5°;\ F'=r^2\left(\frac{1.0019\times K^2+.33143\times K^3+\frac{2}{3}}{K+1}-0.99937\right);$$

Coefficient of K^2, log. 0.000824.

" " K^3, " $\bar{1}.520395$.

$$A'=rt\left(\frac{1.9962\times K}{K+1}\right).$$

$$v=10^\circ\,;\ F'=r^2\left(\frac{1.00748\times K^2+0.32578\times K^3+\frac{2}{3}}{K+1}-0.99746\right);$$

Coefficient of K^2, log. 0.003325.

" " K^3, " $\bar{1}.512918$.

$$A'=rt\left(\frac{1.98481\times K}{K+1}\right).$$

$$v=15^\circ\,;\ F'=r^2\left(\frac{1.01646\times K^2+0.31649\times K^3+\frac{2}{3}}{K+1}-0.99428\right);$$

Coefficient of K^2, log. 0.007088.

" " K^3, " $\bar{1}.500361$.

$$A'=rt\left(\frac{1.96593\times K}{K+1}\right).$$

$$v=20^\circ\,;\ F'=r^2\left(\frac{1.02834\times K^2+0.303785\times K^3+\frac{2}{3}}{K+1}-0.98982\right);$$

Coefficient of K^2, log. 0.012135.

" " K^3, " $\bar{1}.482567$.

$$A'=rt\left(\frac{1.93969\times K}{K+1}\right).$$

$$v=25^\circ\,;\ F'=r^2\left(\frac{1.04246\times K^2+0.28795\times K^3+\frac{2}{3}}{K+1}-0.98408\right);$$

Coefficient of K^2, log. 0.018058.

" " K^3, " $\bar{1}.459319$.

$$A'=rt\left(\frac{1.90631\times K}{K+1}\right).$$

$$v=30^\circ\,;\ F'=r^2\left(\frac{1.05801\times K^2+0.26934\times K^3+\frac{2}{3}}{K+1}-0.97705\right);$$

Coefficient of K^2, log. 0.024490.

" " K^3, " $\bar{1}.430298$.

$$A'=rt\left(\frac{1.86603\times K}{K+1}\right).$$

$$v=35^\circ\,;\ F'=r^2\left(\frac{1.07408\times K^2+0.24836\times K^3+\frac{2}{3}}{K+1}-0.96871\right);$$

Coefficient of K^2, log. 0.031035.

" " K^3, " $\bar{1}.395084$.

$$A'=rt\left(\frac{1.81915\times K}{K+1}\right).$$

$$v=40^\circ\,;\quad F'=r^2\left(\frac{1.0896\times K^2+0.22548\times K^3+\frac{2}{3}}{K+1}-0.95905\right);$$

Coefficient of K^2, log. 0.037273.

" " K^3, " $\overline{1}.353105$.

$$A'=rt\left(\frac{1.76604\times K}{K+1}\right).$$

$$v=45^\circ\,;\quad F'=r^2\left(\frac{1.10355\times K^2+0.20118\times K^3+\frac{2}{3}}{K+1}-0.94806\right).$$

Coefficient of K^2, log. 0.042792.

" " K^3, " $\overline{1}.303594$.

$$A'=rt\left(\frac{1.70711\times K}{K+1}\right).$$

$$v=50^\circ\,;\quad F'=r^2\left(\frac{1.1148\times K^2+0.17599\times K^3+\frac{2}{3}}{K+1}-0.935715\right);$$

Coefficient of K^2, log. 0.047199.

" " K^3, " $\overline{1}.245498$.

$$A'=rt\left(\frac{1.64279\times K}{K+1}\right).$$

$$v=55^\circ\,;\quad F'=r^2\left(\frac{1.1223\times K^2+0.15043\times K^3+\frac{2}{3}}{K+1}-0.922004\right);$$

Coefficient of K^2, log. 0.050106.

" " K^3, " $\overline{1}.177328$.

$$A'=rt\left(\frac{1.57358\times K}{K+1}\right).$$

$$v=60^\circ\,;\quad F'=r^2\left(\frac{1\frac{1}{8}K^2+\frac{1}{8}K^3+\frac{2}{3}}{K+1}-0.90690\right);$$

$$A'=rt\left(\frac{\frac{3}{2}K}{K+1}\right).$$

$$v=65^\circ\,;\quad F'=r^2\left(\frac{1.122\times K^2+0.1002\times K^3+\frac{2}{3}}{K+1}-0.89037\right);$$

Coefficient of K^2, log. 0.049995.

" " K^3, " $\overline{1}.000885$.

$$A'=rt\left(\frac{1.42262\times K}{K+1}\right).$$

$$v=70^\circ\,;\ F'=r^2\left(\frac{1.11253\times K^2+0.0765\times K^3+\frac{2}{3}}{K+1}-0.872404\right);$$

Coefficient of K^2, log. 0.046310.

" " K^3, " $\bar{2}.883661$.

$$A'=rt\left(\frac{1.34202\times K}{K+1}\right).$$

$$v=75^\circ\,;\ F'=r^2\left(\frac{1.09592\times K^2+0.0543\times K^3+\frac{2}{3}}{K+1}-0.85296\right).$$

Coefficient of K^2, log. 0.039778.

" " K^3, " $\bar{2}.734794$.

$$A'=rt\left(\frac{1.25882\times K}{K+1}\right).$$

$$v=90^\circ\,;\ F'=r^2\left(\frac{K^2+\frac{2}{3}}{K+1}-0.78540\right);$$

$$A'=rt\left(\frac{K}{K+1}\right).$$

From (60) we have calculated table DD, giving what we may regard as the actual thrust of the semicircular arch, surcharged horizontally, under the conditions expressed at the head of this article. The table also gives the maximum effect of the surcharge of any constant depth, t, above the summit of the arch. In drawing up the table we have reduced (60) to its numerical form for every value of v, in whole numbers, from 40° to 75°, inclusive. But knowing the resulting maximum thrusts to be somewhat greater than they need be in heavy arches, we have supposed $v=60^\circ$ for all values of K exceeding 1.22.

Being once on the track we have generally found the maximum value of F', corresponding to any particular value of K, by three or four substitutions.

Column 1 gives the value of $K=1+\frac{d}{r}$.

" 2 " " $\frac{2r}{d}$, or ratio of the span to the thickness.

" 3 " angle of maximum thrust down to $K=1.22$, $v=45°$; below that, v is assumed at 60°.

" 4 " maximum value of F' down to $K=1.22$; below that the value of F' corresponding to $v=60°$.

" 5 " for the purpose of comparison, from table D, the maximum and actual thrust in the case of rupture and fall.

" 6 " $\delta=\frac{F}{F_2}$, or ratio of these two thrusts, properly the coefficient of stability.

" 7 " the value of A, or maximum effect of the surcharge, $v=0$.

" 8 " for the purpose of comparison, from table F, the values of A_2, or maximum effect of the surcharge in case of rupture and fall.

" 9 " $\delta'=\frac{A}{A_2}$, or ratio of these two effects.

CALCULATION OF THE MAXIMUM THRUST OF THE ROOF-SHAPED SEMICIRCULAR ARCH; THE CURVE OF PRESSURE PASSING AT $\frac{1}{3}$ THE LENGTH OF THE JOINT FROM THE EXTRADOS AT THE KEY, AND FROM THE INTRADOS AT THE JOINT OF GREATEST THRUST.

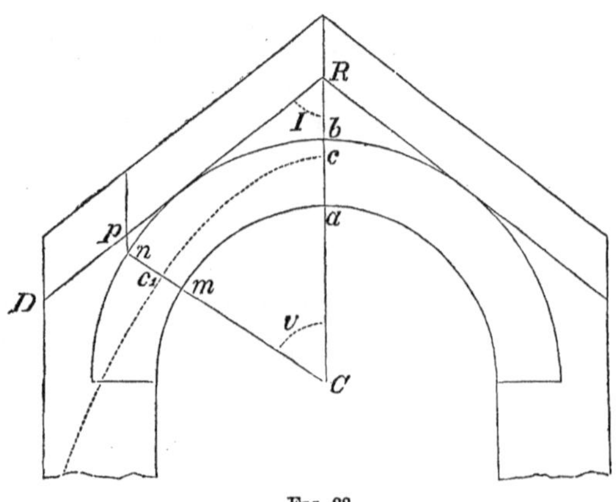

FIG. 33.

117. R=the radius of the extrados; r=the radius of the intrados; d=the thickness of the arch at the key; $K=\frac{R}{r}=1+\frac{d}{r}$; I=the angle between the roof and a vertical; v=the angle between any joint and a vertical.

By a course of investigation similar to that referred to, art. 116, we find, as the general expression of the horizontal force, F' which, applied at c, on the central joint, $a\,b$, $c\,b=\frac{1}{3}a\,b$, shall hold in equilibrium any segment, $a\,m\,n\,p\,R\,a$, on c_1, a point of the lower joint $m\,n$, $m\,c_1=\frac{1}{3}m\,n$,—

$$F'=\tfrac{1}{2}r^2\sin.^2 v\times\left(\frac{\frac{K^2\times 2(2-\sin.(I+v))-K^3(1-\sin.(I+v))}{\sin. I}-\frac{v(K+2)}{\sin. v}+\frac{1}{\cos.^2\frac{1}{2}v}}{K(2-\cos. v)+1-2\cos. v}\right). \quad (62)$$

In like manner we find, under the same supposition as to the curve of pressure, as a general expression of A', the addition to the thrust caused by a surcharge of the constant depth t, above the tangent roof, $D\,R$,—

$$A' = \tfrac{1}{2} rtK \sin.^2 v \frac{(4-K)}{K(2-\cos. v)+1-2\cos. v} \tag{63}$$

of which the maximum value is

$$A = rt \times \frac{4K-K^2}{K+2} \times \frac{2K+1-\sqrt{3K^2-3}}{K+2}, \tag{64}$$

corresponding to an angle whose cosine is

$$\cos. v = \frac{2K+1-\sqrt{3K^2-3}}{K+2} \tag{65}$$

From (62), (64), and (65), we have calculated table FF, giving, directly or by proportional parts, under the conditions expressed at the head of this article, the actual thrust in all the isolated magazine arches in common use. In drawing up the table we have reduced (62) to its numerical form for values of I respectively equal to 60°, 55°, 50°, and 45°, and for values of v increasing by $2\frac{1}{2}$°, from 30° to 60°, that is, as far as necessary, both ways, to ascertain the maximum thrust.

The results under each value of I, are not exactly the maximum thrust, but, in general, a little less; the difference, however, is practically nothing.

EXPLANATION OF TABLE FF.

Column 1 gives the value of $K = 1 + \frac{d}{r}$.

" 1, under each value of I, gives the angle of greatest thrust.

" 2, under each value of I, gives the decimal C; F=the thrust$=r^2 C$.

" 3, under each value of I, gives the coefficient of stability, δ, or ratio of the actual thrust to the diminished thrust at the moment of rupture and fall, the latter being obtained from table F.

" 1, under "surcharge," gives the angle of maximum thrust of the surcharge.

" 2, under "surcharge," gives the decimal C; $A = rtC$=the maximum effect of the surcharge.

REMARKS.

It will be seen that the angle which renders the effect of surcharge a maximum, differs but a few degrees from the angle of maximum thrust in the arch proper; consequently the error, in excess, which we commit, by adding the two maxima together, and taking their sum as the actual thrust of the arch and its load, is exceedingly small, and the table may be regarded as practically exact.

It will also be seen that the coefficient of stability, δ, is nearly the same, for the same values of K, in all the arches; consequently, we can obtain, from table F, the actual thrust, on the conditions announced at the head of this article, for values of I some degrees above 60°, by multiplying the thrust, computed from that table, by the value of δ found opposite the given value of K in table FF.

The maximum effect of surcharge, given by the last column of FF, is independent of I, and the same in all arches.

For rules for using table FF, see rules for using table F, arts. 61, 62.

CALCULATION OF THE THRUST OF THE SEMI-CIRCULAR ARCH SURCHARGED HORIZONTALLY; THE CURVE OF PRESSURE PASSING AT $\frac{1}{3}$ THE LENGTH OF THE JOINT FROM THE EXTRADOS AT THE KEY, AND FROM THE INTRADOS AT THE JOINT OF GREATEST THRUST.

118. This is a particular case of the roof-shaped arch discussed in art. 117. We need not repeat that discussion. Formulæ (62), (63), (64), and (65), remain the same. In the first it is only necessary to make $I=90°$ which reduces (62) to

$$F'=\tfrac{1}{2}r^2\sin.^2 v\frac{K^2\times 2(2-\cos.v)-K^3(1-\cos.v)-\dfrac{v(K+2)}{\sin.v}+\dfrac{1}{\cos.^2\frac{1}{2}v}}{K(2-\cos.v)+1-2\cos.v} \quad (62)'$$

From this formula and from other sources, we have calculated table DDD, giving the maximum or actual thrust of the arch in question under the conditions stated above.

EXPLANATION OF TABLE DDD.

The 1st column gives the value of $K=1+\frac{d}{r}$; d=the thickness at the key.

The second column gives the decimal C; $F=r^2C$=the thrust on the condition stated at the head of the table.

The 3d column gives the decimal C; $A=rtC$=the addition to the thrust caused by a surcharge of the constant depth t above the key.

$F+A$=the entire thrust, with an excess arising from adding two maxima together.

The 4th column gives the joint of rupture or angle of greatest thrust on the supposition of actual rupture and fall, from table D.

The 5th column gives the angle of greatest thrust on the supposition that the curve of pressure is at $\frac{1}{3}$ the length of the joint from the extrados at the key, and from the intrados at the joint of greatest thrust, calculated at intervals of $2\frac{1}{2}$ degrees.

The 6th column gives the angle of greatest thrust on the supposition that the curve of pressure is at the center of the joints of the key and of greatest thrust, taken from table DD. Below $K=1.22$ the angle is not given.

The 7th column gives the coefficient of stability, δ, or the ratio of the actual thrust, on the conditions stated at the head of the table, column 2, to the calculated thrust at the instant of rupture and fall, table D.

The 8th column gives the coefficient of stability on the supposition that the curve of pressure passes through the middle of the joints, from table DD.

REMARKS ON TABLE DDD.

Columns 6 and 8 have been taken from table DD. They are added here that the reader may see at a glance, how the angles of greatest thrust and the thrusts themselves vary with the suppositions which we make upon the curve of pressure.

The greatest value of δ in column 7, is 1.92; in column 8, it is 2.59.

CALCULATION OF THE THRUST OF SEGMENTAL ARCHES, SURCHARGED HORIZONTALLY, THE CURVE OF PRESSURE PASSING THROUGH THE MIDDLE OF THE KEY, AND THE MIDDLE OF THE JOINT OF GREATEST THRUST, WHICH IS GENERALLY AT THE SPRINGING LINE.

119. If the semi-angle at the center be as great, or nearly as great, as the angle of maximum thrust in table DD, art. 116, we shall find in that table the actual thrust on the condition announced above. This table may, indeed, be used in all cases without any great error; for we have shown that the curve of pressure, passing through the middle of the joint at the key and the middle of the joint of greatest thrust, will continue near the centers of all intermediate joints. The error will, of course, be always in excess.

The exact thrust, when it is less than that given in DD, will be obtained from equation (60) art. 116, when we have substituted for the constants which enter into that formula, their known values.

The effect of a surcharge of constant depth may also be obtained from table DD, with an error, always in excess.

CALCULATION OF THE THRUST OF SEGMENTAL ARCHES, SURCHARGED HORIZONTALLY, THE CURVE OF PRESSURE PASSING AT $\frac{1}{3}$ THE LENGTH OF THE JOINT, FROM THE EXTRADOS AT THE KEY, AND FROM THE INTRADOS AT THE JOINT OF GREATEST THRUST, WHICH IS GENERALLY AT THE SPRINGING LINE.

120. Notation: s=the span; f=the rise; r=the radius of the intrados; d=the thickness of the arch at the key; $K=1+\frac{d}{r}$; C=the decimal in the first column under each value of v; F=the thrust$=r^2C$; v=the semi-angle of the whole arch.

If one half the angle subtended by the given arch be as great, or nearly as great, as the angle of maximum thrust in column 5, table DDD, we can obtain the required thrust directly from that table. But if this half-angle, v, be less than the angle of maximum thrust, substitute its known value, and the value of K in (62)′: the resulting value of F' will be the actual thrust on the condition stated above.

To obtain the effect of a surcharge of the constant depth t above the key: if v be as great, or nearly as great, as the angle which renders the effect of surcharge a maximum, see last column but one of table FF, the required addition will be obtained from the last column of that table, or from the 4th column of table EE.

But if v be less than the angle in question, the required effect of surcharge must be computed from formula (63). The sum, $F+A$, as usual, will be the entire thrust.

Table EE gives, either directly or by proportional parts, the actual thrust of segmental arches in common use.

EXPLANATION OF TABLE EE.

Column 1 gives the value of $K=1+\frac{d}{r}$.

" 1, under each value of v, gives the decimal C; $F=r^2C=$the thrust of the arch loaded up to the level of the extrados at the key.

" 2, under each value of v, gives the ratio, δ, of this actual thrust to the thrust of the same arch at the moment of rupture and fall, taken from table E′.

" 3, under each value of v, gives the decimal C; $A=rtC=$the addition to the thrust caused by a surcharge of the uniform depth t.

ELLIPTICAL ARCHES.

121. In the first part of this paper, section V., art. 90, and following, we have shown how to obtain the ultimate thrust of the elliptical arch, loaded and unloaded. The actual thrust may be found in a similar manner.

ELLIPTICAL ARCHES SURCHARGED HORIZONTALLY.

Let us compare the given arch with a circular arch, surcharged in like manner horizontally, having the same span, and a thickness at the key as much greater than the thickness of the elliptical arch as the half-span is greater than the rise. Through c, the middle of $a\,b$, and c_3, the mid-

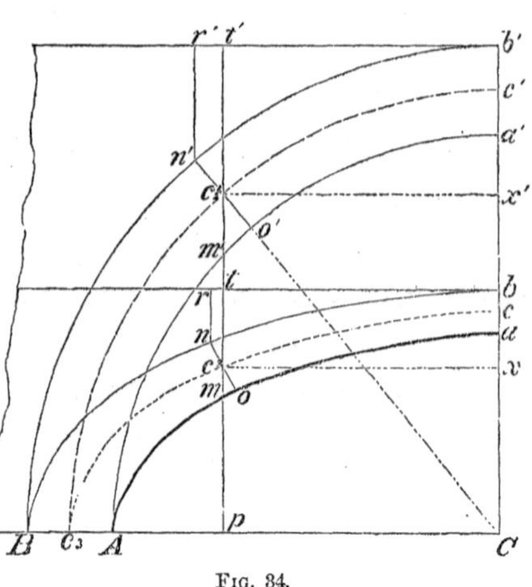

FIG. 34.

dle of A B, draw the ellipse $c\ c_2\ c_3$ similar to the intrados. This curve will cut the several joints of the elliptical arch near their central points, and will never pass within the inferior limit, one-third the length of a joint from the intrados, unless we give an unnecessary extension of these joints at the reins. Draw the curve $c'\ c'_2\ c_3$, dividing into equal parts the joints of the auxiliary circular arch, supposed here to be of equal thickness throughout. Drawing any vertical $t'\ t\ p$, let S=the surface $m\ t\ b\ a$, S'=the surface $m'\ t'\ b'\ a'$, $y=c\ x$, or vertical distance between c and c_2, $y'=c'\ x'$, p=the horizontal distance between the vertical $t\ p$ and the center of gravity of S, p'=the corresponding distance in the circular arch.

The horizontal force F which, applied at c, shall hold in equilibrium the surface S, in relation to c_2, as the center of rotation, is $F=\frac{S\times p}{y}$; in like manner, we have $F'=\frac{S'\times p'}{y'}$.

But wherever the vertical be drawn, the depths $m\ t$, $m'\ t'$, stand in the constant relation of the rise to the half-span, or f to r; the surfaces S, S', and the lever-arms y and y' stand in the same relation; the centers of gravity of S and S' are on the same vertical line, so that $p=p'$. We have, therefore,

$$S : S' :: y : y', \text{ and } \frac{Sp}{y}=\frac{S'p'}{y'}, \text{ or } F=F'.$$

These surfaces having the same thrusts wherever the vertical be drawn, their maximum thrusts will also be the same; and we arrive at this result:

The actual thrust of an elliptical arch sustaining a load of masonry or of equal weight with masonry, rising to the horizontal line tangent to the extrados at the key, is nearly equal to the thrust of the semicircular arch, loaded in like manner, having the same span, and a thickness at the key as much greater than the thickness of the elliptical arch, as the half-span is greater than the rise.

We shall, therefore, be able to obtain immediately from table DD, the actual thrust of the elliptical arch.

Strictly speaking, a slight correction—addition—would be necessary, as we have disregarded the influence of the small surfaces $c_2\, n\, r\, t$, $c'_2\, n'\, r'\, t'$; but on the other hand we have provided for some exaggeration of the thrust, by supposing the curve of pressure to pass through the middle of the key, and near the middle of the joint of greatest thrust.

Example. Central arch of the London Bridge. $r=$ half-span$=76'$; $f=$the rise$=38'$; $d=$the thickness at the key$=5'$; $D=$the thickness of the auxiliary circular arch$=\frac{r}{f}\times d=10'$; $K=1+\frac{D}{r}=1.1316$; hence from the 4th column of table DD, by proportional parts, $F=r^2\times.16723=$ 966.45 cubic feet. Suppose a surcharge one foot deep above the key, $t=1'$; the corresponding surcharge of the auxiliary circular arch is $\frac{r}{f}t=2'$, and its effect is, 7th column of table DD, $A=2'\times76'\times1.0617=161.38$.

THE COEFFICIENT OF STABILITY.

122. In the first part of this paper, we have shown how to find, by tables or calculation, the actual thrust of most arches at the supposed moment of rupture and fall, when all the forces in the system act upon three points or edges of masonry; viz., the extrados at the key, the intrados at the reins, and the exterior lower edge of the semi-arch or pier. We have shown, art. 109, that this ultimate thrust is also the minimum or least possible thrust that can ever exist in the arch.

This minimum, Audoy, Poncelet, and others, multiply by what they call the coefficient of stability: 2, or some smaller number, according to the proportions of the arch;—and they determine the thickness of pier on the condition that the resultant of the thrust thus increased, and of the weight of the semi-arch and pier, shall pass through the exterior edge of the base of the pier.

The value of this coefficient was determined by an examination of a powder-magazine of Vauban, which, having stood the test of ages, was presumed to have all the necessary elements of stability. The value of the co-efficient thus determined, was found to be about 2; and this is evidently applicable to all similar structures, that is, to structures identical, or nearly so, with the magazine of Vauban, in all their proportions, and only different in their absolute dimensions. The rule has been of great service, for it so happens that most magazines have been modeled after that of Vauban.

But the idea was entirely empirical, and was so understood by its authors. The co-efficient of stability thus defined and used, is by no means a correct index or measure of the stability of any pier. In piers of great height, it will generally give results too small,—in piers of small height, results too large; nor is it sure to give correct results in any work not strictly similar to that of Vauban from which the rule was deduced. The proper value of this coefficient will change, not only with every variation of the proportions of the arch, but, in the same arch, with every increase or reduction of the height of the pier. Nor is it possible to know this proper value without first learning the actual thrust of the well-established arch; and when we have attained this knowledge, we have only to make proper use of it: the coefficient has become useless. We know the thrust itself.

As it is evident that the curve of pressure in the arch should be everywhere traced between two other curves which divide the joints into three equal parts,—so, in the pier, this curve must lie between corresponding lines; and at the base, where it approaches nearest to the exterior face, it must not come nearer than $\frac{1}{3}$ the length of the lower joint, or $\frac{1}{3}$ the thickness of pier. This conclusion is inevitable, if we admit the principle of Navier as to the distribution of the pressures upon the joints; and this principle is generally admitted, we believe, by engineers.

123. Let us examine the magazine of Vauban anew, fig. 13. Its dimensions are: Radius of the intrados$=r=$ $12'.50$; radius of the extrados$=R=15'.50$; $K=\frac{R}{r}=1.24$; inclination of the roof to a vertical$=I=49° 7' 17''$; height of the pier from the base to the springing line$=h=8'$; thickness of pier given by Vauban$=8'$; on the exterior face, counterforts $6'$ long and $4'$ deep, with intervening spaces of $12'$; whole thickness of pier and counterfort$=12'$.

The ultimate thrust of this arch, arts. 48, 63, is $F=r^2\times 0.2294$. But we learn from table FF that its least actual thrust, consistent with the condition that no joint shall open at either the extrados or intrados, is $r^2\times 0.3496$. Substituting this value in formula $(31\frac{1}{3})'$ art. 66, we obtain, as the least thickness of a solid pier whose lowest joint will not open on the inside, $10'.56$. The mean thickness of Vauban's wall is $9'.33$, and the thickness given by the rule of Audoy, $\delta=2$, formula $(31)'$, art. 66, is $9'.23$.

We come at once to this unexpected result,—that the rule of Audoy does not in this case give a pier of sufficient thickness to withstand the thrust of the arch without any openings of the joints. We are authorized and compelled to conclude, that the magazine of Vauban derived some additional stability from adhesion of mortar in the arch or pier, or both.

During the construction of an arch it is almost impossible to prevent cracks or openings at the reins, and although they may close on the removal of the center, still the adhesion of mortar must be forever impaired or destroyed. It would be unwise to rely upon any adhesion of mortar *in the arch.*

On the other hand, the pier is subject to no disturbance during its construction; its mortar has time to set; and we may in some cases rely with confidence upon this element of stability.

The calculation of the effective resistance of the piers in Vauban's magazine is complicated by the existence of abutments. Let us still assume that the lowest joint, under the action of the horizontal thrust, is on the point of opening at its inner edge, where the pressure is consequently zero, and that the pressure increases uniformly from that point to the exterior edge of the abutments. The mean pressure will be represented by the ordinates of the opposite Figure, and the point of application of the resultant of all the pressures will be at C, $B\,C=5'.255$.

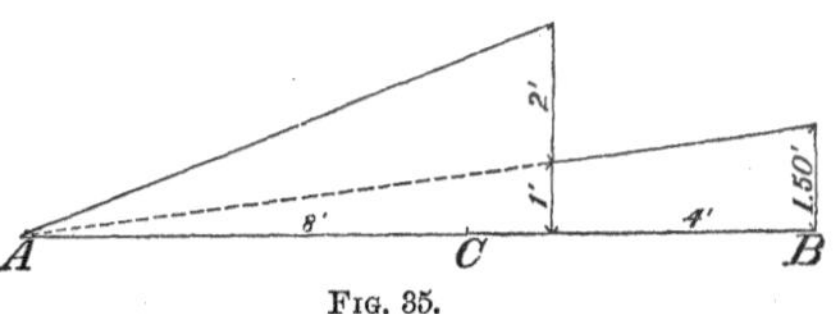

Fig. 35.

The mean center of gravity of the pier is $7'.143$ from B, the exterior edge. Taking the moment of the pier and of the semi-arch in relation to C, we find the thrust, acting horizontally one foot below the extrados at the key, which stands in equilibrium with these elements of resistance, to be $52.70 = r^2 \times 0.3373$, less than the actual thrust before given by $r^2 \times 0.0123$. The supposition of a very slight adhesion of mortar upon the base of the pier, viz., $1\frac{1}{2}$ pounds per square inch, not more than a fifteenth part of the adhesion of good mortar, will equalize the two thrusts.

It thus appears that the magazine of Vauban illustrates and confirms in a remarkable manner the new theory of the arch. Its piers present almost precisely the resistance which this theory requires.

COEFFICIENT OF STABILITY—NEW DEFINITION.

124. The coefficient of stability is the ratio of the actual thrust of the well-established arch to the ultimate thrust existing at the moment of rupture and fall, or the quotient of the former divided by the latter.

This ultimate thrust for most arches likely to occur in practice, is given by the tables which belong to the first part of this paper, viz., A, C, D, E, E′, F, and G.

If we had tables equally extensive of the actual thrust, we should no longer need this coefficient. But at present such is not the case. M. Cavallo has given an extensive table of the actual thrusts of semicircular arches, based on the supposition of vertical joints, and of a surcharge bounded horizontally at top with a depth on all vertical lines bearing a constant ratio to the depth of the arch proper on the same lines. And we have given in this paper tables of the actual thrusts of the unloaded circular ring, AA, art. 114; the magazine or roof-shaped arch, FF, art. 117; the semicircular arch surcharged horizontally, DDD, art. 118, the segmental arch surcharged horizontally, EE, art. 120; all based on the supposition of joints of equal length perpendicular to the intrados, and of a curve of pressure at the key $\frac{1}{3}$ the length of the joint from the extrados, and at the joint of greatest thrust $\frac{1}{3}$ the length of the joint from the intrados; also, a table, DD, art. 116, of the actual thrusts of semicircular arches surcharged horizontally, with joints as above, and with a curve of pressure passing through the middle of the key-stone and weakest joint.

We have given in all of these tables the value, δ, of the coefficient, as defined above, to show at a glance how the actual compares with the ultimate thrust when both are known, and to exhibit a guide which may lead to the former when the latter only is known.

For instance, we learn, from table FF, that the value

of δ, corresponding to $K=1.20$, is 1.47 when $I=45°$; 1.46 when $I=50°$; 1.46 when $I=55°$; 1.45 when $I=60°$; and we learn from table DDD that the value of δ is 1.47 when $K=1.20$ and $I=90°$; we may thence conclude, by analogy, that δ does not exceed 1.47 for roofs of any inclination between a horizontal and 45°. In like manner we learn the value of δ for other values of K, and may deduce the actual thrust from table F, when the given value of I does not place the case in table FF.

In all this we use the ultimate thrust as a convenient and almost indispensable standard of comparison; not only because that thrust, as already remarked, has been extensively calculated and published, but also because it can be determined with great accuracy by experiments upon models. The actual thrust cannot, with equal accuracy be thus determined.

Regarding this ultimate thrust as the standard, we may with propriety call the ratio by which it must be multiplied to give the actual thrust, the *coefficient of stability.*

DISCUSSION OF THE COEFFICIENT OF STABILITY, OR RATIO OF THE ACTUAL TO THE ULTIMATE THRUST, WHEN THE CURVE OF PRESSURE LIES, AT THE KEY, $\frac{1}{3}$ THE LENGTH OF THE JOINT FROM THE EXTRADOS, AND AT THE REINS $\frac{1}{3}$ THE SAME DISTANCE FROM THE INTRADOS.

125. *Semicircular arches surcharged horizontally.*—We learn from column 7, table DDD, that this ratio, beginning with 1 for $K=1$, gradually increases by nearly arithmetical differences, to its maximum, 1.92, corresponding to $K=1.35$. It then begins to diminish, and would finally become 1 again.

The magazine arch.—We learn from table FF, that the value of δ constantly increases from $K=1.15$ to $K=$

1.40. It attains, in fact, its greatest value when K slightly exceeds 1.40.

The value of δ corresponding to the usual values of K, say from $K=1.15$ to $K=1.30$ is nearly the same in each horizontal column. We hence infer the constancy of δ for intermediate values of I, and for values somewhat less than 45° or more than 60°.

Comparing together tables FF and DDD, we see that δ up to $K=1.18$, is less with the horizontal than with the inclined roof; that it is about the same with all roofs from $K=1.18$ to $K=1.24$; and that above $K=1.24$, it predominates more and more with the horizontal roof up to $K=1.35$. Above that, its predominance diminishes.

Segmental arches surcharged horizontally.—Table EE. The coefficient δ, beginning with 1 for $K=1$, gradually increases under each value of v, or each ratio of the span to the rise, to its maximum, corresponding to values of K varying from 1.34 to 1.07. The maximum itself diminishes from 1.938 under $s=4f$, to 1.788 under $s=8f$, and then increases to 1.938 under $s=16f$.

The great variation of the coefficient, δ, from the lowest to the higher values of K, viz., nearly from 1 to 2, proves the great inaccuracy of the rule of Audoy, as used by him and others. Even with the same values of K, this coefficient varies largely: opposite $K=1.07$, from 1.177 to 1.938; opposite $K=1.03$, from 1.077 to 1.506; opposite $K=1.34$, from 1.938 to 1.

We have not given the ratio of the actual and ultimate effects of surcharge upon the thrust; but in tables F and FF have given the effects themselves, from which the corresponding ratios may be easily determined: In general they differ but little from the coefficient of stability of the arches to which they belong. This last remark is also applicable to segmental arches.

THE COEFFICIENT OF STABILITY, OR RATIO OF THE ACTUAL TO THE ULTIMATE THRUST, WHEN THE CURVE OF PRESSURE PASSES THROUGH THE MIDDLE OF THE KEY AND THE MIDDLE OF THE JOINT OF GREATEST THRUST.

126. *Semicircular arches surcharged horizontally.*—Table DD. The ratio δ, is seen to increase from 1 opposite $K=1$, to 2.59 opposite $K=1.35$. It then diminishes, and would finally become 1 again.

Opposite $K=1.22$, δ is 1.91. For higher values of K, the thrusts given in that table were calculated on the supposition of a curve of pressure passing through the middle of the key and the middle of the joint 60° from the key. They are consequently a little less than they would have been had we continued to use the angle of maximum thrust.

THICKNESS OF PIER—UNIVERSAL METHOD.

128. We suppose the surcharge, if partly of earth or any light material, to be reduced in height in the proportion of its density compared with the density of the arch proper. Let

h=the mean height of the pier from its base to the surface of the reduced surcharge over its top, $=E'\,D$, fig. 4; $=O\,O'$, fig. 10; $=E'\,D'$, fig. 15; to be estimated if not known.

E=the elevation of the reduced ridge above the springing line, $=C\,a$, fig. 4; $=C\,R'$, fig. 10; $=C\,A'$, fig. 9; $=m'\,R'$, fig. 15.

E'=the depth of the arch and its reduced surcharge at the springing line, $=C\,a=E$, fig. 4; $=A\,a'$, figs. 10, 11; $=m'\,R'=E$, fig. 15.

n=the surface of that part of the arch and its reduced load which lies directly over the half-span.

m=the moment of that surface in relation to the interior edge of the joint of the springing line.

l=the lever arm of the thrust measured from the base to the point of application on the key-stone joint, say $\frac{1}{3}$ its length from the extrados.

F=the actual horizontal thrust however determined.

r=the half-span, whatever be the curve of the intrados.

x=the distance between the exterior edge of the base of the pier and the intersection of this base with the curve of pressure.

e=the unknown thickness of pier.

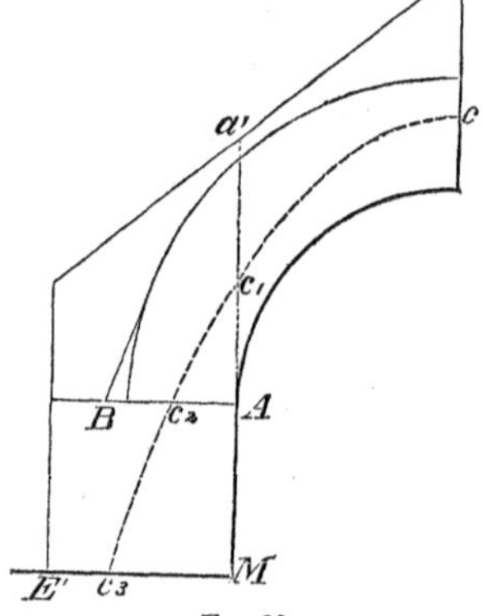

FIG. 36.

Let us determine the thickness of pier on the condition that the lowest joint shall not open at its inner edge, M. We must form the equation of moments in relation to c_3, $E'c_3=\frac{1}{3}E'M=\frac{1}{3}e$. The equation is

$$\tfrac{1}{6}e^2h+\tfrac{2}{3}ne+m=Fl\,; \qquad (66)$$

giving

$$e=-2\frac{n}{h}+\sqrt{4\frac{n^2}{h^2}-6\frac{m}{h}+6\frac{Fl}{h}}. \qquad (67)$$

If we desire the curve of pressure to intersect the base at $\frac{1}{4}e$ from the exterior edge we have the equation of moments,

$$\tfrac{1}{4}e^2h+\tfrac{3}{4}ne+m=Fl\,; \qquad (66\tfrac{1}{4})$$

giving

$$e=-\frac{3}{2}\times\frac{n}{h}+\sqrt{\frac{9}{4}\times\frac{n^2}{h^2}-4\frac{m}{h}+4\frac{Fl}{h}}. \qquad (67\tfrac{1}{4})$$

If we determine the thickness of pier, as in the method of Audoy, on the condition that the curve of pressure shall pass through the exterior edge of the base, we have,

$$\tfrac{1}{2}he^2+ne+m=Fl; \qquad (66\tfrac{0}{})$$

giving

$$e=-\frac{n}{h}+\sqrt{\frac{n^2}{h^2}-2\frac{m}{h}+2\frac{Fl}{h}}. \qquad (67\tfrac{0}{})$$

If the curve of pressure intersect the base at $\frac{2}{5}e$ from its exterior edge, we have the equation of moments,

$$\tfrac{1}{10}e^2h+\tfrac{6}{10}ne+m=Fl; \qquad (66\tfrac{2}{5})$$

giving

$$e=-3\frac{n}{h}+\sqrt{9\frac{n^2}{h^2}-10\frac{m}{h}+10\frac{Fl}{h}}. \qquad (67\tfrac{2}{5})$$

If the curve of pressure intersect the base at any proportional distance $p\times e$ from the exterior edge, we have

$$(\tfrac{1}{2}-p)e^2h+(1-p)ne+m=Fl; \qquad (66p)$$

giving

$$e=-\left(\frac{1-p}{1-2p}\right)\times\frac{n}{h}+\sqrt{\left(\frac{1-p}{1-2p}\right)^2\times\frac{n^2}{h^2}-\frac{2}{1-2p}\times\frac{m}{h}+\frac{2}{1-2p}\times\frac{Fl}{h}}. \qquad (67p)$$

Let the curve of pressure pass through the middle of the base, we have

$$\tfrac{1}{2}ne+m=Fl: \qquad (66\tfrac{1}{2})$$

$$e=2\left(\frac{Fl}{m}-\frac{m}{n}\right). \qquad (67\tfrac{1}{2})$$

The values of e, drawn from (67), $(67\frac{1}{4})$, $(67\frac{0}{})$, $(67\frac{2}{5})$, $(67\frac{1}{2})$, $(67p)$, differ only in the numerical coefficients of

$$\frac{n}{h}, \ \frac{n^2}{h^2}, \ \frac{m}{h}, \ \frac{Fl}{h};$$

so that, having calculated these latter quantities, once for all, we can readily solve all those equations and others of a similar character.

Giving to h and l in (67) the particular values which correspond to the springing line, we learn at once the required thickness of the arch at that place, on the condition that the curve of pressure shall cross the springing line $\frac{1}{3}$ the length of the joint from the exterior edge.

Should the result require an increase of the thickness already adopted, this increase need not extend higher up than, say, 35° from the springing line. We here speak of semicircular and semi-elliptical arches.

Giving to l in ($67\frac{1}{2}$) its value at the springing line, we learn the thickness of arch required at that place when the curve of pressure passes through the middle of the joint.

VALUES OF m AND n IN PARTICULAR CASES: THE ROOF A PLANE SURFACE, THE SEGMENTAL RING EXCEPTED.

129. *The intrados a semi-circle.* We have (see art. 65)

$$n=\tfrac{1}{2}r(E+E')-r^2\times 0.7854.$$
$$m=r^2(\tfrac{1}{3}E+\tfrac{1}{6}E')-r^3\times 0.452065.$$

If the roof be inclined 45°, we have

$$n=r^2(K-0.7854).$$
$$m=r^3(\tfrac{1}{2}K-0.452065).$$

130. *The segmental ring of equal thickness throughout* (art. 72).

$$n=r^2\frac{v}{2}(K^2-1);$$

$$m=\frac{ns}{2}-\tfrac{1}{3}r^3(K^3-1)(1-\cos. v);$$

in which v is the semi-angle at the center and s the span.

131. *Segmental arches surcharged horizontally.*

$$n=\tfrac{1}{2}s(f+d+t)-\tfrac{1}{4}r^2(2v-\sin. 2v);$$
$$m=\tfrac{1}{8}s^2(f+d+t)-r^3(\tfrac{1}{2}v\sin. v+\tfrac{1}{3}\cos.^3 v-\tfrac{1}{3});$$

in which f is the rise, d the thickness of the arch at the key, and t the constant depth of the surcharge.

132. *Segmental arches covered by two symmetrical plain surfaces of any inclination* (art. 89); approximate formulæ.

$$n=\tfrac{1}{4}s(E+E'-\tfrac{4}{3}f);$$

$$m=\tfrac{1}{12}s^2(E+\tfrac{1}{2}E'-\tfrac{5}{4}f);$$

133. *Elliptical arches surcharged horizontally* (art. 107). $E=E'=f+d+t;$

$$n=r\times E-rf\times 0.7854;$$

$$m=\tfrac{1}{2}r^2\times E-r^2\times f\times 0.452065;$$

in which r is the half-span or semi-transverse axis, f the rise or semi-conjugate axis, d the thickness of the arch at the key, t the constant depth of surcharge above the horizontal passing through the extrados at the key.

THICKNESS OF PIER, THE ROOF GREATLY INCLINED, LITTLE OR NO SURCHARGE.

134. When the roof is so steep and the arch so thin that we can regard the triangle $D\,E\,P$, fig. 13, as forming a part of the semi-arch or pier, we can give to n, m, and h, in the formulæ of art. 128, a meaning which, without changing the form or purport of any of those equations, shall render their application somewhat easier.

Let n'=the surface of the whole semi-arch and its reduced load, and of that part of the pier which lies above the springing line.

m'=the moment of that surface in relation to the interior edge of the joint of the springing line.

h'=the height of the pier from its base *to the springing line.*

Let E, l, F, r, x, e remain the same as in art. 128.

Let I, as usual represent the angle between the roof and a vertical. We have

$n'=\frac{1}{2}$ tang. $I\times E^2-r^2\times 0.7854.$

$m'=\frac{1}{2}$ tang. $I\times E^2(r-\frac{1}{3}$ tang. $I\times E)-r^3\times 0.452065$;

To determine the thickness of pier we have, for

$$x=\tfrac{1}{3}e;\ \tfrac{1}{6}h'e^2+\tfrac{2}{3}n'e+m'=Fl; \qquad (66)'$$

$$e=-2\frac{n'}{h'}+\sqrt{4\frac{n'^2}{h'^2}-6\frac{m'}{h'}+6\frac{Fl}{h'}}; \qquad (67)'$$

$$x=\tfrac{1}{4}e;\ \tfrac{1}{4}h'e^2+\tfrac{3}{4}n'e+m'=Fl, \qquad (66\tfrac{1}{4})'$$

$$e=-\tfrac{3}{2}\times\frac{n'}{h'}+\sqrt{\tfrac{9}{4}\times\frac{n'^2}{h'^2}-4\frac{m'}{h'}+4\frac{Fl}{h'}}, \qquad (67\tfrac{1}{4})'$$

$$x=0;\ \tfrac{1}{2}h'e^2+n'e+m'=Fl, \qquad (66\tfrac{0}{-})'$$

$$e=-\frac{n'}{h'}+\sqrt{\frac{n'^2}{h'^2}-2\frac{m'}{h'}+2\frac{Fl}{h'}}, \qquad (67\tfrac{0}{-})'$$

$$x=\tfrac{2}{5}e;\ \tfrac{1}{10}h'e^2+\tfrac{6}{10}n'e+m'=Fl, \qquad (66\tfrac{2}{5})'$$

$$e=-3\frac{n'}{h'}+\sqrt{9\frac{n'^2}{h'^2}-10\frac{m'}{h'}+10\frac{Fl}{h'}}; \qquad (67\tfrac{2}{5})'$$

$$x=\tfrac{1}{2}e;\ \tfrac{1}{2}n'e+m'=Fl, \qquad (66\tfrac{1}{2})$$

$$e=2\left(\frac{Fl}{n'}-\frac{m'}{n'}\right) \qquad (67\tfrac{1}{2})'$$

To (67) and (67)′ we should generally look for the thickness of pier.

THE THICKNESS OF PIER—EXAMPLES.

135. Example I. Powder magazine, roof inclined 45°, no surcharge. $r=10'$; $R=12'$; $K=\frac{R}{r}=1.20$; $I=45°$; $h'=10'$; $l=h'+r+\frac{2}{3}(R-r)=21'.3333..$; F, table FF,$=r^2\times 0.3790=37.90$; n', art. 134,$=65.46$; m', art. 134,$=173.356$; from these data we obtain

$$\frac{n'}{h'}=6.546\,;\ \frac{n'^2}{h'^2}=42.85\,;\ \frac{m'}{h'}=17.3356\,;\ \frac{Fl}{h'}=80.8533,$$

and, by (67)′ art. 134, $e=10'.41$.

The rule of Audoy, art. 67, example 1, gives $e=8'.79$.

For $h'=5'$ (67)′ gives $e=8'.75$; the rule of Audoy gives for $h=5'$, $e=8'.19$.

For $h=0$, (66)′ gives $e=5'.87$; the rule of Audoy gives $e=6'.81$.

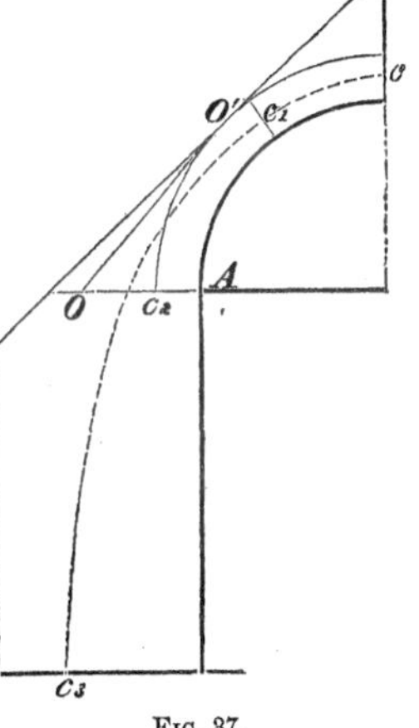

Fig. 37.

From the value of e at the springing line, $5'.87$, we learn that the curve of pressure passes through c_2 at the distance $\frac{2}{3}e=3'.91$ from A, the interior edge of the joint. This is entirely outside of the arch proper, supposed to be of equal thickness throughout. Hence, making $A\ O=5'.87$, the arch must be extended to the line $O\ O'$, either straight or slightly convex on the upper side, joining the proper extrados about 40° from the springing line, where the curve of pressure will obviously pass near the middle of the joint. The point c_1 where this curve comes nearest to the intrados, is, table FF, about $37\frac{1}{2}°$ from the vertical. In practice, it would be better to make the whole lower part of the arch, out as far as the roof, one solid piece of masonry.

Example 2. The magazine of Fort Jefferson, fig. 12. $r=14'$; $R=17'.50$; $K=1.25$; $I=56°\ 3'\ 23''=55°+$

$1^\circ.0564$; $t=5'.90$; $h=16'.50$ below the springing line$+$ $13'.50$ above,$=30'$; $l=16'.50+14'-\frac{2}{3}\times5'.50=32'.8333$.

$E=\frac{R}{\sin. I}+t=27'$; $E'=E-r$ cotang. $I=17'.58$; $F^*=$

114.7128; n, art. 129,$=158.12$; m, art. 129,$=1097.82$; $\frac{n}{h}=5.27$; $\frac{n^2}{h^2}=27.78$; $\frac{m}{h}=36.594$; $\frac{Fl}{h}=125.5468$; $\frac{m}{n}=$ 6.943. With these data we obtain:

(67), art. 128, $x=\frac{1}{3}e$, ... $e=14'.85$
The rule of Audoy gave, art. 67, ex. 2, . . $e=11'.88$
To obtain the required thickness at the springing line, make $h=13'.50$; $l=16'.3333$; and we have, (67), ... $e=6'.47$
The rule of Audoy gives, ... $e=7.33$

Example 3. Arch in the citadel of Fort Porter, fig. 11, art. 63, ex. 3, art. 67, ex. 3. $r=6'$; $R=7'.668$, $K=1.278$; $I=86^\circ\ 46'$; $t=6'.60$; $h=18'$ below the springing line$+$ $12'$ above,$=30'$; $l=18'+r+\frac{2}{3}(R-r)=25'.112$; $E=$ $14'.28$; $E'=12'.59$; $n=52.3356$; $m=149.254$.

This case does not come directly under table FF; but, comparing that with table DDD, we infer that the coefficient of stability is about 1.69; the ultimate thrust of the arch, without including the effect of the surcharge 6'.6

---

* Table FF, $K=1.25$, $I=55^\circ$, ... $F=r^2\times0.2916$ 0.2916
Table FF, $K=1.25$, $I=60^\circ$, ... $F=r^2\times0.2529$

Difference for the interval of 5° in I, . $=r^2\times0.0387$
$5^\circ : 0.0387 :: 1^\circ.0564 : x=$ 0.0082

Hence the thrust of the arch without surcharge, . . . $=r^2\times0.2834=55.5464$
Add for surcharge, last column of table FF, $A=14'\times5.90\times0.7163$. $=59.1664$

Total thrust$=F=114.7128$

The ultimate thrust, art. 67, ex. 2, is 74.86; the coefficient of stability, table FF, $K=1.25$, $I=55^\circ$, 60°, is 1.53. 74.86×1.53 . . . $=114.5358$

deep, art. 63, ex. 3, is 5.0126, which, multiplied by 1.69, gives, ... 8.4713

Add for surcharge, table FF, $A=rtC=6' \times 6'.6 \times 0.705$, ... $=27.9180$

Total thrust, $F=36.3893$

$\frac{n}{h}=1.7445$; $\frac{n^2}{h^2}=3.0435$; $\frac{m}{h}=4.975$; $\frac{Fl}{h}=30.4603$; $\frac{m}{n}=2.852$.

With these values we obtain from (67)—$x=\frac{1}{3}e$, $e=9'.36$

The rule of Audoy gave, art. 67, ... $e=6'.65$

To obtain the required thickness at the springing line, make $h=12'$; $l=7'.112$, we find, ... $e=2'.72$

The rule of Audoy gives at the springing line, $e=2.85$

By comparing tables FF and DDD, we find that the angle of greatest thrust of the arch without surcharge, is about . . . . 55°

The angle of the maximum effect of the surcharge, table FF, is . . . . 48°

Taking both into view, the angle of greatest thrust is, therefore, about . . . . 50°

We now have three points of the curve of pressure in the arch, one at the key $\frac{1}{3}$ the length of the joint below the extrados; one at 50° from the key, the same distance from the intrados; and one at the springing line $\frac{2}{3} \times 2'.72=1'.82$ from the intrados. Between the first and the second, the curve is near the middle of the joints; below the second, it gradually departs from the intrados and passes through the middle of some joint about 60° from the key, and at the springing lines passes entirely outside of the arch proper; hence the necessity of enlarging the arch at that line, as far as $e=2'.72$, or a little further, the enlargement diminishing as we ascend, and becoming nothing about 60° or 65° from the key.

Example 4. The magazine of Vauban, fig. 13, arts. 63,

67. $r=12'.50$: $R=15'.50$; $K=1.24$; $I=49°\ 7'\ 17''=50°-0°.8786$; $h'=8'$; $l=h'+r+\frac{2}{3}(R-r)=22'.50$; $E=20.50$; n', art. 134, $=120.039$; m', art. 134, $=235.06$.

Table FF, $K=1.24$, $I=$
45°, . . $F=r^2\times 0.4076$

Table FF, $K=1.24$, $I=$
50°; . . $F=r^2\times 0.3372=r^2\times 0.3372$

Difference for the interval 5° in I, . $r^2\times 0.0704$

$5°:0.0704::0°.8786:x=$ . . $r^2\times 0.0124$

Therefore, for $K=1.24$,
$I=49°\ 7'\ 17''$ . . . $F=r^2\times 0.3496=54.625$

$$\frac{n'}{h'}=15.005\,;\ \frac{n'^2}{h'^2}=225.1463\,;\ \frac{m'}{h'}=29.3825\,;\ \frac{Fl}{h'}=153.633.$$

Substituting these values in (67)′, art. 134, we find . . . . $e=10'.56$

The rule of Audoy gave . . . . . . $e=\ 9'.23$

To obtain the required thickness at the springing line, make $h'=0$, and $l=14'.50$ in (66)′ art. 134, we find $e=6'.96$

The rule of Audoy gives, under the same circumstances, ... $e=7'.30$

Example 5. Chester Bridge, Harrison, architect: Span$=s=200'$; rise$=f=42'$; d=thickness at the key$=4'$; d'=thickness at the spring$=6'$; r=radius of the intrados$=140'$, nearly; $s=4.76\times f$; $K=1+\frac{d}{r}=1.0286$. We have no certain information as to the load borne by this arch; it had necessarily some surcharge at the crown; let us suppose its cover of earth and masonry to have the density of the arch, and to rise to a horizontal plane one foot above the extrados at the key, $t=1'$. We obtain the thrust, by proportional parts, from table EE.

0.0622 .	. 0.0622	0.0700 .	. 0.0700
0.0529		0.0611	
1 : 0.0093 :: 0.76 :	x=0.0071	1 : 0.0089 :: 0.76 :	x=0.0068
	0.0551		0.0632

0.0632	
0.0551 .	. 0.0551
1 : 0.0081 :: 0.86 :	x=0.0070

Thrust of the arch proper, . $r^2 \times 0.0621 = 1217.16$
Effect of surcharge, $rtC = 140' \times 1' \times 0.88 =$ 123.20

Total thrust, $F = 1340.36$

This thrust corresponds to a curve of pressure at the key, $\frac{1}{3}d$ from the extrados, and, at the spring, the same distance from the intrados. But in consideration of the lightness of the arch, we ought to provide for a larger thrust, corresponding to a curve of pressure passing through the middle of the key, and at least $2' = \frac{1}{3}d'$ from the intrados at the spring.

We learn from table EE, that the actual thrust, when $s = 4.76 \times f$, $K = 1.0286$, exceeds the ultimate thrust by a little more than 9 per cent. It is obvious that if we add $4\frac{1}{2}$ per cent. to the ultimate, or in this case, about 4 per cent. to the actual thrust above given, we shall have nearly the thrust corresponding to a curve of pressure passing through the middle of the joints, here supposed to be equal.

Thus, 1340.36
+4 per cent., 53.61

1393.97

In fact the actual thrust, according to this last supposition, art. 116, $v = 45°$, is . . . . 1377.00, nearly.

The true semi-angle at the center, is $v = 45° \ 35' \ 5''$.

Let us therefore take, as the total thrust, $F=1400$.

The mean pressure per square foot at the key is $\frac{1400}{4}=350$ cubic feet; and the pressure at the upper or most exposed edge we must regard as twice this mean pressure, or 700 per square foot. If we suppose the material to be granite weighing 175 pounds per square foot, this last pressure corresponds to about 850 pounds per square inch, not more, probably, than $\frac{1}{10}$ the ultimate resisting power of good granite.

The pressure at the springing line being the resultant of the thrust, F, and of the weight of the semi-arch and its load, n, determined below, is

$$P=\sqrt{(1400)^2+(1802)^2}=2282 \text{ cubic feet};$$

which gives the pressure at the intrados of the springing line

$$2\times\frac{2282}{6}=760\tfrac{2}{3} \text{ cubic feet}=924 \text{ pounds per square inch.}$$

Suppose we wish to obtain the thickness of an abutment pier 23′ high from the foundation to the springing line. This gives $h=23+47=70'$; $l=67'.666$; n, art. 130, $=1802$; m, art. 130, $=56256$. Hence, by calculation,

$$\frac{n}{h}=25'.74;\ \frac{n^2}{h^2}=662.70;\ \frac{m}{h}=803.66;\ \frac{F\times l}{h}=1353.33.$$

These quantities give us, art. 128,

(67), when $x=\frac{1}{3}e$, $e=25'.65$.
(67¼) " $x=\frac{1}{4}e$, $e=22'.13$.

At the springing line, $l=44.666$, and the thickness when $x=\frac{1}{2}e$, or when the resultant passes through the middle of the base, is $e=2\times\dfrac{Fl-m}{n}=6'.97$.

Example 6. Central arch of the London Bridge. Elliptical. r=half-span$=76'$; f=rise$=38'$; d=thickness at the key$=5'$.

Suppose the load of the density of masonry to rise to the level of the top of the arch, and the curve of pressure from the key to the joint of greatest thrust to continue near the middle of the joints. The thrust already given in art. 121, is $F=r^2\times 0.16723=966.45$; to this, if we suppose a surcharge of 1′, we must add $A=rt\times 1.0617=161.38$; giving, as the total thrust, $F=1127.83$.

Let us assume as the point of application of the thrust, the center of the keystone joint, $2\frac{1}{2}$ feet above the intrados; let us also assume, as the height of the pier from its base to the springing line, 16′. We have $h=16'+38'+5'+1'=60'$; $l=56'.50$; $E=E'=44'$; art. 133, $n=1075.76$, $m=27849$;

$$\frac{n}{h}=17.93\,;\ \frac{n^2}{h^2}=321.46\,;\ \frac{m}{h}=464.15\,;\ \frac{F\times l}{h}=1062.04.$$

These values substituted in (67), $x=\frac{1}{3}e$, give $e=33'.95$.
" " " (67$\frac{1}{4}$), $x=\frac{1}{4}e$, " $e=28'.92$.
" " " (67$\frac{0}{-}$), $x=0$, $e=21'.02$.
At the springing line we have $h=44'$; $l=40'.50$;
giving, when $x=\frac{1}{3}e$, . . . $e=20'.54$.

The true extrados of the arch should extend to B; $A\,B=20'54$.

From the key to $o\,n$, $o\,p$=about $\frac{1}{2}\,a\,C$, the thickness of the arch may remain nearly constant: from $o\,n$ the thickness should gradually increase to $A\,B$; or, what is still better, the lower part of the arch should form one solid mass with the pier up to some joint $t\,s$, more or less elevated, according to circumstances, making $t\,s$ the true springing line.

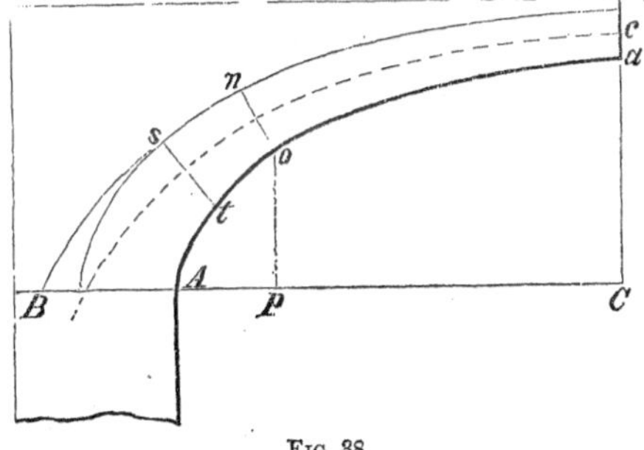

FIG. 38.

THICKNESS OF ARCH.

136. The celebrated Perronet has given the following rule for the thickness, d, at the key in terms of $2r$ the span:

$$d=1'.1''+\tfrac{1}{23}\times 2r=13 \text{ inches}+\tfrac{1}{23} \text{ the span.}$$

He does not seem, however, to have paid much attention to the rule; but has made his bridges much lighter than the rule would require.

The best information on this subject may be obtained from the record of existing structures which have stood the test of time. Table I gives the principal elements of many celebrated bridges, differing widely in their absolute and relative dimensions. Numbers 4, 9, and 19 are remarkable for their lightness; but No. 4 fell on the removal of the center, and it is probable that the other two are near the limits of possibility. The segmental bridges of Rennie and Stevenson are somewhat heavier, but still light. They are admirable works, and show what may be done with good stone.

In these lighter structures, which may be regarded as models of segmental arches, the thickness at the key is found to vary from $\frac{1}{30}$ to $\frac{1}{33}$ the span, and from $\frac{1}{26}$ to $\frac{1}{30}$ the radius of the intrados. The augmentation of thickness at the springing line is made, by the Stevensons, from 20 to 30 per cent.; by the Rennies, about 100 per cent.

The London Bridge, in its plan and workmanship, is, perhaps, the most perfect work of the kind. The intrados is an ellipse; the span, 152′; the rise, $\frac{1}{4}$ as much, the thickness at the key $\frac{1}{30}$ the span. The crown settled down only two inches on the removal of the center.

The proper thickness at the key does not depend upon the rise and span alone, but also upon the load, and upon the resisting power of the material.

The pressure at the extrados of the key, which is in general the most exposed part of that joint, should not, according to the best authorities, exceed $\frac{1}{10}$ the ultimate resisting power of the material. This rule is, without doubt, perfectly safe. In the railway bridge of Maidenhead, No. 13, table I, the ultimate resistance is only $3\frac{1}{2}$ times the calculated actual pressure at the extrados of the key.

Although we may determine the thrust on the supposition of a curve of pressure passing through the middle of the key-stone joint, we ought to admit the possibility of a greater elevation; viz.: to $\frac{1}{3}$ the length of that joint from the extrados. This diminishes the thrust; but the difference in light arches is very small.

Let P=the pressure per unit of surface at the upper edge of the key-stone joint; F=the actual thrust, which, for our present purpose, we may regard as acting $\frac{1}{3}$ the length of the joint from the extrados; d=the length of the key-stone joint. We have, art. 112,

$$P=2\frac{F}{d}.$$

$\frac{F}{d}$ is the mean pressure; which, to state the rule in another way, should not exceed $\frac{1}{20}$ the ultimate resistance of the material.

By two or three trials we can always find a value of d which shall satisfy the condition.

Being once in its neighborhood, we can determine that value directly by an equation of the first degree.

But it is far more satisfactory to make two or three independent trials, and to observe the resulting variations in the thrust and in the pressure per unit of surface.

The load of a bridge is generally fixed by circumstances, and independent, or nearly so, of the thickness of the arch.

Example. The Monocacy stone bridge, art. 73. s=span=$54'$; f=rise=$9'$; r=radius of the intrados=$45'$.

Suppose the load of this aqueduct bridge to rise to a plane $8'$ above the crown of the arch, and to have the density of the latter; $t=8'$.

Assume 4,000 pounds per square inch as the ultimate resisting power of the material = 576,000 pounds per square foot$=P'$. Assume the weight of a cubic foot of materials to be 160 pounds.

First, in table EE, under $s=6f$, make $K=1.05$. We have

$$\frac{F}{d}=\frac{r^2\times 0.0695+r\times t\times 0.8476}{r\times 0.05}=198.166 \text{ cubic feet};$$

which, multiplied by 160, gives . $\frac{F}{d}=31706$ pounds.

But $\frac{1}{20}P'=$ . . . 28800 "

Consequently d must be increased. Make $K=1.06$. We now have $\frac{F}{d}=27082$ pounds. Hence, by proportional parts, the value of K which shall make $\frac{F}{d}=28800$ pounds$=\frac{1}{20}P'$, is $K=1.0563$, giving $d=2'.53$.

In making the above calculations, we have, without doubt, under-estimated the strength of the stone. The mean pressure, $\frac{F}{d}$, corresponding to $d=2'.53$, is probably not more than $\frac{1}{30}P'$.

Some excess of strength at the key may be necessary to keep the pressure per unit of surface at the springing line or weakest joint, within the limits of safety.

Our various tables of the actual thrust furnish the means of solving most questions of this kind in a few minutes. But we ought not to aim at great accuracy of adjustment. The resisting power of stone is imperfectly known.

Very light arches may seem to stand the test above given, and still be impracticable: that is, the curve of pressure, in certain places, may necessarily pass outside of the prescribed limits; and the pressure per unit of surface, at the most exposed edges, may be far more than double the mean pressure.

This will be explained hereafter: see Third mode of rupture, Limit of practicable arches, &c.

INCREASE OF THICKNESS AT THE REINS, OR JOINT OF GREATEST THRUST, AND BELOW THAT JOINT TO THE SPRINGING LINE.

137. It will be shown hereafter that very light arches, otherwise impracticable, may be made practicable, by giving a certain increase of thickness between the key and the joint of greatest thrust, without changing the thickness at either of those joints. In this article we shall have in view larger arches, not in danger of the third mode of rupture.

Semicircular arches. We learn from table DDD, that the joint of greatest thrust is about the same in circular arches of the ordinary proportions, under the three suppositions there made in reference to the curve of pressure.

1st. The curve of pressure passing through b and m, as in the ultimate thrust.

2d. Through c and c_2, $cb=\frac{1}{3}ab$, $mc_2=\frac{1}{3}mn$, as supposed in table DDD.

3d. Through c and c_2, $cb=\frac{1}{2}ab$, $mc_2=\frac{1}{2}mn$, as in table DD.

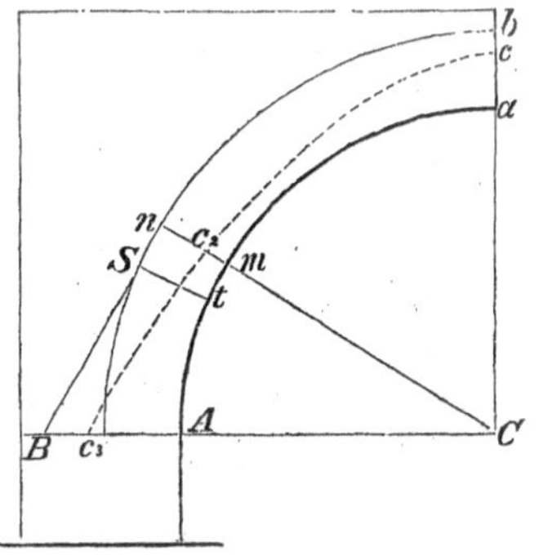

FIG. 39.

We learn, furthermore, that the joint in question is in the neighborhood of 60° from the key.

We also know from observation that the circular arch, if we except those of very light and impracticable proportions, tends to open at the intrados of the key and at the extrados of the reins. We therefore know that the curve of pressure is above the middle of $a\,b$, and inside the middle of $m\,n$.

Any increase of thickness between $a\,b$ and $m\,n$, would

be useless, unless the arch be exceedingly light, so as to change its form by vibration under a variable load. Such increase will have no sensible effect upon the thrust; it will cause no sensible change in the place of the curve of pressure; it will not diminish, but increase, the pressure per unit of surface at m, the edge most exposed. For all these reasons it will be useless. But the curve of pressure, after crossing the weakest joint, at c_2, begins to approach the extrados; some degrees below $m\,n$ it crosses the central line of the joints; it soon passes the exterior limit, and usually runs entirely outside of the circular ring, at some distance above the springing line. It will be enough, therefore, to begin to increase the arch at some joint, $t\,S$, about 25° above the springing line. Find the thickness, $B\,A$, at the springing line, art. 128, (67), on the condition that $B\,c_3 = \frac{1}{3} B\,A$, or $x = \frac{1}{3}e$. $B\,S$ will be the proper extrados of this part of the arch. For greater security we may extend this line out a little further than $B\,S$ as above given.

138. *Elliptical arches.* We have found the actual thrust of the elliptical arch to be about equal to that of a circular arch of the same span, and of a thickness at the key and a thickness of load as much larger than the corresponding parts of the elliptical arch as the half-span is larger than the rise.

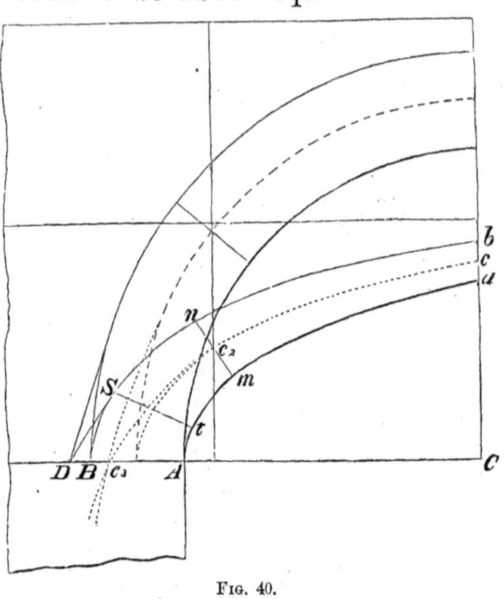

Fig. 40.

Calling $2r$ the span, f the rise, and d the thickness at the key, we have, as the thickness of the auxiliary circular arch, $BA = \frac{r}{f}d$. With one exception, the pressure per unit of surface, the elements of stability are the same in the two arches; their respective curves of pressure have the same relative situations, and these curves finally meet and cross at the springing line. The true extrados should be another ellipse, on the axes BC, Cb, similar to the intrados. But near the springing line the thickness must be increased.

Determine the thickness required at the springing line in order that $Dc_3 = \frac{1}{3}DA$, or $x = \frac{1}{3}e$, art. 128, (67).

The tangent, DS, will be the proper extrados of the lower part of the arch, or some curve near that tangent. This extrados, of course, cannot extend beyond the middle of the pier when the latter supports parts of two arches.

139. *Segmental arches.* Wherever we suppose the curve of pressure to be, the joint of greatest thrust is at the springing line, or but little above it. If the arch be of sufficient weight and size to resist all change of form, its thickness may remain the same throughout. The idea of increasing the thickness in order to equalize the pressure per unit of surface at the key and spring is altogether fallacious.

All observation shows that the segmental, like the circular arch, tends to open at the intrados of the key and the extrados of the joint of greatest thrust. Consequently, the curve of pressure starts above the center of ab, and ends in the arch, within the center of $mn = ab$.

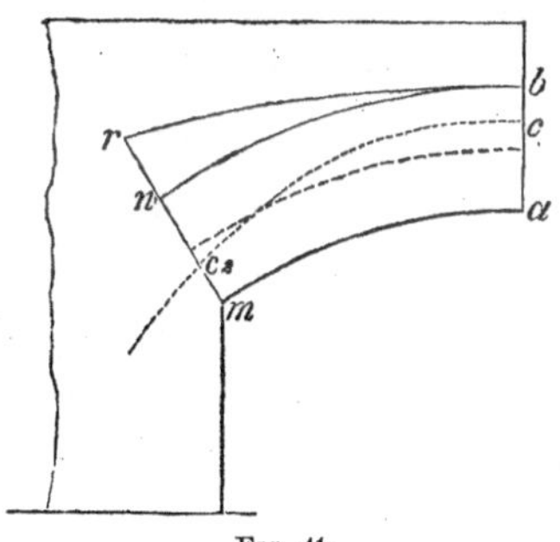

FIG. 41.

Let us first suppose $mc_2 = \frac{1}{3}mn = \frac{1}{3}d$, and the joint mn increased to mr. This increase having no sensible effect upon the thrust, the entire pressure is still borne by *m n;* the extension, *n r*, remains open; the pressure at *n* remains zero; at *m*, as before, it is double the entire pressure, *P*, divided by *mn*, $=\frac{2P}{d}$.

Let us now suppose the curve of pressure to pass through the middle of *m n*, $m c_2 = \frac{1}{2} m n$: the pressure per unit of surface is everywhere $\frac{P}{d}$; increase the joint *m n* to $m r = \frac{3}{2} m n$. The pressure at *r* is zero; at *m* it is $\frac{2P}{\frac{3}{2}d} = \frac{4}{3} \times \frac{P}{d}$. Thus, increasing the joint by one half, we have increased the pressure per unit of surface at *m*, by one third.

Supposing the arch to be of equal thickness throughout, so long as the curve of pressure meets the springing line inside of its middle point, any increase of the joints would be worse than useless.

There are, however, other considerations which, in the case of very light arches, demand a progressive augmentation of thickness from the key to the spring. We allude to stiffness, stability of form under variable loads. No precise rule can be given, but it can hardly ever be necessary to carry the augmentation beyond fifty per cent. This augmentation will give a wide range to the curve of pressure, within the limits of perfect safety to the upper and lower edges of the lower joint.

Such augmentation will, it is true, always increase the pressure per unit of surface at *m*, the intrados of the weakest joint, whatever be the curve of the intrados; but it will diminish the pressure at the exterior edge *n* or *r;* and it may prevent the third mode of rupture.

The most important principle to bear in mind here, is this: if the pressure per unit of surface at *m* is too great, we must increase the thickness of the segmental ring throughout.

RELATIVE PRESSURE, PER UNIT OF SURFACE, AT THE KEY, AND THE WEAKEST JOINT BELOW THE KEY.

140. The pressure, F_2, on any joint $m\ n$, is, $F_2 = \sqrt{F^2+n^2}$, in which expression F represents the horizontal thrust, and n the surface of the arch and its load between the joint $m\ n$ and the summit.

In flat arches n is less than F, and F_2, therefore, less than $1.414 \times F$; if $n=F$, we have $F_2=1.414 \times F$; if $n=1.73 \times F$, or $n^2=3F^2$, we have $F_2=2F$.

It is easy in any arch, to determine the pressure upon every joint; but it is only in reference to the weakest joint that this knowledge is important.

PRESSURE, PER UNIT OF SURFACE, UPON THE LOWEST JOINT OF THE PIER.

141. Referring to the notation of arts. 112, 128, the pressure P, per unit of surface, at the exterior edge of the base, if $x=\frac{1}{3}e$, is

$$P=2 \times \frac{n+eh}{e}.$$

Should this exceed $\frac{1}{10}$ the ultimate strength of the material, it will be necessary to increase e.

The above refers to an abutment. The pressure, per unit of surface, upon the base of a pier supporting two equal arches, is

$$\frac{2n+eh}{e}$$

Let e'=the thickness required at the springing line to support safely the given pressure; h'=the height of pier above the springing line; h=the height below; e= the thickness at bottom.

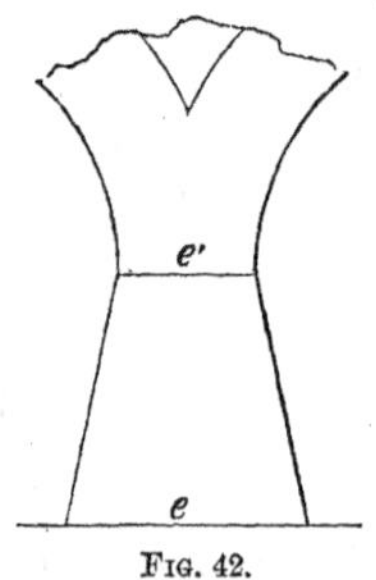

FIG. 42.

Let us determine e so as to equalize the pressure, per unit of surface, upon e' and e; we must have

$$\frac{2n+e'h'}{e'}=\frac{2n+e'h'+\frac{1}{2}h(e'+e)}{e}\text{; giving}$$

$$e=e'\times\frac{2n+e'h'+\frac{1}{2}he'}{2n+e'h'-\frac{1}{2}he'}$$

THIRD MODE OF RUPTURE—LIMIT THICKNESS OF POSSIBLE ARCHES.

142. In article 25, the conditions of this mode of rupture have been briefly pointed out.

The light semicircular arch surcharged horizontally up to the summit of the crown, and without additional surcharge, is the one most exposed to this danger.

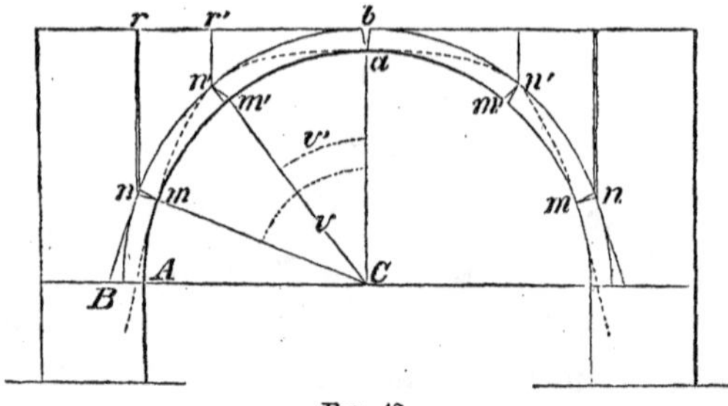

FIG. 43.

In this rupture, the arch rises at the crown and falls in four segments; the upper segments turn outwardly on the hinges n', n'; the lower segments fall towards the center, turning on the hinges m, m. The work below $m\ n$, $m\ n$, is not necessarily disturbed. At the moment of equilibrium preceding the rupture and fall, the points or edges in contact are a, n', n', m, m. The curve of pressure, which necessarily passes through those points, is tangent to the intrados at a, m, m, and to the extrados at n', n'. The joints $m\ n$, $m\ n$ are the lower joints of rupture and the joints of maximum thrust, supposing a to be the point of application of the horizontal thrust.

This rupture can only take place in light arches; and in these the position of $m\ n$ is nearly the same as in the first mode of rupture—ultimate thrust.

Let us determine the limit of possible arches, supposing, for the present, that mere edges of masonry are able to withstand any pressure whatever.

Let F=the maximum thrust of the arch, or horizontal force which, applied at a, shall keep the segment $b\ a\ m\ n\ r\ b$ in equilibrium on m, $m\ n$ being that particular joint which renders F a maximum.

Let F''=the horizontal force which, applied at a, shall be just sufficient to overturn the upper segment of the arch on some point n' of the extrados. It is evident that F, in any arch, must not exceed F''. When these two forces are equal, we shall have the thinnest possible arch, an arch in which the curve of pressure, as already stated, touching the intrados at a and m, is in contact with the extrados at n'. In any thinner arch, the curve of pressure would necessarily pass outside of the ring, either at a or n' or both. In other words, we are not at liberty to suppose a thinner arch.

It is interesting to observe that this kind of rupture may take place without any disturbance of the pier or lower part of the arch—all motion being confined to that part of the arch which lies above the lower and regular joint of rupture, $m\ n$. On the other hand, the first and usual mode of rupture can be developed only by overturning the pier or lower part of the arch. While the first mode of rupture can be prevented by giving to the pier a sufficient mass, or by opposing to the horizontal thrust the similar thrust of another arch, the third can be rendered impossible only by changing the proportions of the arch itself.

Another interesting fact is to be noticed. The third mode of rupture gives rise to two new joints of rupture, each about half way between the key and the lower joints.

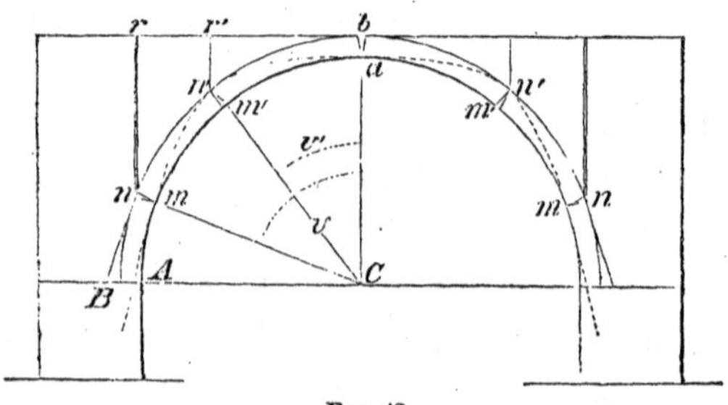

FIG. 43.

Let R=the radius of the extrados; r=the radius of the intrados; $K=\frac{R}{r}$; v=the angle $m\,C\,b$ corresponding to the maximum F; v'=the angle $m'\,C\,b$ corresponding to the minimum F'.

The following table gives the values of F, F', v, v' corresponding to very light arches, or small values of K.

Values of $K=\frac{R}{r}$	Ratio of the diameter to the thickness.	Values of v. and F.		Values of v' and F'.	
		v.	F.	v'.	F'.
1.00		72°	$r^2\times 0.05561$		
1.01	200.0	71	" 0.06214		$r^2\times 0.02177$*
1.02	100.0	70	" 0.06868	23°	" 0.04349
1.03	66.⅔	68	" 0.07526	28	" 0.06452
1.04	50.0	67	" 0.08188	35	" 0.08486

* By the law of differences.

The lowest two numbers in the last column have been taken from the calculations of M. Petit.

Corresponding to $K=1.02$, we see that F is more than half as large again as F'; in other words, an arch of such proportions is far below the limits of possibility. When $K=1.03$, the excess of F over F', is much less. When $K=1.04$, F is less than F'. By proportional parts, we find these two forces to be equal when $K=1.0378$, or when the thickness is $\frac{1}{53}$ of the span. In this case, $v=67°$ and $v'=33\frac{1}{2}°$, nearly.

Any lighter arch surcharged horizontally, will fall by the third mode of rupture whatever be the thickness of the piers.

M. Petit has given an erroneous solution of this question, by supposing the horizontal thrust, acting at the intrados of the key at the moment of rupture, to be generated by the tendency of the whole semi-arch to rotate forward towards the center. In this way he has greatly under-estimated the thrust, and given a limit of thickness nearly as small as $\frac{1}{80}$ the span. Other French writers have fallen into the same error.

But M. Petit made a greater mistake in supposing the question to be more curious than useful. It is the beginning, as we shall see, of a highly important investigation.

No branch of the subject can be more important than that which determines, and shows how to determine, correctly, the limits of practicability. In this country and in Great Britain, these limits are frequently approached—sometimes passed. In France, arches seem to be, in general, of heavier proportions.

LIMIT THICKNESS OF POSSIBLE SEGMENTAL ARCHES.

143. If the arch be segmental, and the semi-angle at the center less than the angle of rupture, the limit will

become smaller, diminishing more and more as the opening diminishes.

The following table gives the limit thickness of segmental arches surcharged horizontally, up to the level of the extrados at the key, on the supposition that mere edges of masonry can withstand any pressure whatever.

F'' and v' are the same as in the preceding table. F is the ultimate thrust in the third mode of rupture, the point of application being at the intrados on the key. It is taken from table E'. Let r=the radius of the intrados; s=the span; f=the rise; C=the coefficient of r^2 in table E'. Then

$$F=r^2\times C(1+\frac{r}{f}(K-1)).$$

The values of K are written at top.

In each horizontal division, will be found the limit value—of K, of the diameter $2r$ in terms of the thickness $d=r\ (K-1)$, and of the span s also in terms of d.

LIMIT THICKNESS OF POSSIBLE SEGMENTAL ARCHES, ON THE SUPPOSITION THAT MERE EDGES OF MASONRY CAN WITHSTAND ANY PRESSURE WHATEVER.

Values of K	1.01	1.02	1.03	1.04
Values of v' Values of F'	18° * $r^2 \times 0.02177$	23° $r^2 \times 0.04349$	28° $r^2 \times 0.06452$	35° $r^2 \times 0.08486$
$s=4f;\ \frac{r}{f}=2.50;\ F=$ Limit $\begin{cases} K=1.0342 \\ 2r=58\frac{1}{2}d \\ s=47 \times d \end{cases}$		$r^2 \times 0.06200$	$r^2 \times 0.06982$	$r^2 \times 0.07758$
$s=5f;\ \frac{r}{f}=\frac{29}{8};\ F=$ Limit $\begin{cases} K=1.0275 \\ 2r=73 \times d \\ s=50d \end{cases}$		$r^2 \times 0.05288$	$r^2 \times 0.06138$	$r^2 \times 0.06982$
$s=6f;\ \frac{r}{f}=5;\ F=$ Limit $\begin{cases} K=1.02207 \\ 2r=90\frac{1}{2}d \\ s=54d \end{cases}$	$r^2 \times 0.03707$	$r^2 \times 0.04600$	$r^2 \times 0.05491$	
$s=7f;\ \frac{r}{f}=\frac{53}{8};\ F=$ Limit $\begin{cases} K=1.0177 \\ 2r=113d \\ s=60d \end{cases}$	$r^2 \times 0.03137$	$r^2 \times 0.04058$	$r^2 \times 0.04974$	
$s=8f;\ \frac{r}{f}=8.50;\ F=$ Limit $\begin{cases} K=1.0144 \\ 2r=139d \\ s=65d \end{cases}$	$r^2 \times 0.02718$	$r^2 \times 0.03654$		
$s=10f;\ \frac{r}{f}=13;\ F=$ Limit $\begin{cases} K=1.0099 \\ 2r=202d \\ s=78d \end{cases}$	$r^2 \times 0.02164$	$r^2 \times 0.03124$		

* v' and F' for $K=1.01$ have been determined by the law of differences.

LIMIT THICKNESS OF PRACTICABLE ARCHES.

144. In the preceding articles 142 and 143, we have treated of the ultimate thrust. At the moment of rupture mere edges or points of masonry were supposed to be in contact, and able to withstand all the pressures that might be thrown upon them. We have given too high a limit, for it is evident that these edges will give way long before the pressures come upon mathematical points.

Let us now determine the least *practicable* thickness of the semicircular arch, surcharged horizontally up to the summit of the extrados, on the condition that the curve of pressure shall be everywhere traced between two other curves which divide the joints into three equal parts. The case is analogous to the one already considered, art. 142, the extrados and intrados of the latter case being now replaced by the limit curves.

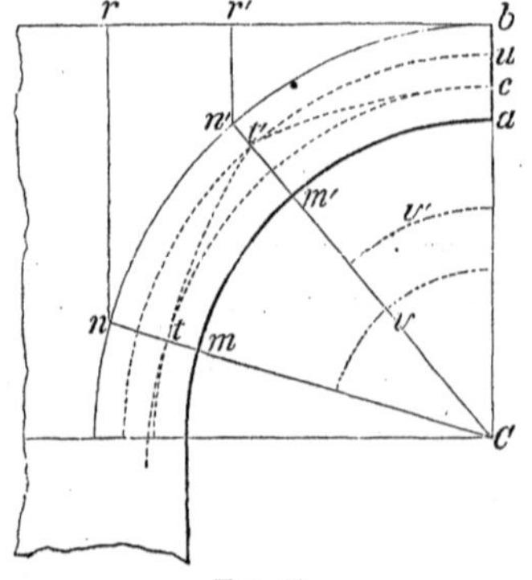

FIG. 44.

The curve of pressure touching the inferior curve at c, on the central joint, and again at t, on the joint of maximum thrust, must not, at any intermediate point, t', pass outside the superior limit.

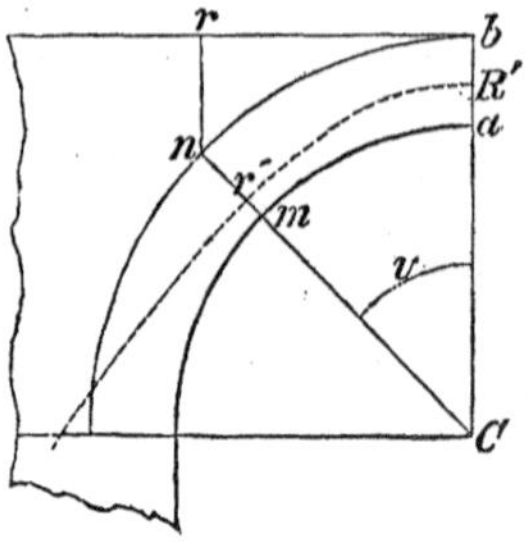

The general expression of the horizontal force F which, applied at any point, R', on the central joint, shall keep the segment $b\,a\,m\,n\,r\,b$ in equilibrium on any point, r', of any joint, $m\,n$, is

FIG. 45.

$$F=\tfrac{1}{6}r^2\frac{\sin.^2 v}{\frac{R'}{r}-\frac{r'}{r}\cos.v}\left\{\frac{K^2}{\sin.I}\left(6\frac{r'}{r}-3K-(3\frac{r'}{r}-2K)\sin.(I+v)\right)-\frac{3v}{\sin.v}\times\frac{r'}{r}+\frac{1}{\cos.^2\frac{1}{2}v}\right\} \qquad (68)$$

in which $R'=CR'$; $r'=Cr'$; v=angle $r'\,C\,R'$ or $m\,C\,b$; I=the angle between the roof and a vertical; r=the radius of the intrados; Kr=the radius of the extrados.

Suppose $I=90°$; $R'=r'=r+\frac{1}{3}r(K-1)=\frac{1}{3}r(2+K)$. Substituting these values, (68) is reduced to

$$F=r^2\left\{\frac{2\cos.^2\frac{1}{2}v(2-\cos.v)K^2-\frac{1}{2}\sin.^2vK^3+1}{K+2}-\frac{1}{2}v\cot.\frac{1}{2}v\right\} \quad (69)$$

The maximum value of this expression evidently gives the actual thrust for the case in hand.

Suppose $R'=\frac{1}{3}r(2+K)$, as above,

and $r'=r+\frac{2}{3}r(K-1)=\frac{1}{3}r(2K+1)$;

(68) reduces to

$$F'=r^2\left\{\frac{\sin.^2v(1-\frac{1}{2}\cos.v)K^2+\frac{1}{2}\sin.^2vK^3-\frac{1}{2}v\sin.v-v\sin.vK+(1-\cos.v)}{(2-\cos.v)-K(2\cos.v-1)}\right\} \quad (70)$$

The minimum value of this expression is the least force which, acting horizontally at c, $b\,c=\frac{2}{3}b\,a$, shall cause the resultant of the force and of the weight of the segment $b\,a\,m'\,n'\,r'\,b$, which corresponds to the minimum, to reach the superior limit. Any greater force would carry this resultant, and consequently the curve of pressure, beyond the superior limit.

It is obvious that the greatest value of F in any arch should not exceed the least value of F'. If these two forces be equal, the curve of pressure will touch the superior limit, as represented in fig. 44.

Let F=the maximum value of F in (69); v=the angle, $m\,C\,b$, corresponding to that maximum; F'=the minimum value of F' in (70); v'=the corresponding angle.

The following table gives the values F, v, F', and v', as far as necessary for the object in view:—

Value of $K=\frac{R}{r}$.	Ratio of the diameter to the thickness.	Values of F and v.		Values of F' and v'.	
		v.	F.	v'.	F'.
1.01	200.00				
1.02	100.00	70°	$r^2\times 0.07012$	15°	$r^2\times 0.03175$
1.03	$66\frac{2}{3}$	68	" 0.07754	20°	" 0.04758
1.04	50.00	67	" 0.08510	22° 30′	" 0.06317
1.05	40.00	65	" 0.09275	25°	" 0.07873
1.06	$33\frac{1}{3}$	64	" 0.10055	30°	" 0.09420
1.07	28.57	62	" 0.10848	32° 30′	" 0.10930
1.08	25.00				

We learn from this table that F is greater than F', that is, that the arch is impracticable, for all values of K less than 1.06; and that F is less than F', or the arch practicable, for $K=1.07$ and all larger values. By proportional parts we find these two forces to be equal when $K=1.06886$, or when the span is about 29 times the thickness. We thus find the least possible arch which can exist without any opening of the joints.

145. If the arch be segmental, and the semi-angle at the center less than the angle of maximum thrust, the limit of practicable arches will of course become smaller, decreasing more and more as the opening diminishes,

The following table gives the limit thickness of segmental arches surcharged horizontally up to the level of the extrados at the key. F' and v' are the same as in the preceding table. F is the actual thrust, on the supposition of a curve of pressure touching the inferior limit at the key and at the springing line. F is obtained from table EE by the following formula. Let $C=$the coefficient of r^2 in that table, $f=$the rise, then

$$F=r^2\times C\left(1+\frac{K-1}{\frac{f}{r}(K+2)}\right)$$

LIMIT THICKNESS OF SEGMENTAL ARCHES, ON THE CONDITION THAT NO JOINT SHALL BEGIN TO OPEN.

Values of K.	1.01	1.02	1.03	1.04	1.05	1.06	1.07
Values of $v'=$ Values of $F'=r^2\times$	12° * 0.01568	15° 0.03175	20° 9.04758	22° 30′ 0.06317	25° 0.07873	30° 0.09420	32° 30′ 0.10930
$s=4f;\ \frac{r}{f}=2.50;\ F=r^2\times$ Limit $\begin{cases} K=1.06521 \\ 2r=31\times d \\ s=25\times d \end{cases}$						0.09756	0.10623
$s=5f;\ \frac{r}{f}=\frac{29}{8};\ F=r^2\times$ Limit $\begin{cases} K=1.0545 \\ 2r=37\times d \\ s=25\times d \end{cases}$				0.07240	0.08157	0.09072	
$s=6f;\ \frac{r}{f}=5;\ F=r^2\times$ Limit $\begin{cases} K=1.0441 \\ 2r=45\times d \\ s=27\times d \end{cases}$			0.05625	0.06564	0.07520	0.08466	
$s=7f;\ \frac{r}{f}=\frac{53}{8};\ F=r^2\times$ Limit $\begin{cases} K=1.03544 \\ 2r=56\times d \\ s=30\times d \end{cases}$		0.04123	0.05083	0.06045			
$s=8f;\ \frac{r}{f}=8.50;\ F=r^2\times$ Limit $\begin{cases} K=1.0288 \\ 2r=70\times d \\ s=33\times d \end{cases}$		0.03707	0.04684				
$s=10f;\ \frac{r}{f}=13;\ F=r^2\times$ Limit $\begin{cases} K=1.01976 \\ 2r=101\times d \\ s=39\times d \end{cases}$	0.02180	0.03160					
$s=16f;\ \frac{r}{f}=32.5;\ F=r^2\times$ Limit $\begin{cases} K=1.0088 \\ 2r=227\times d \\ s=56\times d \end{cases}$	0.01496	0.02503					

* v' and F' for $K=1.01$ determined by the law of differences.

EFFECT OF SURCHARGE UPON THE PRACTICABILITY OF ARCHES.

146. Returning to the semicircular arch surcharged as above, let us illustrate the effect of a surcharge of a constant depth above the extrados at the key.

When $K=1.04$, or the span$=50$ times the thickness, we learn from art. 144, that the arch is impracticable; but adding a surcharge$=\frac{1}{17}$ the radius, or $\frac{1}{34}$ the span, we find the arch to become barely practicable, the lower joint of rupture being 58° from the key, and the upper joint 30°.

The addition of a deeper surcharge up to a certain point, would increase the stability of the arch; that is, cause the curve of pressure to depart less from the central line of the joints.

The addition to the actual thrust caused by a surcharge of constant depth, t, is, for any angle v,

$$A=rtK\frac{\cos.^2 \frac{1}{2}v(4-K)}{K+2}; \tag{71}$$

to be added to the value of F, eq. (69), corresponding to the same value of v. The maximum value of $F+A$ to be obtained, as usual, by variations in v.

In (71) as well as in (69), the point of application of the horizontal thrust at the key is supposed to be at $\frac{1}{3}$ the length of the joint from the intrados, while the curve of pressure is supposed to be at the same distance from the intrados at the joint of maximum thrust.

The effect of surcharge to be added to F', eq. (70), is,

$$A'=\tfrac{1}{2}rtK\frac{\sin.^2 v(2+K)}{(2-\cos. v)-(2\cos. v-1)K}; \tag{72}$$

the minimum of $F'+A'$ to be obtained by variations in v.

In (70) and (72) the point of application upon the key is, as above, at $\frac{1}{3}$ the length of the joint from the intrados, and at the joint of minimum thrust at the same distance from the extrados.

EQUATION OF THE CURVE OF PRESSURE IN THE ARCH.

147. Assume as known the horizontal thrust, F, and R', its point of application.

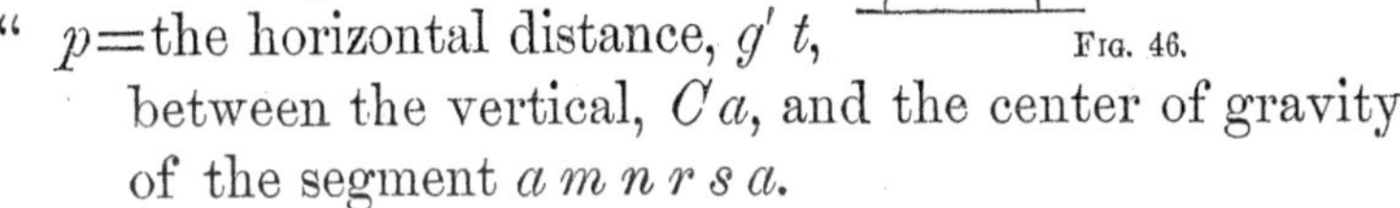

FIG. 46.

Let $R' = C\,R'$.

" $r' = C\,r'$ = the variable distance of the curve of pressure from the center C.

" v = the angle $r'\,C\,R'$.

" p = the horizontal distance, $g'\,t$, between the vertical, $C\,a$, and the center of gravity of the segment $a\,m\,n\,r\,s\,a$.

" S = the surface $a\,m\,n\,r\,s\,a$, bounded by the circular arc $a\,m$, the verticals $C\,R'\,s$, $n\,r$, the joint $m\,n$, of any length, and the upper surface $s\,r$, of any inclination.

As the thrust, F, and the weight, S, are in equilibrium on every point of the curve of pressure, we have the equation of moments,—

$$F(R' - r' \cos. v) = S(r' \sin. v - p),$$

giving

$$r' = \frac{F \times R' + S \times p}{S \times \sin. v + F \times \cos. v}. \qquad (73)$$

F must be found by calculation, or by the tables contained in this paper; it is the actual thrust.

R', the point of application, and the distance $C\,R'$, $= R'$, must be assumed according to the circumstances of the case. Sp is the moment on C of the surface $C\,n\,r\,s\,C$ minus the moment on C of the sector $m\,C\,a$. S is the surface $C\,n\,r\,s\,C$—the sector $m\,C\,a$.

Assuming any particular value of v, Sp and S are easily calculated. A table giving the values of the surface $C\,m\,a = \frac{1}{2} v\, r^2$, and its moment on C, $= \frac{1}{3} r^3 (1 - \cos. v)$, at intervals of 5 or 10 degrees, would greatly facilitate the calculation of r'.

Suppose we are in doubt whether the proposed arch is practicable or not. This doubt need not arise unless the proposed arch is very light, and surcharged horizontally, or nearly so.

Determine the thrust on the condition that the curve of pressure, at the key and the lower joint of rupture, shall touch the inferior limit one-third the length of the joint from the intrados. Still better, ascertain the somewhat larger thrust which is given by table DD, or the formulæ of art. 116, on the supposition of a curve of pressure passing through the middle of the joints in question.

Assume $R'=r+\frac{1}{3}(R-r)$, and compute several values of r' near the bisecting line of the angle $R'\,C\,r'$, $m\,n$ being the joint of greatest thrust.

Should the greatest value of r' exceed $r+\frac{2}{3}(R-r)$, we know that the proposed arch is impracticable.

Should the greatest value of r' be less than $r+\frac{2}{3}(R-r)$ and larger than $r+\frac{1}{3}(R-r)$, we know that the arch is practicable, and are at liberty to suppose a more elevated curve of pressure, so traced as nearly to equalize the pressure inside and outside of the central line of the joints.

POINT OF APPLICATION OF THE THRUST AT THE KEY.

148. The formulæ used in the investigation of circular arches are transcendental in form, so that, in general, practical conclusions can be drawn only from laborious calculations.

We are about to meet with an exception, and shall reach at once some generalizations of great value and interest with little labor.

We have assumed that the point of application of the thrust at the key shall be somewhere in the middle space formed by dividing the vertical joint into three equal parts. We have found in certain cases, that the curve of pressure must start from the lower limit to keep inside the upper-limit curve.

This takes place only in very light arches loaded horizontally or nearly so. As we increase the arch or increase the surcharge, we are evidently at liberty and in fact compelled to suppose the curve to start from a higher point.

Let us now inquire when we are at liberty to suppose this point of departure, or point of application of the thrust at the key, to be as high as the upper limit.

Table DDD gives the thrust corresponding to this supposition for the arch surcharged horizontally, the curve of pressure touching the inferior limit at the joint of greatest thrust. It is obviously necessary that the curve of pressure, starting from the upper limit c, $ca=\frac{2}{3}ba$, should not at any point above the joint of greatest thrust, mn, be found outside of the circular arc of which Cc is the radius. From the point c it should run immediately below, and not above, that arc.

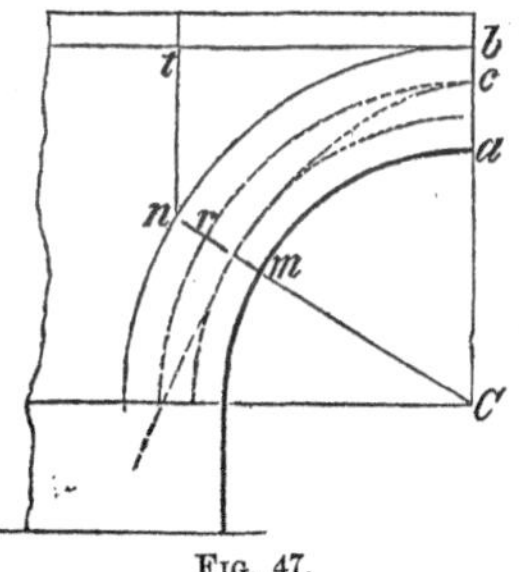

FIG. 47.

In (68) suppose $R'=r'=r+\frac{2}{3}(R-r)=\frac{1}{3}r(1+2K)$; $I=0$, and $v=0$. We have

$$(F)=r^2\frac{K^3+K^2-2K}{1+2K}. \tag{74}$$

Under the same suppositions we find the effect of surcharge to be

$$(A)=tr\frac{2K+K^2}{1+2K}. \tag{75}$$

The 1st column of the following table contains the values of K; the 2d and 3d columns the values of (F) and (A) respectively; the 4th and 5th, the horizontal thrust and the effect of surcharge, both taken from table DDD.

Values of K.	(F) from eq. (74) and (A) " " (75).		Values of F and A from Table DDD.	
	(F)	(A)	F	A
1.02	$r^2\times0.02026$	$rt\times1.0133$	$r^2\times0.0694$	$rt\times0.8971$
1.04	" 0.04106	" 1.0265	" 0.0832	" 0.8612
1.06	" 0.06238	" 1.0396	" 0.0973	" 0.8358
1.08	" 0.08421	" 1.0527	" 0.1112	" 0.8156
1.10	" 0.10656	" 1.0656	" 0.1250	" 0.7988
1.12	" 0.12942	" 1.0785	" 0.1387	" 0.7841
1.14	" 0.15278	" 1.0913	" 0.1523	" 0.7712
1.00	" 0.22588	" 1.1294	" 0.1918	" 0.7387

We learn from this table, that when K is small F is much larger than (F). In such cases, if the curve of pressure were to start at c, it would immediately run above the upper limit. When K=1.14, F is nearly equal to (F); for greater values of K, F is less than (F). Consequently, for all values of K exceeding 1.14, we are at liberty to suppose a curve of pressure starting from the upper limit on the vertical joint.

We have found that when K is less than 1.06886, the arch is impracticable, art. 136; that when K is equal to 1.06886, the arch is barely practicable, the curve of pressure necessarily starting from the lower limit on the key.

Between K=1.06886, and K=1.14, the starting point will gradually rise from the lower to the upper limit.

By comparing the values of (F) given above, with those of F in table EE, segmental arches, we find that the curve of pressure may start from the upper limit on the key, as follows:

$s=$ 5f or v=43° 36′ 10″, when K=1.12, nearly.
$s=$ 6f or v=36° 52′ 10″, " K=1.10, "
$s=$ 7f or v=31° 53′ 27″, " K=1.08, "
$s=$ 8f or v=28° 4′ 20″, " K=1.07, "
$s=$16f or v=14° 15′ 00″, " K=1.02, "

and for all larger values of K.

However small the value of K, by giving to t in (A), and A, a certain value, we shall make $(F)+(A)=F+A$.

Example. When $K=1.02$, suppose $t=r\times 0.42$, we have $(F)+(A)=r^2\times .4458$,
and $F+A=r^2\times .4461$.

When $K=1.04$ and $t=r\times 0.25$, we find the two sums to be nearly equal.

These results agree with those already obtained by independent means, and show that an arch impossible or impracticable without surcharge, may become perfectly safe when a load of sufficient depth has been added.

We will add a word of explanation as to the principle of the demonstration above given.

The quantity which reduces to (F), equation (74), when $v=o$, is the variable horizontal force which, applied at c, $ac=\frac{2}{3}ab$, shall hold any segment $a\,m\,n\,t\,b\,a$ in equilibrium on r, fig. 47, $Cr=Cc=r+\frac{2}{3}(R-r)$. Let $(F)'=$ that variable force.

In like manner, the quantity which reduces to (A), equation (75), when $v=o$, is the variable effect of surcharge under the same supposition as to the points of application. Let $(A)'=$that variable effect.

The sum $(F)+(A)$, corresponding to $v=o$, will either be a maximum or a minimum; generally the latter.

In either case, the sum corresponding to small values of v, will not differ sensibly from $(F)+(A)$, to which it is reduced when $v=0$.

Consequently, if the actual thrust, $(F+A)$, exceed $((F)+(A))$, it will also exceed the neighboring sums of $((F)'+(A)')$, and, so long as this superiority continues, the curve of pressure must run entirely outside the superior limit $c\,r$, $Cr=r+\frac{2}{3}(R-r)$.

On the other hand, if $(F+A)$ be less than $((F)+(A))$ the curve of pressure will remain within the superior limit at all points above the joint of maximum thrust.

POINT OF APPLICATION OF THE ULTIMATE THRUST.

149. By a course of investigation entirely similar to that indicated above, we may prove that the point of application of the ultimate thrust can not always be at the extrados, but must, in many arches, be below it. When $K=1.0378$, this point is necessarily at the intrados, art. 142, and K must be increased to a certain extent before it can rise to the extrados.

Some of the tables of the ultimate and of the actual thrust are based, in reference to light arches, upon an impossible supposition as to this point of application; but their value is not, on that account, seriously impaired, because the thrust is not sensibly affected by small changes in the point of application.

REMARKS ON TABLE I.

150. This table gives the principal elements of many celebrated bridges: the dimensions, the total thrust at the key in terms of the radius of the intrados, the mean pressure, in pounds, on each square foot of the key, and the ratio of the estimated ultimate resisting power of the material, to the pressure on the edge most exposed. This pressure is assumed to be double the mean pressure.

The thrusts have all been obtained from the tables and formulæ contained in this paper,—circular arches, from table DD, No. 3 excepted, which is taken from table DDD; elliptical arches from table DD, as explained in art. 121; segmental arches, from art. 116.

In the absence of definite information as to the load borne by the several arches, it was necessary to make some hypothesis. Very few of them were loaded with masonry over the reins up to the level of the top of the key; but all had some surcharge over the key. It has been assumed in all cases, that the surcharge was equivalent to a load in masonry, rising throughout to the level of of the top of the key-stone.

The results are given as illustrations, and as approximations to the truth. The reader is cautioned against receiving them as fixed or established facts.

No. 1. Bishop Auckland Bridge. $r=68'.29$; $K=1.027$; $s=54.77\times d$; $2r=74.50\times d$; $s=4.57\times f$. When $s=4f$ we have, as the limit of possibility, art. 143, $K=1.0342$; when $s=5f$ we have, at the limit, $K=1.0275$; hence, by proportional parts, the limit corresponding to $s=4.57$, is found to be, $K=1.0304$. Therefore, a bridge of the given dimensions, and of the supposed load, would fall, by the third mode of rupture, whatever the stability of the piers, and whatever the resisting power of the materials.

The date, 1388, renders it probable that this bridge was but lightly loaded at the reins.

No. 2. Llanwast Bridge. $r=33'.24$; $K=1.045$; $s=38\frac{2}{3}d$; $2r=44.30\times d$; $s=3.41f$. The limit values of K are nearly the same as in semicircular arches; viz., the limit of possibility, art. 142, $K=1.0378$; limit of practicability, art. 144, $K=1.06886$. This bridge, therefore, under the supposed load, is impracticable, though not impossible.

It could not exist without considerable cracks at the the key, the springing line, and the intermediate joints of rupture. We have doubtless overestimated the load upon the reins.

No. 3. Westminster Bridge. $r=38'$; $K=1.20$; $2r=10d$. This is a very heavy structure, of three times the required thickness, whether we look at the limit, art. 144, or at the pressure per unit of surface at the key, table I.

No. 4. Taaf Bridge. $r=87'.50$; $K=1.029$; $s=56\times d$; $2r=70\times d$; $s=4f$. Limit of possibility, art. 143, $K=1.0342$. This arch, therefore, under the supposed load, is impossible. In fact, this bridge fell on the removal of the center, but was rebuilt with a diminished load upon the reins.

No. 5. Wellington Bridge, over the Aire. $r=90'.83$; $K=1.033$; $s=33\frac{1}{3}d$; $2r=60.55\times d$; $s=6\frac{2}{3}f$. Limit of possibility, see table in art. 143, $K=1.019$; limit of practicability, see table in art. 145, $K=1.0383$. Not quite practicable under the supposed load, if we suppose the thickness of the arch to be the same throughout, but more than practicable when we take into consideration the rapidly increasing thickness on each side of the key. An increase of $\frac{1}{2}$ instead of $1\frac{1}{3}$ at the springing line, would have made this arch more than practicable and safe under the worst possible load.

No. 6. Waterloo Bridge. $r=60'$; $f=35'$; $d=4'.75$; the thrust, art. 121, is nearly equal to that of a circular arch of the same span, and of a thickness$=\frac{r}{f}d=8'.143$. The curve of pressure has nearly the same relative situation in both, and they are alike exposed to the third mode of rupture. In the circular arch we have $K=1.1357$, which places both arches far above the limits of practicability.

It is worthy of remark, that a segmental arch of the same rise and span, and of the same thickness, equal throughout, would be barely practicable. In this arch we should have $r=68'.93$, and $K=1.0689$.

The intrados of the segmental arch departs more, in its general direction, from the curve of pressure, than the intrados of the ellipse.

No. 7. London Bridge. This bold and beautiful work has the thrust and the general character of stability within itself, of a circular arch of the same span, and of such thickness as to make the ratio K of the two radii equal to 1.1316, or the span about fifteen times the thickness.

A segmental arch of the same rise, span, and thickness, equal throughout, $r=95'$, $K=1.05263$, would not be practicable, but might be made so by increasing the thickness gradually on each side of the key, to $7'.50$ at the spring.

No. 8. Staines Bridge. Span=8 times the rise; $K=1.038$. More than practicable and secure without any increase of thickness between the key and the spring (see art. 145).

No. 9. Chester Bridge. $r=140'$. nearly; $K=1.0286$; mean value of $K=1.0357$, nearly; $s=50\times d$; $2r=70\times d$; $s=4.76f$. Impracticable and but little more than possible, if loaded according to our supposition. We are told that the crown settled only $2\frac{1}{2}$ inches on the removal of the center. This is no proof of excellence of workmanship. This arch is near the third and not the first mode of rupture. The crown tends to rise, or has little tendency to settle down, on the removal of the center.

No. 11. Hutcheson Bridge. $s=5.925\times f$; $K=1.0537$. Perfectly secure without any increase of thickness between the key and the spring.

No. 12. Whitadder Bridge. $s=6.52f$; $K=1.0374$; mean value of $K=1.0411$. Nearly practicable without any increase of thickness between the key and the spring.

No. 13. Railway Bridge at Maidenhead. This remarkable structure is made of bricks. It has the span and thickness at the key, of the celebrated bridge of Neuilly, and a rise considerably less. It is, perhaps, the boldest work of which we have any record. It has the thrust and the general stability of form of a circular arch of the same span, and of a thickness$=13'.86$ throughout, corresponding to $K=1.2165$.

The ultimate resisting power of the material is only $3\frac{1}{2}$ times the actual pressure at the most exposed edges.

No. 14. Bridge of Neuilly. Very similar in its proportions, to the London Bridge, but a little bolder when we take into consideration the strength of the material (see the last column).

It has nearly the thrust and stability of a circular arch of the same span, and of the constant thickness of $10\frac{1}{2}$ feet, corresponding to $K=1.164$.

No. 15. The Bridge of Pesmes. $r=67'.11$; $s=11.67\times f$; $K=1.057$. A very heavy work. One half the thickness would have been ample. The more flat the arch over a given span, the less the thickness required for stability of form.

No. 16. A very heavy work, whether we look to the stability of form or to the ratio of pressure to resisting power.

No. 17. This work has ample stability of form, and a pressure, per unit of surface, at the key, nearly equal to the limit prescribed by engineers. The least thickness required for stability of form, would have been $2'.53$, corresponding to $K=1.0214$; but this would have caused too great a pressure, per square foot, at the key.

No. 18. Nemours. $r=96'.394$; $K=1.033$; $s=14.2\times f$. This arch is extremely flat. The thickness required for stability of form, is only $1'.18$ (see the table in art. 145), corresponding to $K=1.0122$. This thickness should be increased until the mean pressure at the key does not exceed $\frac{1}{20}$ the resisting power, or until the ratio in the last column is not less than 10.

No. 19. Turin. $r=160'.29$; $K=1.0296$; $s=8.20f$. The thickness required for practicability (art. 145), is about $3\frac{1}{4}$ inches less than the thickness given. The pressure at the key comes up to the limit.

GENERAL REMARKS UPON THE DETERMINATION OF THE THRUST AND UPON THE THICKNESS OF THE ARCH AT THE KEY.

151. Given the span, the rise, and, approximately, the load. Assume a thickness at the key in view of the strength of the material, the probable character of the workmanship, the load, and all other circumstances.

If the arch be of light proportions, look for its thrust to those formulæ, tables, or geometrical methods, which suppose the curve of pressure to pass through the middle of the key and the middle of the weakest joint, or joint of greatest thrust.

On the other hand, if the arch be of heavy proportions, look for its thrust to those methods which suppose the curve of pressure to start one third the length of the joint from the extrados of the key and to pass at the same distance from the intrados of the weakest joint.

Having found the thrust in cubic feet, divide it by the length of the vertical joint, or thickness of the arch at the key, and multiply the quotient by the weight of a cubic foot of the material. The result will be the mean pressure at the key in pounds. If this mean pressure exceed $\frac{1}{20}$ the ultimate resisting power of the material, make a new supposition,—increase the thickness, find the thrust and mean pressure anew; and so on until the results seem to be satisfactory.

We cannot draw the line precisely between light and and heavy arches. Most of the arches of table I are light. With one exception, their thrusts were calculated on the first supposition mentioned above. The exception is the

Westminster Bridge, whose thrust has been calculated on the second supposition.

We have shown, art. 148, that in the worst possible case, that of a semicircular arch surcharged horizontally up to the extrados of the key, we are at liberty to determine the thrust on the second supposition when $K=1.14$ or more, or when the span is 14.29 times the thickness, or less.

We may therefore adopt this value of K as the dividing point between light and heavy semicircular arches.

In segmental arches, a smaller value of K will give the limit, art. 148. When the span is six times the rise, the limit is $K=1.10$; and this may be taken as the general limit of *light* segmental arches.

In elliptical arches, it would be well, perhaps, to raise the limit; say to regard all as light in which the rise is five times the thickness at the key, or more.

In speaking above of the worst possible case, we have omitted one of occasional occurrence, viz., that in which the load upon the reins rises higher than the key, the latter being uncovered. It would be well in such a case to raise the limit.

152. The investigation of the arch indicated in the preceding article will not in all cases be sufficient. The mean pressure at the key may be within the prescribed limits, while the arch is impracticable and even impossible. We have shown briefly how to investigate this case, and have given the limits below which it need not be investigated.

Very light arches, only, require such investigation. Their thrust should always be determined on the first supposition of art. 151. Having obtained a thickness which satisfies all the conditions, we must, if the arch be very light, make some further provision for the change of form which is sure to take place after the removal of the center.

If we knew the compressibility of granite and other materials under a given pressure, it would be possible to estimate the change of form and consequently the required increase of thickness.

In the absence of such information, we can only study the proportions of existing arches. There are two ways of making the increase.

1st. We can add an equal thickness to the arch throughout.

2d. We can gradually increase the thickness from the key to the spring, or to the weakest joint.

The first method will be the best when the arch is covered by a heavy load; the second, when it is lightly covered as in most bridges.

This increase need not in general exceed 50 per cent. at the weakest joint, and at the intermediate joint of rupture, about half way between the key and the former, it must be sufficient to keep the curve of pressure within the prescribed limits.

In assuming that the curve of pressure shall pass through the middle of the key and the middle of the weakest joint, we make, in fact, an impossible supposition; for when we reflect upon the effect of pressure and compression at the several joints between the key and the regular lower joint of rupture, we see at once that the curve of pressure must run in the aggregate about equally on both sides of the central line, inclining to that side, generally the upper, on which the particular pressures are the least.

That supposition gives, however, the proper thrust a little in excess; and as to the curve of pressure we have only to suppose it lowered or changed until the proper disposition is attained. Here we see the advantage of giving to the very light arch a gradual increase of thickness on both sides of the key. We thus attain room for the curve of pressure, and make practicable perhaps what might otherwise have been an impossible arch.

This increase above the lower joint of rupture is only useful when the arch is inclined to the third mode of rupture; and, instead of a gradual and uniform augmentation from the key to that joint, it would perhaps be better to increase the thickness more rapidly to the intermediate joint of rupture, then more slowly or not at all to the lower joint.

The thickness at that intermediate joint must be more than equal to a constant thickness large enough to secure the practicability of the work.

The magazine or roof-covered arch is not inclined to the third mode of rupture. We may always take its thrust, including the effect of surcharge, from table FF.

GEOMETRICAL METHODS.

153. Poncelet has given a geometrical solution of the ultimate thrust, No. 12 Mémorial de l'Officier du Genie; and his method might be modified, with little change, so as to give the actual thrust of the arch. We follow his method, in its first stages; but by introducing some of the properties of the curve of pressure, we have been able to make a more simple, direct, and comprehensive solution. In one or two hours, a person a little familiar with the geometrical method, can lay down on paper, and verify, all the elements of the most complex case. This method is entirely independent of all particulars, and is consequently especially useful when irregularities of outline or construction place the arch almost beyond the reach of calculation.

The method is the same in all cases; but to explain it more fully, we shall apply it to loaded and unloaded full circle and segmental arches.

Allusion may be made occasionally to letters and lines which, to avoid confusion, have not been written and traced on the diagrams; but the places of such letters and lines can not be mistaken.

A brief demonstration or justification of the several steps will be given.

THE UNLOADED ARCH.

154. Let figure 48, plate XII., represent the proposed arch, of any intrados and extrados. The semi-arch is limited by the indefinite horizontal, CE, of the springing line; the indefinite vertical, CK, passing through the center of the key; the outline $i\, i_1\, i_2 \ldots i_6$ of the intrados; and the outline $e\, e_1\, e_2 \ldots e_6$ of the extrados.

I. *Point of application of the thrust.* This must be between c and c', points which divide the joint of the key into three equal parts. In heavy arches, loaded or unloaded, we generally assume the upper limit, c, as the point of application; in light arches, so loaded as to be in danger of the third mode of rupture, the crown rising, we generally assume c', the lower limit, as the point of application.

The same lower limit should be assumed in the gothic arch.

II. *Nearest approach of the curve of pressure to the intrados and to the extrados.* Draw the curves $c', c'_1, c'_2 \ldots c'_6$; $c, c_1, c_2 \ldots c_6$, dividing the joints of the arch into three equal parts. The curve of pressure must not pass outside of these limits between the key and the joint of greatest thrust.

III. *Division of the arch into fictitious voussoirs.* Divide the semi-arch into 4, 6, 8, or 10 segments, according to its absolute size, and to the degree of accuracy which we wish to attain. Let these segments have a common altitude, so chosen as to effect the desired division. Make the division as follows: from e, with the common altitude as a constant radius, describe a small arc and draw the joint $i_1\,e_1$ tangent thereto. The joints are generally perpendicular to the intrados. Next, from e_1 as a center and with the same radius, describe another arc, and draw the joint $i_2\,c'_2\,c_2\,e_2$ tangent thereto...and so on to the springing line. We need not waste time in trying to make this division come out exact. The last segment, fig. 50, may have an altitude, $e_5\,p$, a little more or less than the *constant*, $a\,p$.

IV. *Partial and total areas of the fictitious voussoirs.* Draw the parallels $i\,d_1$ to $e\,i_1$, meeting $e_1\,i_1$ prolonged at d_1; $i_1\,d_2$ to $e_1\,i_2$ meeting $e_2\,i_2$ prolonged at d_2...and so on to the springing line. If the last altitude, $e_5\,p$, fig. 50, comes out unequal, lay off $p\,a$ on $p\,e_5$, prolonged if necessary, $p\,a$ being the constant altitude, which we will designate by a. Draw $i_5\,a'$ parallel to $e_5\,i_6$; then $e_5\,d_6$ parallel to $a\,a'$, and $e_5\,d'_6$ parallel to $a\,e_6$. The surface $i_5\,i_6\,e_6\,e_5$ is measured by $a \times \frac{1}{2}\,d_6\,d'_6$. The area of any other segment, as $i_2\,i_3\,e_3\,e_2$, is measured by $\frac{1}{2}a \times d_3\,e_3$. It will be seen that we regard the right lines supposed to connect $i\,i_1$, $i_1\,i_2$... $e\,e_1$, $e_1\,e_2$, &c., as representing the outlines of the arch. This supposition is generally, in practice, favorable to stability.

On the vertical $C\,K$, from the assumed point of application of the thrust, which, in fig. 48, is c, the upper limit, lay off $c\,s_1 = \frac{1}{2}d_1\,e_1$, $s_1\,s_2 = \frac{1}{2}\,d_2\,e_2$, and so on to the springing line. Then the partial segments will be measured as follows, viz.: the surface $i\,i_1\,e_1\,e$ by $a \times c\,s_1$, surface $i_1\,i_2\,e_2\,e_1$ by $a \times s_1\,s_2$, &c.; and the total segments, $i\,i_2\,e_2\,e$ by $a \times c\,s_2$, $i\,i_3\,e_3\,e$ by $a \times c\,s_3$, &c. Area of the entire semi-arch $=$ $a \times c\,s_6$, or $a \times c\,s_8$,...as the segments may be 6, 8, &c., in number. If the line $c\,s_6$ or $c\,s_8$...is found to extend too far on the drawing for convenience, all the distances $c\,s_1$, $s_1\,s_2\ldots s_5\,s_6$ may be reduced by one half, in which case the areas of the several segments will be measuredby $c\,s_1$, $s_1\,s_2\ldots c\,s_2$, &c., multiplied by $2a$; that is, by a into the reciprocal of the fraction of reduction.

Draw the indefinite horizontals $s_1\,u_1$, $s_2\,u_2\ldots s_6\,u_6$.

V. *Centers of gravity of the partial segments or voussoirs.* Of any quadrilateral, fig. 49, draw the diagonals intersecting at m; lay off $e_4\,a=m\,i_3$, $i_4\,p=m\,e_3$, and mark c, the middle of $e_4\,i_3$, and n, the middle of $i_4\,e_3$; join $a\,n$, $c\,p$; their intersection, o_4, is the center of gravity of the figure. This point is sometimes given more conveniently by taking $c\,o_4=\frac{1}{3}\,c\,p$, or $n\,o_4=\frac{1}{3}\,n\,a$. In this manner, or in any other more expeditious manner, determine the centers of gravity o_1, o_2, o_3, &c., of all the segments.

VI. *Centers of gravity of the total segments.*

Draw a horizontal through some point, K', about as far below the point of application of the thrust as the extreme center, o_6, is distant from the vertical $C\,c$.

Project vertically on that horizontal the centers o_1, o_2, o_3, ... respectively at o'_1, o'_2, o'_3, &c. Prolong $o'_1\,c$ until it intersects the horizontal through s_1 at m_1; thence draw $m_1\,m_2$, parallel to $o'_2\,c$, meeting $s_2\,u_2$ at m_2; thence $m_2\,m_3$, parallel to $o'_3\,c$, meeting $s_3\,u_3$ at m_3, and so on to the springing line.

Project o_1 vertically on the horizontal $c\,n_7$ at n_1. Lay off $c\,K=c\,K'$; draw $K\,n_2$ parallel to $m_2\,c$ meeting $c\,n_7$ at n_2; $K\,n_3$ parallel to $m_3\,c$, meeting $c\,n_7$ at n_3; and so on to n_6, corresponding to m_6, and to the springing line.

The points, n_1, n_2, n_3, n_4, &c., on the direction of the horizontal thrust, are directly over the centers of gravity of the total segments, n_2 corresponding to $i\,i_2\,e_2\,e$, or segments 1 and 2 combined; n_3 to segments 1, 2, and 3 combined, etc.; n_6 is over the center of gravity of the whole semi-arch. (a)

VII. *The actual thrust.* Let us determine the horizontal force, which, acting at c, shall hold the first segment in equilibrium on c'_1, $i_1 c'_1 = \frac{1}{3} i_1 e_1$. $n_1 c'_1$ is obviously the direction of the resultant of this force and of the weight of the segment, represented by $c\,s_1$. Draw $c\,t_1$ parallel to $c'_1 n_1$, meeting $s_1 m_1$ at t_1; $s_1 t_1$ is the force required. In like manner draw $c\,t_2$ parallel to $c'_2 n_2$, meeting $s_2 m_2$ at t_2; $c\,t_3$ parallel to $c'_3 n_3$ meeting $s_3 m_3$ at t_3; and so on, until the ordinates $s_1 t_1$, $s_2 t_2$, &c., having attained their maximum, begin to diminish. Draw a vertical, $u_1 u_6$, tangent to the curve $t_1 t_2 t_3 t_4 \ldots$ If t_3 be the point of tangency, and t=the greatest horizontal ordinate of the curve (in this case $t = s_3 t_3$), the actual thrust expressed in cubic feet, or cubic units, if other than feet be used, will be $F = a \times t$. We must not forget to double a if the lines $c\,s_1$, $s_1 s_2$, &c., have been reduced by $\frac{1}{2}$.. See IV.

VIII. *The curve of pressure.* Mark $u_1, u_2, u_3, \ldots u_6$, the intersections of the vertical just mentioned with $s_1 m_1$, $s_2 m_2$, $s_3 m_3, \ldots s_6 m_6$. Draw $n_1 x_1$ parallel to $u_1 c$, meeting the joint $i_1 e_1$ at x_1; $n_2 x_2$ parallel to $u_2 c$, meeting $i_2 e_2$ at x_2 $\ldots n_6 x_6$ parallel to $u_6 c$, meeting the springing line at x_6.

(a) Let s_1, s_2, s_3, &c.,=the areas of the combined segments, 1; 1 & 2; 1, 2, & 3, &c.
" m_1, m_2, m_3, &c.=mom'ts on C " " " " " "
Then $s_2 - s_1$=area of the 2d segment; $s_3 - s_2$=area of 3d segment, &c.
" $m_2 - {}_1m$=mom't " " $m_3 - m_2$=mom't " " "
We have, by construction,

$$cK' : K'o'_1 :: cs_1 : s_1m_1 = \frac{K'o'_1 \times cs_1}{cK'} = \frac{m_1}{cK'}.$$

$$cK' : K'o'_2 :: s_1s_2 : s_2m_2 - s_1m_1 = \frac{K'o'_2 \times s_1s_2}{cK'} = \frac{m_2 - m_1}{cK'}.$$

Hence, $s_2m_2 = \frac{m_2}{cK'}$. In like manner $s_3m_3 = \frac{m_3}{cK'}$, &c. We also have $cs_2 : s_2m_2 :: cK : cn_2 = \frac{cK \times s_2m_2}{cs_2} = \frac{m_2}{s_2}$. In like manner, $cn_3 = \frac{m_3}{s_3}$, $cn_4 = \frac{m_4}{s_4}$, &c.

The curve of pressure passes through the points c, x_1, x_2, $x_3 \ldots x_6$. (*b*) It cannot come within the inferior limit, c', c'_1, c'_2, &c.; but it will generally approach the outer limit above the springing line, if the arch be full circle.

If the curve of pressure runs above the upper limit immediately after leaving the key, we must regard the assumed point of application of the thrust as impracticable. A lower point must be taken. If the curve corresponding to this last point still pass beyond the outer limit *before touching the inner*, a still lower point must be taken. If the curve of pressure, starting from the upper limit at the key, fall immediately below the upper limit curve, we need not investigate the thrust or the point of application any further.

IX. *Changing the point of application of the thrust.* Suppose we have obtained, as above, the actual thrust and the curve of pressure corresponding to any point of application, say c, $ic=\frac{2}{3}ie$, and wish to determine the variations in both, consequent upon a change to any other point of application, say c', $ic'=\frac{1}{3}ie$.

Project the points n_1, n_2, n_3, n_4, etc., already determined, vertically on the horizontal passing through the new point of application, c'. Mark these projections as n'_1, n'_2, n'_3, etc. Determine a new curve of thrusts (VII.) by drawing ct'_1 parallel to $c'_1\, n'_1$, meeting $s_1\, m_1$, at t'_1; ct'_2 parallel to $c'_2\, n'_2$, meeting $s_2\, m_2$ at t'_2, etc.

Draw a vertical tangent to the new curve t'_1, t'_2, t'_3, etc., and mark its intersections, u'_1 with $s_1\, m_1$, u'_2 with $s_2\, m_2$, etc.

The greatest horizontal ordinate of this curve $=s_1\, u'_1=$

(*b*) We have $cs_3=$the vertical force due to the total segment $i\, i_3\, e_3\, e$; $s_3\, u_3=$the actual thrust or constant horizontal force. The diagonal $u_3\, c$ is the direction of the resultant; n_3 is one point in it.

The same considerations apply to the other points.

$s_2\, u'_2$, etc., is the actual thrust under the conditions imposed.

Determine the new curve of pressure by drawing $n'_1\, x'_1$, parallel to $u'_1\, c$, meeting $i_1\, e_1$ at x'_1; $n'_2\, x'_2$ parallel to $u'_2\, c$, meeting $i_2\, e_2$ at x'_2 and so on, to the springing line. These changes are made in a few minutes by a repetition of steps already explained. The points s_1, s_2, s_3, ... m_1, m_2, etc., are laid off once for all. To avoid confusing the diagram, the new curves of thrust and of pressure, are not indicated in fig. 48. In like manner, any number of points of application may be assumed and their corresponding thrusts and curves determined. But it will rarely be necessary to assume more than two or three points.

X. *Limits of possible and practicable arches.* If we suppose the curve c', c'_1, c'_2, ... which marks the nearest approach of the curve of pressure to the intrados, to be the intrados itself, and, assuming i, the lowest point of the key, as the point of application, find the resulting curve of pressure to pass outside of the extrados between the key and the joint of greatest thrust, we know the arch to be *impossible*, whatever the resisting power of the materials.

If the curve of pressure starting from c', the lower limit, and touching that limit again at the joint of greatest thrust, is found, at some intermediate joint, to pass beyond the upper or outer limit, we regard the arch as impracticable.

The curve of pressure can not, in such a case, be confined within two other curves which divide the joints into three equal parts, and the joints of the arch must open at the intrados, or extrados, or both.

XI. *The case of two unequal arches, or arches bearing unequal loads, with a common key.*

Figure 48 representing the semi-arch of least thrust, let $s_1\, u''_1$=the thrust of the other part. First, to test the possibility of the smaller semi-arch, assume i as the point of application; on a horizontal passing through i project n_1, n_2, n_3, n_4, etc., already determined in relation to any other point of application. Call these projections n''_1, n''_2, n''_3, etc. Continue the vertical through u''_1 meeting $s_2 m_2$ at u''_2, $s_3 m_3$ at u''_3, etc. Construct the curve of pressure in the usual manner, by drawing $n''_1 x''_1$ parallel to $u''_1 c$ meeting $i_1 e_1$ at x''_1; $n''_2 x''_2$ parallel to $u''_2 c$ meeting $i_2 e_2$ at x''_2, etc. If this curve pass outside of the extrados, the arch is impossible.

Second, to test the practicability of the semi-arch, assume c', $i c' = \frac{1}{3} i e$, as the point of application. On the horizontal through c' project vertically the points n_1 at n'_1, n_2 at n'_2, n_3 at n'_3, etc., and determine points in the curve of pressure by drawing, from these last points, parallels $n'_1 x'_1$ to $u''_1 c$, meeting $i_1 e_1$ at x'_1, $n'_2 x'_2$ to $u''_2 c$, etc. If the curve thus determined, pass beyond the outer limit, c, c_1, c_2, c_3, ... etc., the arch is impracticable. At the point where it crosses that limit, it will be necessary to begin to increase the thickness of the arch.

XII. *Direction and magnitude of the pressure upon the several joints.* As the actual thrust, $s_3 t_3$, fig. 48, is the constant horizontal force acting upon all the joints, while $c s_1$, $c s_2$, $c s_3$. . etc., represent the surfaces or weights of the total segments, 1; 1 and 2; 1, 2, and 3, etc., it is obvious that the diagonals, u_1c, u_2c, u_3c, u_4c, etc., represent, both in magnitude and direction, the resultants which press upon the several joints; viz., u_1c on i_1e_1, u_2c on i_2e_2, u_3c on i_3e_3, etc.

If the angle between any one of these resultants and the corresponding joint should be less than the complement of the angle of friction, say less than 60°, rupture may take place by sliding. Lay off these diagonals from the same point on any line, as $c' u'_5$, fig. 54; make $uv = ie$; continue the line $c' v$. The intercepted ordinates, $u'_2 v_2$, $u'_3 v_3$, etc., will give the required lengths of joint on the condition that these shall be proportional to the resultants.

XIII. *The thrust by sliding.* The horizontal force P' necessary to hold any surface S in equilibrium on a joint making the angle v with a vertical is, a being the angle of friction, $P'=S\times$cotang. $(a+v)$. Assume $a=30°$. Then $P'=S\times$tang.$(60°-v)$.

Draw the line Cv, fig. 48, 60° from a vertical; draw $c\,t''_1$—angle $s_1\,c\,t''_1=$ang. $v\,C\,i_1=60°-v$, meeting $s_1\,m_1$ at t''_1; $c\,t''_2$—ang. $s_2\,c\,t''_2=v\,C\,i_2$, meeting $s_2\,m_2$ at t''_2, and so on.

The greatest horizontal ordinate of the curve $t''_1\,t''_2\,t''_3$..., is the thrust by sliding. The corresponding joint of greatest thrust is generally inclined about 30° to the vertical. It would be well to interpolate one or two joints near 30°, with altitudes$=\frac{1}{2}\,a$.

Should the thrust due to sliding exceed that due to rotation, the former will be the actual thrust. The point of application may be assumed, generally, as near the center of the key, and the curve of pressure may be determined precisely as in XI.

XIV. *Thickness of Pier.* Continue $n_6\,x_6$, corresponding to the springing line, fig. 48, to the base, x_7. $A\,B=\frac{3}{2}\,A\,x_7$ will, if the height of the pier be small, be very nearly the thickness required on the condition that the curve of pressure shall meet the base at one third its length from the exterior edge. $2\times A\,x_7=A\,B_1$, is the thickness required in order that the curve of pressure shall pass through the middle of the base. The exact distance may be obtained most easily by a curve of errors. Let $x=$the distance between the exterior edge of the base of the pier and the intersection of this base with the curve of pressure; $e=$the required thickness of pier; $p=$the ratio of x to e; so that $x=p\times e$. p is usually assumed at one third, sometimes as large as one half. Having already obtained the provisional thickness $A\,B_1$, mark r_1 such that $r_1\,x_7=p\times r_1\,A$. If $p=\frac{1}{3}$, $r_1\,x_7=\frac{1}{2}x_7\,A$.

AB_1 being too large, lay off the error $B_1\,r_1$ above B_1; this gives f_1. Assume AB_2 as another thickness. Determine the distance $B_2\,d_7$, precisely as if the surface $AB_2\,E_2\,i_6$ were a segment of the arch, such that $a\times\frac{1}{2}B_2\,d_7=A\,B_2\times B_2\,E_2$. Lay off $\frac{1}{2}B_2\,d_7$ from s_6 reaching to s_7, draw the horizontal $s_7\,u_7$. Project the center of gravity of $A\,B_2\,E_2\,i_6$ on $K'o'_6$ at o'_7; draw $m_6\,m_7$ parallel to o'_7c, meeting $s_7\,u_7$ at m_7; draw Kn_7 parallel to m_7c, thence $n_7\,x_8$ parallel to u_7c. This gives x_8. Mark r_2 such that $r_2\,x_8=p\times r_2A$, and, AB_2 being too small a thickness, lay off the error, $B_2\,r_2$, below B_2.. giving f_2. Join $f_1\,f_2$ meeting the line of the base at B. AB is the thickness required, very nearly. Verify this by assuming AB as the thickness; determine s_7, m_7, n_7, and x_8 anew; this will at least give a new point in the curve of errors very near the base. Connect this point with the more distant f_1 or f_2 and mark the new intersection with the base. Further trial will rarely be necessary.

If we wish to cover the pier above the springing line, by a mass of masonry sloping gradually to the extrados of the arch, we must take into account this new surface and its moment as a part of the pier, adding its surface to cs_7, projecting its center of gravity on $K'o'_7$, and so on, in the usual order to the intersection of the curve of pressure with the base.

XV. *The pressure per unit of surface.* The pressure at the key being $F=t\times a$, the mean pressure at that joint, d representing its length, is, $\frac{t\times a}{d}$; multiplying this by w, the weight of a cubic unit, we have the pressure in pounds $=W=\frac{t\times a\times w}{d}$. The mean pressure at any other joint, as $i_4\,e_4$, fig. 48, is $\frac{u_4c\times a\times w}{i_4e_4}$. The mean pressure should not exceed $\frac{1}{20}$ the ultimate resisting power of the material.

The greatest danger will be at the joints of rupture, so called, where the curve of pressure approaches nearest to the outlines of the arch. We here use the pressure or resultant itself, not its normal component.

We might, with more accuracy, use the latter, if we took notice also of the component parallel to the joint which generally tends to cause the rupture which we wish to prevent.

XVI. *Increase of the arch below the joint of greatest thrust.* The proper thickness of the full circle or semi-elliptical arch at the springing line, we can best estimate after laying off the curve of pressure down to the joint above.

The last exterior segment must be at least equal to one third the length of the joint.

THE LOADED ARCH.

155. Let fig. 51 represent the proposed arch, with any intrados and extrados, and sustaining any load rising to p, p_1, p_2, etc. As to the point of application and the situation or range of the curve of pressure (see I. and II. of the preceding article.

III. *Division of the arch into fictitious voussoirs or segments.* Divide the semi-arch into 4, 6, 8, or 10 segments, with a common altitude drawn from the upper angle of each perpendicular to the opposite side or joint, precisely as in the preceding article. From the points of the extrados thus determined, raise the verticals $e p$, $e_1 p_1$ $e_2 p_2$, etc., through the mass of the surcharge, supposed to have the density of the arch proper. Bear in mind the last part of III., 154.

IV. *Partial and total areas.* Draw the parallels, $i\, d_1$ to $e\, i_1$, meeting $e_1\, i_1$ at d_1; $i_1\, d_2$ to $e_1\, i_2$, meeting $e_2\, i_2$ at d_2, and so on to the springing line. Draw the parallels $p\,k_1$ to $e\,p_1$, meeting $e_1\,p_1$ at k_1, thence $k_1\,d'_1$ to $e_1\,e$, meeting $i_1\,e_1$ at d'_1; $p_1\,k_2$ to $e_1\,p_2$, meeting $e_2\,p_2$ at k_2, thence $k_2\,d'_2$ to $e_1\,e_2$, meeting $i_2\,e_2$ at d'_2, and so on, to the springing line.

On the vertical $C c$ passing through the middle of the key, beginning at c, the assumed point of application of the thrust, lay off $c\,s_1 = \frac{1}{2} d_1\,d'_1$, $s_1\,s_2 = \frac{1}{2} d_2\,d'_2$, and so on to the springing line. Then, area of the 1st segment including its load $= a \times c\,s_1$; area of 2d segment $= a \times s_1\,s_2$, etc.; 1st and 2d combined $= a \times c\,s_2$; 1st, 2d, and 3d combined $= a \times c\,s_3$, etc.

In fig. 51, for want of room, we have reduced these distances, $c\,s_1$, $s_1\,s_2$, $s_2\,s_3$, etc, by one half, so that, in the formulæ just given, a must be replaced by $2a$.

Draw the indefinite horizontals $s_1\,u_1$, $s_2\,u_2$, $s_3\,e_3$, etc.

V. *Centers of gravity of the partial segments.* Determine o', fig. 52, the center of gravity of any segment of the arch proper (see V. 154); and 0, the center of gravity of the superincumbent load. Drawing perpendiculars $o'a'$, $o\,a$, to the line $o\,o'$, make $o'\,a' = e_3\,d'_3$, $o\,a = d_3\,e_3$; join $a\,a'$ meeting $o\,o'$ at o_3. This gives the center of gravity, o_3, of the 3d segment and its load. (a)

In like manner the other centers, o_1, o_2, o_4, o_5, etc., may be found.

All the remaining parts of the construction are precisely the same as in the preceding article, except—

XIV. *Thickness of Pier.* $A\,B$ being the line of the base, add to the semi-arch that part of the pier which underlies the assumed thickness at the springing line. Lay off $s_5\,s_6$ representing its surface; project its center of gravity at o'_6, and determine in the usual manner the corresponding points, m_6, n_6 and finally x_6.

(a) The parallels $o'\,a'$, $o\,a$, are not necessarily perpendicular to $o\,o'$ but may be drawn in any other more convenient direction.

Mark r_1, $r_1 x_6 = \frac{1}{2} x_6 A$. On the line $e_5 B_1$, above B_1 if $A B_1$ be too large, below if too small, lay off the error $B_1 f_1 = B_1 r_1$. Assume another thickness, say $A r_1$, and, corresponding to the addition thus made to the pier, $B_1 r_1 p_6 p_5$, determine the suite of points o'_7, s_7, n_7, x_7 Lay off $x_7 r_2 = \frac{1}{2} A x_7$ and $r_1 f_2 = r_1 r_2$, the corresponding error. f_2 would have been laid off above the base if the supposed thickness had been too great.

If $A B_1$ had been too great, the line $r_1 p_6$ would have been on the right of B_1, $s_6 s_7$ laid off from s_6 downwards, $m_6 m_7$ drawn backwards, parallel to $c o'_7$. Continue $f_1 f_2$, meeting the line of the base at B. $A B$ is the required thickness, nearly, corresponding to $x = \frac{1}{3} e$, or $p = \frac{1}{3}$ (see XIV., art. 154). In like manner the thickness required for any other value of p, may be determined. In general,

$$x_6 r_1 = \frac{p}{1-p} \times x_6 A, \; x_7 r_2 = \frac{p}{1-p} \times x_7 A.$$

SEGMENTAL ARCHES.

156. These may be treated precisely as semicircular or semi-elliptical arches. Light arches, however, loaded or unloaded, admit of a more simple method, of which the only error consists of a slight exaggeration of the thrust, and of the dangers to which the structure is exposed.

This method is recommended for universal use in light arches of large span. We have taken for illustration, an arch which Capt. Meigs is now building on the Washington aqueduct; fig. 53 representing the arch as unloaded; fig. 54, the same with its final load. The span is $s = 220$ feet; the rise $f = 57'.266$; the thickness, at the key $d = 4$ feet, at the spring $d' = 6$ feet; the semi-angle of the opening $v = 55°$; the load, supposed to rise to a horizontal, and to have the density of the arch, is 12 feet deep over the key, $t = 12'$.

157. *The unloaded segmental arch*, fig. 53.

Divide the arch by vertical lines $i_1\,e_1$, $i_2\,e_2$, $i_3\,e_3$, etc., at equal horizontal distances apart, into four, six, or more segments, according to the extent of the angle and to the absolute size of the structure. Midway between these joints lay off, through the arch, the verticals $d_1\,d'_1$, $d_2\,d'_2$, $d_3\,d'_3$, etc.

Points in the direction of all these verticals may be obtained at once by dividing the half-span, or any equal and parallel line, into twice as many equal spaces as we make segments in the semi-arch.

Calling a the common horizontal distance between the joints $i_1\,e_1$ and $i_2\,e_2$, etc., any one of the segments, as $i_3\,i_4\,e_4\,e_3$, will be measured by $a \times d_4\,d'_4$. At the same time, these midway mean depths of the segments pass very nearly through their centers of gravity; we assume them to pass through these centers, the error here, too, being in favor of stability. Project vertically on the horizontal through K', d_1 at o'_1, d_2 at o'_2, d_3 at o'_3, etc. Trace the curves $c'\,c'_1\,c'_2\,c'_3\ldots$, $c\,c_1\,c_2\,c_3\ldots$ dividing the actual joints (perpendicular to the intrados) into three equal parts. Make $c\,s_1 = d_1\,d'_1$, $s_1\,s_2 = d_2\,d'_2$, etc. All the remaining steps are precisely as in art. 154.

In this particular case we see that the curve of pressure starting (as it generally may in the unloaded arch) from the upper limit, and touching the lower curve at the joint of greatest thrust between i_4 and i_5, passes over to the upper limit again at the springing line. The arch is practicable, and that is all.

All the error we commit in supposing the joints to be vertical, is that of neglecting the little surface $c'_6\,d'\,e_6$, which tends to diminish the thrust, and adding the effect of the still smaller surface $d\,c'_6\,i_6$. At other joints the error will be still less.

The thickness of pier may be obtained by construction, as already explained, or by the formulæ of art. 128; in using the latter, remember that $n = c\,s_6 \times a$, $m = n \times Pn_6$.

158. *The loaded segmental arch*, fig. 54.

Divide the semi-arch precisely as in 157, the vertical joints $i\,e$, $i_1\,e_1$, $i_2\,e_2$, etc., being at equal horizontal distances apart, and the broken lines $d_1\,d'_1$, $d_2\,d'_2$, $d_3\,d'_3$, etc., midway between the former, extending from the chords $i\,i_1$, $i_1\,i_2$, $i_2\,i_3$, etc., to the upper surface of the surcharge. On the horizontal $K'\,o'_5$ project vertically d_1 at o'_1, d_2 at o'_2, d_3 at o'_3, etc.; lay off $c'\,s_1=d_1\,d'_1$; $s_1\,s_2=d_2\,d'_2$, etc.; extend $o'_1\,c'$ to m_1, thence draw $m_1\,m_2$ parallel to $o'_2\,c'$, etc., all precisely as in art. 154.

For want of room, we have reduced $c'\,s_1$, $s_1\,s_2$, etc., by one half.

Knowing, in advance, that arches of this kind are inclined to the third mode of rupture, we assume c', the lower limit, as the point of application. The resulting curve of pressure justifies the assumption.

It nearly touches the outer limit midway between the key and the spring, while at these points it coincides with the lower limit. Comparing the unloaded and the fully loaded arch, figs. 53 and 54, we see that the curve of pressure has made the greatest possible change in its place, consistent with the condition of remaining within the prescribed limits. In this case the intrados and extrados are parts of different circles, and it is obvious that no catenarian curves could furnish a more economical structure. Whatever curves be adopted, allowance must be made for variations in the curve of pressure corresponding to variations in the load, bearing in mind all partial removals for repairs, which may be made at a future day.

The thrust $F=2a\times t=2\times\frac{1}{5}$ the half span $\times\,s_5\,t_5=2706$, taken from the drawing, is about four per cent. more than the thrust computed from art. 116, $v=55°$, $K=1.0298=1+\frac{d}{r}$. This, if we suppose each cubic foot to weigh 170 pounds, gives a mean pressure at the key, of 115,000 pounds per square foot=1,600 pounds per square inch, and a pressure of 3,200 pounds per square inch at the edge of the key most exposed.

This is more than twice as great as any pressure given in table I, but is little over one tenth the strength of the material as determined by Capt. Meigs. The pressure at the spring, $F_5 = 2a \times c' t_5$, gives a somewhat larger pressure per unit of surface.

Were this arch, after the removal of the center, loaded progressively in horizontal layers, it would, at one stage, be surcharged horizontally up to the level of the top of the key, or nearly to that level. At that stage it would be far from practicable and barely possible (arts. 143, 145). It would undoubtedly fall. Hence the necessity of putting on the load in due proportion at the reins and at the key simultaneously.

Ordinary prudence would require a larger arch, and in fact the plan of Capt. Meigs provides for a larger arch of rubble masonry resting on the cut stone of the inner arch.

159. We have supposed the curves, which mark the nearest approach of the curve of pressure to the outlines of the arch, to divide the joints into three equal parts.

The geometrical method does not, however, in any measure depend upon these proportions. We can adopt any other proportions; for example, lay off the limit curves each at one tenth the thickness of the joint from the central point, leaving the exterior parts each two fifths the joint.

RUPTURE OF MASONRY BY COMPRESSION.

160. Let the vertical $a\,b$ rising from a solid foundation, and the indefinite horizontal $b\,f$, be the outline of a piece of masonry supporting a weight or pressure distributed

uniformly and indefinitely along the upper surface $b\,f$.

The width measured at right angles to the plane of the section=one unit.

p=the pressure per unit of surface on $b\,f$.

h=the height $a\,b$.

S=the surface $a b n$ corresponding to any line of rupture $a\,n$.

p'=the weight of each unit square in S.

v=the angle $b\,a\,n$.

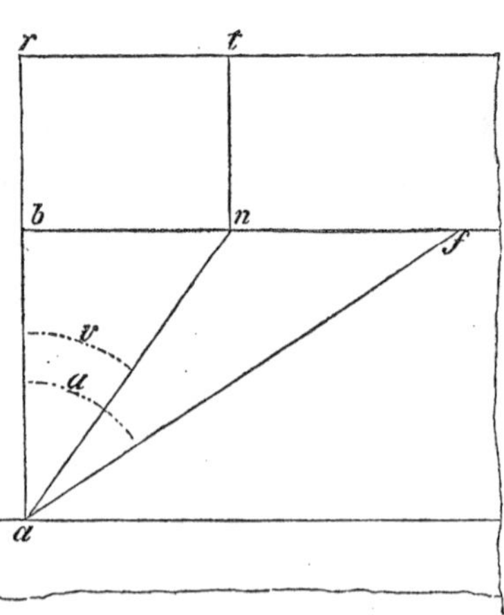

FIG. 55.

f=friction=cot. a.

a=the angle $b\,a\,f$ between the vertical and the natural slope=90°−the angle of friction; f=cot.a=the ratio of friction to pressure.

g=the coherence of the material, per unit of surface, or the force which, acting along any line $a\,n$, shall tear asunder one unit in length.

$W=p\times h\times \text{tang. } v$=the whole weight or pressure on $b\,n$.

P=the horizontal force which, assisted by friction and coherence, shall hold in equilibrium the weights $S\times p'$ and W corresponding to any prism $a\,b\,n$.

We have, parallel to $a\,n$, the components $P\times\text{sin. } v$, $W\times\text{cos. } v$, $S\times p'\times\text{cos. } v$, $g\times\dfrac{h}{\text{cos. } v}$; and, perpendicular to $a\,n$, $P\times\text{cos. } v$, $W\times\text{sin. } v$, $S\times p'\times\text{sin. } v$. For equilibrium we have $P \text{ sin. } v+g\times\dfrac{h}{\text{cos. } v}+(P \text{ cos. } v+W \text{ sin. } v+S\times p'\times\text{sin. } v)\,f=W \text{ cos. } v+S\times p' \text{ cos. } v$, which, substituting for W, $ph\times\text{tang. } v$; and for S, $\frac{1}{2}h^2$ tang. v gives

$$P=ph \text{ tang. } v\times\text{tang. }(a-v)+\tfrac{1}{2}p'h^2 \text{ tang. } v\times \text{tang. }(a-v)-\frac{gh \text{ sin. } a}{\text{cos. } v\times\text{cos. }(a-v)}. \qquad (76)$$

We readily find, by the calculus, or trigonometry, or plane geometry, that tang. $v \times$ tang. $(a-v)$ and cos. $v \times$ cos. $(a-v)$ are both maxima when $v=\frac{1}{2}a$. Hence, the greatest horizontal force which the weights W and $S \times p'$ can cause, is

$$P=ph \text{ tang.}^2 \tfrac{1}{2}a+\tfrac{1}{2}p'h^2 \text{ tang.}^2 \tfrac{1}{2}a-2gh \text{ tang. } \tfrac{1}{2}a. \quad (77)$$

If p or W be nothing, we have the thrust of an embankment of earth; and we see that the angle of greatest thrust is not affected by any supposed cohesion in the mass.

If W be so large that S in comparison may be neglected, we have the thrust of a column.

$$P=ph \text{ tang.}^2 \tfrac{1}{2}a-2gh \text{ tang. } \tfrac{1}{2}a. \quad (78)$$

Let b=the width of the column$=h$ tang. $\frac{1}{2}a$. We have

$$P=W \times \text{tang. } \tfrac{1}{2}a-2gb \quad (79)$$

Let us suppose the weight or pressure W just sufficient to overcome the tenacity of the material; we have

$$P=0, \text{ and } W \times \text{tang.} \tfrac{1}{2}a=2gb; \quad (80)$$

giving the weight that may be supported when the tenacity and the angle of friction are known, and either of the latter when the other and the weight are known.

The angle of friction in stone, is from 30° to 36°, giving $a=60°$ to 54°, and the angle of rupture or angle of least resistance from 30° to 27°.

We are at liberty to suppose the line $a\,b$ to be the surface of an arch—the intrados or the extrados, $b\,n$ any joint of the arch, W the pressure at that joint; and we learn, from the above, that the masonry, if too weak to withstand the thrust, will give way, by sliding, in a direction inclined about 25° or 30° to the line of the intrados or extrados.

We are indebted to Mosely for the application of this principle to columns, and to experiments to determine the resistance of materials to crushing, as it has been improperly called. He has, in substance, given (79); and his remarks thereon have suggested the whole of this article.

THE CURVE OF PRESSURE IN THE PIER.

161. The equation of that curve, art. 64, is

$$x=\frac{\frac{1}{2}he^2+ne+m-Fl}{eh+n}; \tag{32}$$

Suppose h as well as x variable, e constant, d the constant difference between l and h, so that $l=h\pm d$.

Develop (32), for x substitute $x'+\frac{1}{2}e-\frac{F}{e}$, and for h, $h'-\frac{n}{e}$. There results

$$x'h'=\tfrac{1}{2}n+\frac{m}{e}+\frac{F}{e}\left(\frac{n}{e}\mp d\right)=a \text{ constant.}$$

This is the equation of an equilateral hyperbola referred to a horizontal axis $\frac{n}{e}\mp d$ above the point of application of the thrust, and to a vertical axis $\frac{F-\frac{1}{2}e^2}{e}$ outside the exterior face of the pier, inside, should that quantity be negative. If $F=\frac{1}{2}e^2$ or $e=\sqrt{2F}$ the vertical asymtote will coincide with the exterior face which the curve of pressure will meet at an infinite distance.

If F be less than $\frac{1}{2}e^2$ the asymtote will be within the pier. Mosely, in a different manner, has obtained the same result, a fact of which we were not aware in writing the above.

162. The curve of pressure in an arch very heavily loaded, is very nearly the common parabola.

The most economical curves of the intrados and extrados would, in this case, also be parabolas.

At the other extreme, an unloaded arch infinitely thin, the curve of equilibrium is the catenary.

ACTUAL THRUSTS.

TABLE AA.

Table of Thrusts of the Unloaded Circular Ring.

The first column gives the ratio of R, the radius of the extrados, to r, the radius of the intrados.

The second column gives the ratio of the diameter, $2r$, to the thickness at the key.

The third column gives the new thrust based on the condition that no joint shall open; the curve of pressure approaching the extrados at the key, within one third the length of the joint, and the intrados at the reins within one third the length of the joint; this thrust$=F$.

The fourth column gives the thrusts of table A, for the same values of K, calculated on the supposition of actual rupture, the curve of pressure passing through the extrados at the key and the intrados at the reins; this thrust$=F'$.

The fifth column gives the ratio $\delta=\frac{F}{F'}$, of these two thrusts.

The values of F and δ are a little in excess, the excess increasing with K.

$\frac{R}{r}=K$ (1)	$\left(\frac{2r}{R-r}\right)$ (2)	Values of F. (3)	Values of F' from Table A. (4)	$\frac{F}{F'}=\delta$ (5)	K (1)	$\frac{2r}{R-r}$ (2)	Values of F. (3)	Values of F' from Table A. (4)	$\frac{F}{F'}=\delta$ (5)
1.01	200.00	$r^2\times0.00946$	$r^2\times0.00889$	1.065	1.21	9.52	$r^2\times0.16437$	$r^2\times0.11516$	1.427
1.02	100.00	0.01818	0.01691	1.075	1.22	9.09	0.17151	0.11887	1.443
1.03	66.66	0.02693	0.02459	1.095	1.23	8.69	0.17860		1.464
1.04	50.00	0.03504	0.03139	1.116	1.24	8.33	0.18555	&c., as in	1.482
1.05	40.00	0.04348	0.03813	1.140	1.25	8.00	0.19255	table A.	1.499
1.06	33.33	0.05178	0.04455	1.162	1.26	7.69	0.20012		1.521
1.07	28.57	0.05988	0.05065	1.182	1.27	7.40	0.20624	Angles of rup-	1.536
1.08	25.00	0.06804	0.05649	1.204	1.28	7.14	0.21281	ture the	1.554
1.09	22.22	0.07607	0.06177	1.232	1.29	6.89	0.21925	same as in	1.565
1.10	20.00	0.08369	0.06754	1.239	1.30	6.66	0.22632	table A.	1.579
1.11	18.18	0.09105	0.07273	1.252	1.31	6.45	0.23338		1.608
1.12	16.66	0.09845	0.07789	1.264	1.32	6.26	0.24050		1.638
1.13	15.38	0.10587	0.08254	1.283	1.33	6.06	0.24965		1.676
1.14	14.28	0.11335	0.08729	1.298	1.34	5.88	0.25501		1.689
1.15	13.33	0.12076	0.09176	1.316	1.35	5.71	0.26236		1.716
1.16	12.50	0.12826	0.09593	1.337	1.36	5.55	0.26784		1.730
1.17	11.76	0.13553		1.352	1.37	5.40	0.27533		1.757
1.18	11.11	0.14281	&c., as in	1.371	1.38	5.26	0.28286		1.785
1.19	10.53	0.15024	tablo A.	1.392	1.39	5.13	0.28849		1.801
1.20	10.00	0.15727		1.412	1.40	5.00	0.29616		1.822

TABLE DD.

Table of the actual thrusts of semicircular arches surcharged horizontally, the curve of pressure passing through the middle of the key and the middle of the weakest joint (see art. 116, an explanation of the columns).

Val's. of $K = 1+\frac{d}{r}$	Ratio of the span to the thickness at the key $=\frac{2r}{d}$	Angle of maxim'm thrust down to 45°. Below that, $v=60°$.	Values of $F=$ the maximum thrust down to $v=60°$.	Values of F_2 from table D= the maximum thrust in the case of rupture and fall.	$\delta=\frac{F}{F_2}$ or coefficient of stabil'y.	Values of $A=$ the maximum effect of a surcharge of constant depth t.	Values of A_2 from table $F_1=$ the maximum effect of the surcharge in the case of rupture and fall.	Values of $\delta'=\frac{A}{A_2}$
1.00		73°	$r^2 \times 0.05563$	$r^2 \times 0.05547$	1.00	$rt \times 1.0000$		1.00
1.01	200.00	71	0.06315	0.06132	1.03	1.0050		1.16
1.02	100.00	70	0.07083	0.06647	1.06	1.0099	$rt \times 0.8187$	1.23
1.03	66.67	69	0.07865	0.07185	1.09	1.0148		1.30
1.04	50.00	67	0.08668	0.07686	1.13	1.0196	0.7531	1.35
1.05	40.00	66	0.09484	0.08175	1.16	1.0244		1.40
1.06	33.33	65	0.10317	0.08638	1.19	1.0291	0.7059	1.46
1.07	28.57	63	0.11165		1.22	1.0338		1.50
1.08	25.00	62	0.12029	&c., from 4th column of table D.	1.27	1.0385	0.6678	1.55
1.09	22.22	61	0.12908		1.30	1.0431		1.60
1.10	20.00	59	0.13801		1.34	1.0476	0.6353	1.65
1.11	18.18	58	0.14709		1.38	1.0521	0.6206	1.70
1.12	16.67	57	0.15633		1.43	1.0566	0.6068	1.74
1.13	15.38	56	0.16571		1.47	1.0610	0.5936	1.79
1.14	14.28	55	0.17522		1.51	1.0654	0.5810	1.83
1.15	13.33	53	0.18490		1.56	1.0698	0.5690	1.88
1.16	12.50	52	0.19471		1.60	1.0741	0.5575	1.93
1.17	11.76	51	0.20468		1.65	1.0783		1.97
1.18	11.11	50	0.21479		1.70	1.0826		2.02
1.19	10.53	49	0.22504		1.75	1.0868	&c., from the 18th column of table F.	2.07
1.20	10.00	47	0.23544		1.80	1.0909		2.12
1.21	9.52	46	0.24598		1.86	1.0950		2.17
1.22	9.09	45	0.25667		1.91	1.0991		2.22
1.23	8.69	60	0.25960		1.91	1.1031		2.27
1.24	8.33	60	0.26935		1.96	1.1071		2.32
1.25	8.00	60	0.27916		2.01	1.1111		2.37
1.26	7.69	60	0.28900		2.07	1.1150		
1.27	7.40	60	0.29893		2.12	1.1189		
1.28	7.14	60	0.30889		2.18	1.1228		
1.29	6.89	60	0.31892		2.24	1.1266		
1.30	6.67	60	0.32899		2.30	1.1304		
1.31	6.45	60	0.33911		2.36	1.1342		
1.32	6.26	60	0.34929		2.42	1.1379		
1.33	6.06	60	0.35952		2.49	1.1416		
1.34	5.88	60	0.36980		2.55	1.1453		
1.35	5.71	60	0.38013	$r^2 \times 0.14666$	2.59			
1.36	5.55	60	0.39051	0.15111	2.58			
1.37	5.40	60	0.40095		2.58			
1.38	5.26	60	0.41143	&c., from 5th column of table D.	2.57			
1.39	5.13	60	0.42196		2.56			
1.40	5.00	60	0.43254		2.56			

TABLE FF. (*See art.* 117.)

THE MAGAZINE OR ROOF-COVERED CIRCULAR ARCH OF 180°, WITH A LOAD OF MASONRY, OR OF EQUAL WEIGHT WITH MASONRY, RISING, ON EACH SIDE OF THE CENTRAL RIDGE, TO A ROOF TANGENT TO THE EXTRADOS.

Actual thrust in four systems, the curve of pressure passing at one third the length of the joint from the extrados at the key, and from the intrados at the joint of greatest thrust.

[I=the angle between the roof and a vertical; r=the radius of the intrados; R=the radius of the extrados; d=the thickness of the arch proper at the key; $K=\frac{R}{r}=1+\frac{d}{r}$; C=the decimal; F=the thrust$=r^2\times C$; A=the addition to the thrust caused by a surcharge of the constant depth t above the tangent roof; C=the decimal in the last column; $A=rtC$; δ=the coefficient of stability= the quotient of the thrust in this table, divided by the thrust of the same arch in table F=the ratio of the actual thrust, on the conditions expressed above, to the theoretic thrust at the instant of rupture and fall. The angle of maximum thrust is measured from a vertical.]

Value of $K=\frac{R}{r}=1+\frac{d}{r}$	$I=60°$			$I=55°$			$I=50°$			$I=45°$			Surcharge.	
	Angle of max. thrust.	F= thrust = r^2C. C	δ	Angle of max. thrust.	F= thrust= r^2C. C	δ	Angle of max. thrust.	F= thrust= r^2C. C	δ	Angle of max. thrust.	F= thrust= r^2C. C	δ	Angle of max. thrust.	A= effect of surch'ge $=rtC$. C
1.40	50°	0.3549	1.84	50°	0.3961	1.81	47½°	0.4523	1.78	47½°	0.5273	1.76	52°	0.6622
1.39	"	0.3482	1.82	"	0.3892	1.78	"	0.4452	1.76	"	0.5196	1.75	"	0.6654
1.38	"	0.3415	1.79	"	0.3823	1.76	"	0.4381	1.74	"	0.5119	1.72	51	0.6687
1.37	"	0.3347	1.77	"	0.3754	1.74	"	0.4308	1.72	45	0.5042	1.71	"	0.6720
1.36	47½°	0.3281	1.75	"	0.3685	1.73	45	0.4234	1.71	"	0.4968	1.69	"	0.6753
1.35	"	0.3214	1.73	47½	0.3615	1.71	"	0.4159	1.69	"	0.4893	1.67	"	0.6788
1.34	"	0.3147	1.71	"	0.3546	1.69	"	0.4089	1.67	"	0.4818	1.66	50	0.6822
1.33	"	0.3079	1.69	"	0.3476	1.67	"	0.4018	1.65	"	0.4742	1.65	"	0.6857
1.32	"	0.3011	1.67	"	0.3406	1.65	"	0.3946	1.64	"	0.4666	1.63	"	0.6893
1.31	"	0.2943	1.65	"	0.3336	1.63	"	0.3873	1.62	42½	0.4590	1.61	49	0.6929

Value of $K=\frac{\frac{R}{r}}{1+\frac{d}{r}}$	$I=60°$			$I=55°$			$I=50°$			$I=45°$			Surcharge.	
	Angle of max. thrust.	$F=$ thrust $=r^2C$. C	δ	Angle of max. thrust.	$F=$ thrust $=r^2C$. C	δ	Angle of max. thrust.	$F=$ thrust $=r^2C$. C	δ	Angle of max. thrust.	$F=$ thrust $=r^2C$. C	δ	Angle of max. thrust.	$A=$ effect of surch'ge $=rtC$, C
1.30	47½°	0.2874	1.63	45°	0.3266	1.61	45°	0.3798	1.60	42½°	0.4517	1.60	49°	0.6966
1.29	45	0.2805	1.61	"	0.3196	1.60	42½	0.3729	1.59	"	0.4443	1.59	"	0.7004
1.28	"	0.2737	1.59	"	0.3126	1.58	"	0.3658	1.58	"	0.4369	1.57	48	0.7042
1.27	"	0.2669	1.57	"	0.3056	1.56	"	0.3586	1.56	"	0.4294	1.56	"	0.7082
1.26	"	0.2599	1.55	"	0.2986	1.55	"	0.3514	1.55	40	0.4219	1.54	"	0.7122
1.25	42½	0.2529	1.53	42½	0.2916	1.53	"	0.3440	1.53	"	0.4148	1.53	47	0.7163
1.24	"	0.2461	1.52	"	0.2846	1.52	40	0.3372	1.52	"	0.4076	1.52	"	0.7205
1.23	"	0.2392	1.50	"	0.2776	1.50	"	0.3303	1.50	"	0.4003	1.50	"	0.7249
1.22	"	0.2323	1.48	"	0.2706	1.49	"	0.3233	1.49	"	0.3930	1.49	46	0.7293
1.21	"	0.2253	1.47	"	0.2636	1.47	37½	0.3161	1.48	37½	0.3860	1.48	"	0.7339
1.20	40	0.2184	1.45	40	0.2566	1.46	"	0.3089	1.46	"	0.3790	1.47	45	0.7387
1.19	"	0.2115	1.44	"	0.2498	1.45	"	0.3023	1.45	"	0.3720	1.46	"	0.7435
1.18	"	0.2045	1.42	"	0.2430	1.43	35	0.2956	1.44	35	0.3650	1.44	44	0.7486
1.17	37½	0.1976	1.41	"	0.2362	1.42	"	0.2889	1.43	"	0.3584	1.43	"	0.7539
1.16	"	0.1907	1.40	"	0.2294	1.41	"	0.2820	1.42	"	0.3518	1.42	43	0.7594
1.15	"	0.1837	1.38	35	0.2226	1.40	"	0.2750	1.41	32½	0.3451	1.41	"	0.7651
1.14	35	0.1770	1.37	"	0.2164		32½	0.2690		"	0.3389	1.40	42	0.7712
1.13	32½	0.1701	1.36	"	0.2100		"	0.2629		"	0.3327	1.39	41	0.7775
1.12	"	0.1635	1.35	"	0.2036		30	0.2567		30	0.3266	1.38	"	0.7841
1.11	30	0.1568	1.34	"	0.1971		"	0.2505		"	0.3211	1.37	40	0.7912
1.10	"	0.1504	1.33	30	0.1904		"	0.2441		"	0.3155	1.35	39	0.7988

Table DDD.

Table of the actual thrusts of semicircular arches surcharged horizontally, the curve of pressure passing at $\frac{1}{3}$ the length of the joint from the extrados at the key, and from the intrados at the joint of greatest thrust, &c., &c. See the explanation in art. 118.

Values of $K=\frac{R}{r}=1+\frac{d}{r}$.	$F=r^2C$. C.	$A=rtC$. C.	Angle of maximum thrust. In the case of actual rupture and fall. Table D.	The curve of pressure at one third the length, &c., as above.	Curve of pressure at the middle of the joints, &c., Table DD.	δ, or coef't of stability. Curve of pressure at one third the length of the joints, &c. as above.	Curve of pressure at the middle of the joints, &c., Table DD.
(1)	(2)	(3)	(4)	(5)	(6)	(7)	(8)
1.00	0.0556	1.0000	75°	72° 30′	73°	1.000	1.00
1.01	0.0625	0.9248	74	"	71	1.020	1.03
1.02	0.0694	0.8971	73	70°	70	1.040	1.06
1.03	0.0763	0.8772	71	67° 30′	69	1.060	1.09
1.04	0.0832	0.8612	70	"	67	1.080	1.13
1.05	0.0903	0.8476	69	"	66	1.100	1.16
1.06	0.0973	0.8358	68	65°	65	1.126	1.19
1.07	0.1042	0.8252	67	"	63	1.140	1.22
1.08	0.1112	0.8156	66	"	62	1.170	1.27
1.09	0.1181	0.8069	66	62° 30′	61	1.190	1.30
1.10	0.1250	0.7988	65	"	59	1.220	1.34
1.11	0.1319	0.7912	65	"	58	1.240	1.38
1.12	0.1387	0.7841	64	60°	57	1.260	1.43
1.13	0.1455	0.7775	64	"	56	1.290	1.47
1.14	0.1523	0.7712	64	"	55	1.310	1.51
1.15	0.1590	0.7651	64	"	53	1.340	1.56
1.16	0.1657	0.7594	64	"	52	1.360	1.60
1.17	0.1723	0.7539	64	"	51	1.390	1.65
1.18	0.1788	0.7486	63	57° 30′	50	1.410	1.70
1.19	0.1853	0.7435	63	"	49	1.440	1.75
1.20	0.1918	0.7387	63	"	47	1.470	1.80
1.21	0.1982	0.7339	63	"	46	1.490	1.86
1.22	0.2046	0.7293	63	"	45	1.520	1.91
1.23	0.2109	0.7249	63	"		1.550	1.91
1.24	0.2171	0.7205	62	"		1.580	1.96
1.25	0.2233	0.7163	62	"		1.610	2.01
1.26	0.2294	0.7122	62	"		1.640	2.07
1.27	0.2355	0.7082	62	"		1.670	2.12
1.28	0.2415	0.7042	62	"		1.700	2.18
1.29	0.2475	0.7004	61	"		1.730	2.24
1.30	0.2534	0.6966	61	"		1.770	2.30
1.31	0.2593	0.6929	61	"		1.800	2.36
1.32	0.2651	0.6893	61	"		1.830	2.42
1.33	0.2709	0.6857	61	"		1.870	2.49
1.34	0.2766	0.6822	60	"		1.910	2.55
1.35	0.2823	0.6788	60	"		1.920	2.59
1.36	0.2879	0.6753	60	"		1.900	2.58
1.37	0.2935	0.6720	60	"		1.880	2.58
1.38	0.2990	0.6687	59	"		1.870	2.57
1.39	0.3045	0.6654	59	"		1.850	2.56
1.40	0.3099	0.6622	59	"		1.830	2.56

Table EE.

Segmental Arches Loaded up to the Level of the Top curve of pressure passing within one third the and from the intrados at the springing line or

[C=the decimal in any column; r=the radius of the caused by a surcharge of the constant depth t above the key; $1+\frac{d}{r}$; d=the thickness at the key. See art. 120.

$K=1+\frac{d}{r}$.	$s=4f$; $r=2\frac{1}{2}f$; $v=53°\ 7'\ 30''$.			$s=5f$; $r=3\frac{5}{8}f$; $v=43°\ 36'\ 10''$.			$s=6f$; $r=5f$; $v=36°\ 52'\ 10''$.			$s=7f$; $r=6\frac{5}{8}f$; $v=31°\ 58'\ 27''$.		
	$F=r^2\times C$.		$A=rtC$.	$F=r^2\times C$.		$A=rtC$.	$F=r^2\times C$.		$A=rtC$.	$F=r^2\times C$.		$A=rtC$.
	C.	δ	C.	C.	δ	C.	C.	δ	C.	C.	δ	C.
1.40	0.3091	1.827	0.6624	0.2938	1.736	0.6470	0.2700	1.596	0.6067	0.2441	1.443	0.5563
1.39	0.3036	1.845	0.6654	0.2887	1.754	0.6511	0.2655	1.613	0.6115	0.2403	1.460	0.5615
1.38	0.2982	1.862	0.6687	0.2836	1.771	0.6552	0.2610	1.630	0.6163	0.2364	1.477	0.5668
1.37	0.2926	1.880	0.6720	0.2784	1.789	0.6593	0.2564	1.648	0.6212	0.2325	1.494	0.5723
1.36	0.2871	1.900	0.6753	0.2732	1.808	0.6635	0.2518	1.666	0.6262	0.2285	1.512	0.5778
1.35	0.2814	1.918	0.6788	0.2679	1.826	0.6677	0.2471	1.684	0.6313	0.2244	1.530	0.5835
1.34	0.2758	1.938	0.6822	0.2626	1.846	0.6720	0.2424	1.705	0.6365	0.2203	1.548	0.5893
1.33	0.2700	1.909	0.6857	0.2572	1.865	0.6764	0.2376	1.723	0.6418	0.2162	1.568	0.5952
1.32	0.2643	1.876	0.6893	0.2518	1.886	0.6807	0.2327	1.743	0.6471	0.2120	1.588	0.6012
1.31	0.2584	1.842	0.6929	0.2463	1.906	0.6852	0.2278	1.763	0.6526	0.2078	1.608	0.6074
1.30	0.2526	1.809	0.6966	0.2407	1.926	0.6897	0.2229	1.783	0.6581	0.2035	1.628	0.6138
1.29	0.2466	1.775	0.7004	0.2351	1.893	0.6942	0.2178	1.804	0.6638	0.1991	1.650	0.6202
1.28	0.2407	1.745	0.7042	0.2294	1.859	0.6988	0.2127	1.826	0.6695	0.1946	1.670	0.6269
1.27	0.2346	1.714	0.7082	0.2237	1.826	0.7035	0.2076	1.849	0.6754	0.1901	1.693	0.6337
1.26	0.2285	1.683	0.7122	0.2179	1.793	0.7082	0.2023	1.870	0.6814	0.1855	1.715	0.6406
1.25	0.2224	1.654	0.7163	0.2120	1.761	0.7130	0.1970	1.883	0.6875	0.1808	1.737	0.6478
1.24	0.2162	1.623	0.7205	0.2061	1.730	0.7179	0.1916	1.850	0.6937	0.1761	1.761	0.6551
1.23	0.2099	1.594	0.7249	0.2001	1.700	0.7228	0.1862	1.817	0.7001	0.1712	1.785	0.6627
1.22	0.2036	1.566	0.7293	0.1940	1.668	0.7278	0.1806	1.781	0.7066	0.1663	1.810	0.6704
1.21	0.1972	1.538	0.7339	0.1878	1.636	0.7329	0.1750	1.748	0.7132	0.1613	1.835	0.6784
1.20	0.1907	1.510	0.7387	0.1816	1.606	0.7380	0.1692	1.713	0.7200	0.1561	1.830	0.6865
1.19	0.1842	1.482	0.7435	0.1753	1.575	0.7432	0.1634	1.680	0.7269	0.1509	1.794	0.6950
1.18	0.1776	1.456	0.7486	0.1689	1.546	0.7485	0.1575	1.646	0.7340	0.1456	1.756	0.7036
1.17	0.1710	1.429	0.7539	0.1624	1.515	0.7539	0.1514	1.611	0.7413	0.1401	1.719	0.7125
1.16	0.1643	1.403	0.7594	0.1558	1.485	0.7594	0.1453	1.578	0.7487	0.1346	1.682	0.7218
1.15	0.1575	1.377	0.7651	0.1492	1.456	0.7651	0.1391	1.544	0.7564	0.1289	1.644	0.7313
1.14	0.1506	1.351	0.7712	0.1425	1.425	0.7712	0.1327	1.510	0.7642	0.1231	1.607	0.7411
1.13	0.1437	1.326	0.7775	0.1356	1.397	0.7775	0.1263	1.477	0.7722	0.1171	1.568	0.7512
1.12	0.1367	1.301	0.7841	0.1287	1.368	0.7841	0.1197	1.442	0.7804	0.1110	1.529	0.7617
1.11	0.1296	1.276	0.7912	0.1216	1.338	0.7912	0.1129	1.408	0.7888	0.1047	1.489	0.7726
1.10	0.1225	1.250	0.7988	0.1145	1.310	0.7988	0.1061	1.374	0.7975	0.0983	1.450	0.7839
1.09	0.1152	1.226	0.8069	0.1072	1.279	0.8069	0.0991	1.339	0.8064	0.0917	1.409	0.7956
1.08	0.1079	1.199	0.8156	0.0998	1.251	0.8156	0.0919	1.304	0.8156	0.0849	1.367	0.8077
1.07	0.1005	1.177	0.8252	0.0923	1.221	0.8252	0.0846	1.268	0.8252	0.0779	1.325	0.8203
1.06	0.0930	1.151	0.8358	0.0847	1.191	0.8358	0.0771	1.232	0.8358	0.0707	1.283	0.8334
1.05	0.0855	1.128	0.8476	0.0770	1.163	0.8476	0.0695	1.196	0.8476	0.0633	1.239	0.8470
1.04	0.0778	1.103	0.8612	0.0691	1.133	0.8612	0.0616	1.160	0.8612	0.0556	1.196	0.8612
1.03	0.0700	1.077	0.8772	0.0611	1.103	0.8772	0.0536	1.124	0.8772	0.0477	1.150	0.8772
1.02	0.0622	1.054	0.8971	0.0529	1.073	0.8971	0.0453	1.084	0.8971	0.0395	1.103	0.8971
1.01	0.0542	1.027	0.9248	0.0446	1.042	0.9248	0.0368	1.042	0.9248	0.0310	1.055	0.9248
1.00	0.0462		1.0000	0.0361		1.0000	0.0281		1.0000	0.0222		1.0000

TABLE EE.

OF THE KEY. ACTUAL THRUST IN SEVEN SYSTEMS: THE LENGTH OF THE JOINT FROM THE EXTRADOS AT THE KEY, JOINT OF GREATEST THRUST.

intrados; F=the thrust; A=the addition to the thrust $F=r^2 \times C$; $A=rt \times C$; s=the span; f=the rise; K=

$K=1+\frac{d}{r}$.	$s=8f$; $r=8\frac{1}{2}f$; $v=28° 4' 20''$.			$s=10f$; $r=13f$; $v=22° 37' 10''$.			$s=16f$; $r=32\frac{1}{2}f$; $v=14° 15'$.		
	$F=r^2 \times C$.		$A=rtC$.	$F=r^2 \times C$.		$A=rtC$.	$F=r^2 \times C$.		$A=rtC$.
	C.	δ	C.	C.	δ	C.	C.	δ	C.
1.40	0.2188	1.293	0.5038	0.1745	1.095	0.4070	0.1276	1.000	0.3538
1.39	0.2156	1.310	0.5092	0.1722	1.112	0.4123	0.1240	1.000	0.3512
1.38	0.2123	1.326	0.5148	0.1699	1.129	0.4178	0.1204	1.000	0.3487
1.37	0.2090	1.343	0.5205	0.1676	1.146	0.4235	0.1168	1.000	0.3462
1.36	0.2056	1.361	0.5264	0.1652	1.165	0.4294	0.1132	1.000	0.3437
1.35	0.2022	1.378	0.5324	0.1628	1.183	0.4354	0.1097	1.000	0.3411
1.34	0.1988	1.398	0.5385	0.1603	1.203	0.4417	0.1062	1.000	0.3386
1.33	0.1953	1.416	0.5448	0.1578	1.222	0.4481	0.1027	1.000	0.3361
1.32	0.1917	1.436	0.5513	0.1553	1.243	0.4548	0.0993	1.000	0.3335
1.31	0.1881	1.456	0.5579	0.1527	1.265	0.4617	0.0958	1.000	0.3310
1.30	0.1844	1.475	0.5647	0.1501	1.287	0.4688	0.0924	1.000	0.3285
1.29	0.1807	1.497	0.5717	0.1474	1.310	0.4762	0.0891	1.000	0.3260
1.28	0.1769	1.519	0.5789	0.1447	1.335	0.4838	0.0857	1.000	0.3234
1.27	0.1739	1.541	0.5863	0.1418	1.358	0.4918	0.0824	1.000	0.3209
1.26	0.1690	1.562	0.5940	0.1389	1.383	0.5000	0.0791	1.000	0.3184
1.25	0.1649	1.585	0.6019	0.1360	1.411	0.5085	0.0773	1.020	0.3159
1.24	0.1608	1.608	0.6101	0.1330	1.438	0.5173	0.0762	1.050	0.3133
1.23	0.1566	1.633	0.6185	0.1298	1.465	0.5266	0.0749	1.080	0.3134
1.22	0.1523	1.657	0.6271	0.1267	1.496	0.5364	0.0736	1.112	0.3220
1.21	0.1479	1.683	0.6361	0.1234	1.527	0.5465	0.0723	1.147	0.3312
1.20	0.1434	1.707	0.6454	0.1200	1.558	0.5571	0.0709	1.184	0.3410
1.19	0.1388	1.735	0.6550	0.1166	1.593	0.5681	0.0694	1.222	0.3516
1.18	0.1341	1.760	0.6650	0.1131	1.627	0.5797	0.0679	1.264	0.3629
1.17	0.1293	1.788	0.6754	0.1094	1.663	0.5918	0.0663	1.310	0.3750
1.16	0.1243	1.788	0.6861	0.1055	1.699	0.6045	0.0646	1.357	0.3880
1.15	0.1192	1.748	0.6971	0.1015	1.738	0.6180	0.0629	1.410	0.4022
1.14	0.1140	1.706	0.7086	0.0974	1.777	0.6321	0.0611	1.469	0.4175
1.13	0.1086	1.663	0.7207	0.0931	1.818	0.6470	0.0592	1.534	0.4342
1.12	0.1030	1.619	0.7333	0.0886	1.805	0.6627	0.0570	1.597	0.4524
1.11	0.0972	1.575	0.7464	0.0839	1.751	0.6794	0.0547	1.668	0.4725
1.10	0.0913	1.529	0.7601	0.0791	1.701	0.6971	0.0523	1.749	0.4947
1.09	0.0852	1.484	0.7744	0.0740	1.644	0.7160	0.0496	1.830	0.5192
1.08	0.0789	1.440	0.7894	0.0686	1.584	0.7360	0.0467	1.930	0.5467
1.07	0.0723	1.390	0.8051	0.0630	1.525	0.7574	0.0436	1.938	0.5775
1.06	0.0654	1.340	0.8216	0.0570	1.462	0.7804	0.0400	1.843	0.6125
1.05	0.0583	1.287	0.8389	0.0507	1.397	0.8050	0.0361	1.752	0.6524
1.04	0.0509	1.235	0.8572	0.0440	1.329	0.8315	0.0316	1.637	0.6984
1.03	0.0432	1.180	0.8765	0.0368	1.256	0.8601	0.0265	1.506	0.7521
1.02	0.0351	1.125	0.8971	0.0291	1.173	0.8911	0.0206	1.373	0.8155
1.01	0.0267	1.068	0.9248	0.0209	1.094	0.9248	0.0135	1.205	0.8916
1.00	0.0178		1.0000	0.0121		1.0000	0.0051		1.0000

Elements of particular Bridges—the dimensio

[r=the half-span in elliptical arches

	NAME OR SITUATION.	Date.	Architect.	Intrados.	Rise.	Span.	Thickness		Ratio of the	
							at the key.	at the reins or spring.	span to the thickness.	diam. curv. o the intrados at the the ke to the thick'ss
					Feet.	Feet.	Feet.	Feet		
1	Bishop Auckland, over the Wear................	1388	....	Segmental...	22.00	$100\frac{5}{12}$	$1\frac{10}{12}$	$1\frac{10}{12}$	54.77	74.5
2	Llanwast, in Denbighshire.	1636	Inigo Jones....	do ...	17.00	58.00	1.50	.....	38.66	44.3
3	Westminster Bridge, central arch................	1750	Labelye.......	Semicircle...	38.00	76.00	7.60	14.00	10.00	10.0
4	Taaf, South Wales........	1755	Edwards......	Segmental...	35.00	140.00	2.50	2.50	56.00	70.0
5	Wellington Bridge, over the Aire, at Leeds..........	....	Rennie........	do ...	15.00	100.00	3.00	7.00	$33\frac{1}{3}$	60.5
6	Waterloo Bridge, nine equal arches...............	1811	do	Semi-ellipse..	35.00	120.00	4.75	8.00	25.26	.....
7	London Bridge, central arch	1831	George Rennie.	do	38.00	152.00	5.00	10.00	30.40	.....
8	Staines Bridge, five equal arches....	1832	Rennie........	Segmental...	9.25	74.00	3.00	6.0	$24\frac{2}{3}$	52.4
9	Chester Bridge...........	1825	Harrison......	do ...	42.00	200.00	4.00	6.0	50.00	70.C
10	Edinburgh.....	....	Mylne........	Semicircle...	36.00	72.00	2.75	.....	26.18	26.1
11	Hutcheson Bridge, Glasgow	....	Robt. Stevenson	Segmental...	$13\frac{4}{12}$	79.00	3.50	4.50	22.57	37.2
12	Whitadder Bridge, Allanton..................	1842	Do & Sons.....	do ...	11.50	75.00	2.50	3.00	30.00	53.5
13	Railway Bridge, at Maidenhead............	....	Brunel........	Semi-ellipse..	24.25	128.00	5.25	7.16	24.38	.....
14	Bridge at Neuilly, over the Seine, five equal arches..	1774	Perronet......	do	32.00	128.00	5.25	.....	24.38	.....
15	Bridge of Pesmes, on the Ougnon..............	1772	Bertrand... ...	Segmental...	$3\frac{10}{12}$	44.75	$3\frac{10}{12}$	.....	11.67	35.0
16	Chateau Thierry.........	1786	Perronet......	Semi-ellipse..	17.00	51.00	4.00	.....	12.75	.....
17	Louis XIX...............	1791	do	Segmental...	9.75	94.00	$3\frac{87}{12}$	.....	25.64	64.4
18	Nemours.................	1805	do	do ...	3.75	53.25	$3\frac{2}{12}$	.....	16.81	60.8
19	Turin...............		Mosca........	do ...	18.00	147.60	$4\frac{3}{4}$	.....	31.07	67..

COMPILED MAINLY FROM CRESY'S ENCYCLOPEDIA.

r = the radius of the intrados in segmental arches.]

Thrust at the key for each foot of bridge in width.	Mean pressure in pounds on each square foot at the key.	Nature of of the material when known.	Supposed ultimate resisting power of the material per sq. inch.	Ratio of ult. resisting power of the material to the pressure.	REMARKS.
$r^2 \times 0.06356$	25869	....	4000	11.00	Probably with little surcharge.
0.08960	10560	....	4000	27.00	"The road-way approached a horizontal line" in consequence of the substitution of vehicles for pack horses.
0.19180	5908	....	4000	49.00	Thickness taken from the drawing in Cresy's Encyclopedia. Surcharged horizontally.
0.07157	35072	....	4000	8.00	Fell on the removal of the center, the crown rising; but stood after being rebuilt with hollow spaces in the surcharge over the reins.
0.05764	25362	....	4000	$11\frac{1}{3}$	Surcharged horizontally.
0.17113	21905	Granite.	6000	20.00	Counter arch over the piers to receive the horizontal thrust. Settled but a few inches on removing the center.
0.16723	30926	do	6000	14.00	Settled at the key only 2″ on removing the center. Counter arches 6 feet thick over the piers.
0.05721	18862	....	5000	20.00	
0.06406	50223	....	6000	$8\frac{6}{10}$	The crown settled only $2\frac{1}{2}$ inches on removing the center.
0.11683	8809	....	4000	33.00	
0.07810	15177	....	4000	19.00	
0.06195	17740	....	4000	16.00	
0.25292	24666	Brick.	1200	$3\frac{1}{2}$	Six longitudinal walls support the railway.
0.19870	24804	....	4000	11.61	Settled 2 feet at the crown on removing the center.
0.06726	12644	....	4000	23.00	Settled considerably at the crown on removing the center, the abutments moving laterally.
0.26476	6886	....	4000	42.00	
0.04513	27493	....	4000	$10\frac{1}{2}$	In calculating the last column, the pressure, per unit of surface, at the extrados of the key, has been assumed at twice the mean pressure.
0.03877	18200	....	4000	16.00	
0.04887	42294	....	6000	$10\frac{1}{5}$	The weight of a cubic foot of stone is assumed to be 160 pounds. Brick masonry 125 pounds per cubic foot.

INDEX.

www.ingramcontent.com/pod-product-compliance
Lightning Source LLC
LaVergne TN
LVHW010252110826
845151LV00004B/1452

9781425523176